The Blue Devil "Battle Mountain" Regiment in Italy

....a history of the
350th Infantry Regiment
1944-1945

John E. Wallace

THE BATTERY PRESS
NASHVILLE

© 1977 by John E. Wallace

First Edition
1977

Second Edition Published by
THE BATTERY PRESS, INC.
P. O. Box 3107, Uptown Station
Nashville, Tennessee 37219 U.S.A.
Seventh in the Combat Arms Series
1981
ISBN: 0-89839-052-4

Contents

Foreword

Some thirty years after the event, World War II still holds an intense fascination for the ordinary history buff as well as for the historians and especially for the veterans who fought its battles. No other theater of operations of World War II has continued to be more controversial than the Italian Campaign. The combat veterans who slugged through the mountain chains of the Appenines forged bonds of comradeship that time scarcely loosens.

For most of those veterans places like Cassino, Minturno, Battaglia, and Monterumici remain names where acts of heroism and courage have etched their memories forever on their minds. Men of the 350th Infantry Regiment of the 88th Infantry Division remember these and other important battle sites somewhat as isolated engagements. At the time of battle men no doubt pondered the significance of particular battles in the over-all plans for the victory against Nazism. This present history of the "Blue Devil Battle Mountain Regiment" attempts to place in perspective the action of the 350th Infantry relative to the over-all strategy in the Italian Campaign.

At the same time the author has attempted to include the personal element into the narrative. From records in the National Historical Archives in Washington, D.C.; from materials from Fort Benning, Georgia; and from personal interviews and correspondence, he has included detailed actions of a number of individuals; other actions of equal heroism could have been included had the materials been available. The fact that they are excluded does not detract from the valor of the Blue Devils of the Battle Mountain Regiment.

It would be impossible to list the names of all those who have aided in the completion of this history. From the present vantage point in history all those who participated in the grueling Italian Campaign share in its remembered trials as well as its glories, The history is thus dedicated to all the Blue Devils, living and dead, of the gallant 350th who, unlike veterans of American wars of the 1950's and 1960's, had the good fortune of knowing that the war was being waged for complete victory over the enemy and of scourging the world of virulent Nazism. To have shared in the common effort forever cements the bonds of comradeship among the Blue Devils of the 350th Infantry.

It is hoped that the maps, illustrations, pictures, and narrative will make clear to the children of 350th Infantry veterans and their children the part played by their fathers and grandfathers in the battles in Italy during 1944-1945.

Dr. John E. Wallace
University of Southern Mississippi
Gulf Park
Long Beach, Mississippi

August, 1977

SWITZERLAND

AUSTRIA

FRANCE

JUGOSLAVIA

BRENNER PASS

2 MAY 45   BOLZANO
            CAVALESE
1 MAY 45   ARSIE   PRIMOLANO
                     VICENZA
26 APR 45   VERONA   SAN MARTINO
24 APR 45   PO RIVER CROSSING

30 OCT 44   M. ADONE   BOLOGNA
            MONTE RUMICI
            M. CERRERE
            M. CUCCOLI
            M. DELLA TOMBA   M. BATTAGLIA
            M. DELLA VALLE   BORGO S. LORENZO
14 SEP 44   M. BRUNO
            M. ALTO   FLORENCE
            M. ALUTO

6 JUL 44   VOLTERRA
            POMERANCE

ADRIATIC

SEA

PO VALLEY CAMPAIGN

NORTH APPENINES CAMPAIGN   FORMELLO
                             ROME
ROME – ARNO CAMPAIGN
                       4 JUN 44

                             NETTUNO
                             R. CASTELLONE
                             BOL CABELLA
                             M. ALTO
                             FONDI
                             ITRI
                             M. ROTONDI
                             M. CERRI
                             HILL 216
                             M. CIANELLI
                       MINTURNO   PIEDMONTE

                 5 MAR 44   NAPOLI
                       1 MAR 44

ROAD TO VICTORY

PATH OF THE FIGHTING
350 TH INFANTRY REGIMENT

BELL

Chapter One

First Taste of Combat,
February - May, 1944

The entrance of the 88th "Blue Devil" Infantry Division into the lines in defensive positions in the Minturno area on the left flank of Fifth Army positions in March, 1944, was the culmination of several months of waiting and expectations after the division had been in transit to the battle area since October 25, 1943. As the first all-selective service unit to enter combat during World War II, the 88th Division was the first fresh division sent to Italy since the invasion at Salerno. Initially the Blue Devils were attached to II Corps, February 23, 1944. The old gripe of G-I's that the military had them always "to hurry up and wait" was voiced succinctly by Pvt. Frank Caccitore of the 350th Infantry while his regiment was sailing from North Africa to Naples: "I'm nerveous—sure I am; we've waited an awful long time for this. And we're still waiting."[1]

On February 27 the 88th Division received orders to move to the southern flank of the main Fifth Army line to relieve the British Fifth Division in the Minturno area. In this Garigliano River bridgehead, the British X Corps had successfully maintained its gains from the January offensive against the Gustav Line, although other attacking units in the Cassino area eastward had failed to reach their objectives in that offensive. From this exposed position the 88th Division in May, 1944, would successfully pierce the strong German Gustav Line positions in a decisive battle on Mt. Damiano that would aid

immeasurably in prying loose the Krauts' formidable fortifications.

By 1100 hours, March 5, 1944, control of the former British
sector passed to the 88th Division, with the forward command
post located in the village of Carano and the rear echelon
positioned in the village of Casanova. On this same day the 88th
Division was detached from II Corps and attached to British X
Corps. With the 350th Infantry on the left flank on the seacoast,
the 351st in the center sector, and the 349th on the right flank,
the division held a 10,000 yard front, stretching from the
seacoast to the heights of Mt. Damiano near Castelforte. The
division would occupy and maintain this sector until early May,
with primary mission of conducting a holding and harassing
action. To permit each regiment to familiarize itself with the
entire front, the commanding general inaugurated the system
of rotating each regiment to a different sector periodically.
When the 339th Infantry of the 85th Division was attached to the
88th and went into the line on March 17, the Blue Devils now had
enough units in the line to allow one reg iment at a time to rest
and recuperate in preparation for the "Big Push."

Enemy units facing the 350th Infantry and 88th Division included elements of the 94th, 71st, and 44th Divisions of the XIV
Corps, astride the Ausente River. (See Map 1.) The American-
held terrain north of the Garigliano River below Minturno
comprised some flat country, that is, what little there was in
that part of Italy, up to the Nazi-held foothills. (See Map 2.) At
this period of defensive warfare, the G-I's sported British
helmets and tin hats of World War I vintage to confuse the
enemy about new units in the line.

Although artillery fire was constant and heavy, the ground
troops engaged mainly In patrolling and feeling out the enemy.
The prisoners taken by these patrols talked freely. This information was supplemented and checked somewhat by
refugees from Gaeta who came into the 88th Division's lines.
One sure technique of eliciting information was to threaten the
prisoners with turning them over to the Russians in Naples if
they did not talk.

A number of G-I's during this static period of fighting
exemplified the dictum that the American soldier relies on his
own initiative in times of crises. Lt. Jasper D. Parks of
Oklahoma City and Sgt. W.A. Trapp of Wagoner, Oklahoma,

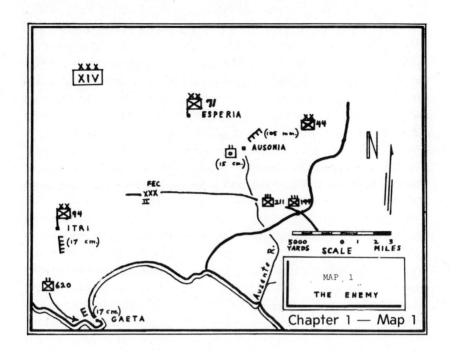

XXX
XIV

⊠ 71
ESPERIA

(105 mm.)

⊠ 44

⊡ ■ AUSONIA
(15 cm.)

FEC
XXX
II

⊠ 2/1 ⊠ 1/94

⊠ 94
ITRI
Ɛ (17 cm.)

Ausente R.

5000 YARDS   0 1 2 3 MILES
SCALE

⊠ 620

Ɛ (17 cm.)
GAETA

MAP 1
THE ENEMY

Chapter 1 — Map 1

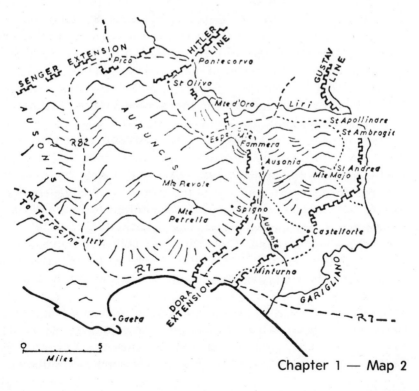

SENGER EXTENSION

Pico

HITLER LINE

Pontecorvo

St Olivo

GUSTAV LINE

Mte d'Oro   Liri

St Apollinare

A U R U N C I S

St Ambrogio

Espe.Mte
Fammera

Ausonia

St Andrea
Mte Majo

AUSONIS

R82

Mte Revole

Mte Petrella

Spigno

Ausente

Castelforte

R7
To Terracina

Itry

R7

DORA EXTENSION

Minturno

GARIGLIANO

R7

Gaeta

0 _____ 5
Miles

Chapter 1 — Map 2

rescued two soldiers after the wounded men had spent six days and nights in a wrecked building in No Man's Land. They found the wounded intoxicated - in the absence of water to drink, they had lived on wine found in the cellars of a wrecked building. When Kraut artillery blew up the ammunition dump, 1st Sgt. Chester W. Pastuszynski of Buffalo, New York, and Cpl. Archie A. Berry of Cincinnati, Ohio, made the term "field expedient" more than just a manual phrase. Since the only mortar ammo available was British mortar shells, they acquired a gadget from a field range, filed it down for use, and soon had their mortars lobbing British shells into German lines.

By the beginning of May the 88th Division's sector had narrowed to a two-regiment front with the arrival of the rest of the 85th Division in Italy, which went into the line on the left flank in the coastal sector. During this period also the 350th Infantry received a new regimental commander when Colonel James C. Fry of Washington, D.C., and Sandpoint, Idaho, replaced Colonel Charles P. Lynch, who left his son in command of the same company that he had served during World War I. The new commander, a West Point graduate, had formerly served as assistant to Generals Douglas MacArthur and Dwight Eisenhower in Hawaii and the Philippines; had been assistant military attache' in Turkey; and had later been stationed in Egypt in the same capacity. Just prior to his assignment to the 350th Infantry, Colonel Fry had commanded the 69th Armored Regiment in the States until he requested overseas assignment. [2]

The overall plan of attack in which the 350th Infantry would perform a vital role by its capture of Mt. Damiano (Cianelli) had been instituted in April, 1944, after the failure of the Allies to break through at Cassino. For the coming offensive General Harold Alexander, commander of Allied Forces in Italy, had concentrated thirteen divisions for a massive blow at the formidable Gustav Line. The Fifth Army sector consisted of a narrow strip 13 miles between the sea and the Liri River close to Cassino. The supply dumps to support this attack had been shifted from Route 6, the highway through the Liri valley, to Highway 7 running close to the sea. The new inter-army boundary between Fifth and Eighth Armies was placed in effect on March 26, and three days later the French Expeditionary Corps and II Corps, the latter on the left, officially

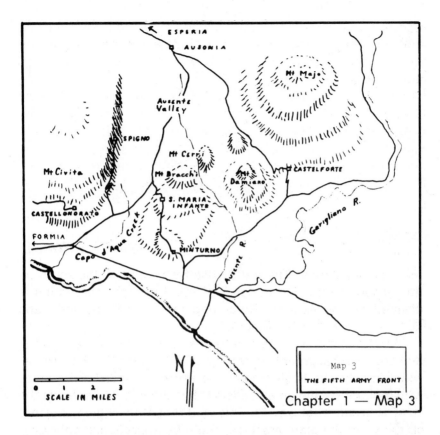

Map 3

THE FIFTH ARMY FRONT

Chapter 1 — Map 3

relieved the British X Corps in the Garigliano sector; X Corps was relieved from Fifth Army on March 31, 1944. [3]

The terrain over which the French Expeditionary Corps and II Corps would advance was a chain of steep and rugged mountains running northwest about 60 miles and averaging 15 miles in width between the sea and the Liri-Sacco Valley, including first the Aurunci Mountains, then the Aussoni, and finally the Lepini. (See Maps 3 & 4). Beginning in the French zone and extending westward into the 350th Infantry and II Corps area, a number of well-fortified mountain peaks dominated three distinct hill masses - Mt. Majo to the east, 940 meters; on the west, Mt. Civita, the critical feature of the major range which rose to a maximum elevation of 1533 meters before dropping in a sheer cliff to the floor of the central Ausente Valley; and in the valley itself, a group of lower but equally steep hills extending from Minturno to Mount Bracchi, which reaches a height of 205 meters before dropping off into

Page 5

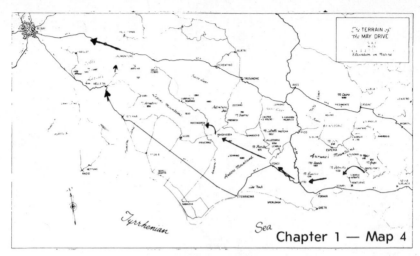

the Ausonia Valley. The Valley itself was split in the south by this group of hills. To the east of this hill mass the valley is drained by the Ausente River and to the west by the Capo D'Aqua Creek.[4] (See Map 3.)

The western side of this valley is sharply delimited by the high fault escarpment of Mt. La Civita and Mt. Fammera, which marks the beginning of the Petrella massif-a region of wild mountains and upland basins stretching on six miles to the Itri-Pico road, Highway 82. This wild mountain region, a prime objective in the plan of attack, could be approached only by a few trails that gave access to the interior. The plan of attack had been modified by May 11 to include the passage of the French Goumiers (mountain fighters) and the French Expeditionary Corps over this seemingly impassable chain. The plan of attack further included employment of the 350th, which would play a significant role in helping to open up this area to advance by the FEC. (See Map 5.)

The area around Spigno on the east of the Petrella massif would be the zone assigned to the 350th Infantry. Except at this village, a steep cliff barred entry into the massif. On the more gentle northern and western sides, a few trails gave access to the interior of the massif. Another possible route hugged the southern side of Mt. Petrella and continued on to Mt. Ruazzo. The high mountain chain could be approached thus from only a few roads on the flanks.

In the simultaneous attack of both armies, the Eighth and the Fifth, planned by General Alexander early in April, the Fifth

Army would capture the Ausonia Defile. The plans called for smashing German forces between Cassino and the sea and driving them back over 200 miles to the Rimini-Pisa line.[5]

In the plan of attack to drive to the Itri-Pico road, Field Order No. 6 limited the attack and divided it into four phases. In Phase I, the capture of the Ausonia-Formia road, the French were to take Mount Majo and areas on the right, while II Corps gained more limited objectives-Hill 413 (Mt. Damiano) just west of Castelforte, known as "Little Cassino," the S Ridge running southwest from Santa Maria Infante, Mount dei Bracchi, and San Martino Hill. From these points it could cut the lower reaches of the Ausonia road. In Phase II the French troops were to move on to Mount Revole and exploit in the Ausonia Valley, with the assistance from II Corps principally in the capture of Mount La Civita and Spigno. American troops would also take Mount I Cerri and Castellonorato.[6]

For co-ordination of the advance in Phase III, the French received orders to cut the Itri-Pico road in the vicinity of Itri and fan out from there. Parts of II Corps were to take Mount

Scauri and Mount Campese, while other units were to advance across the mountains south of Mount Petrella and cut the Itri-Pico road near Itri. Plans for further advance from the Itri-Pico road constituted Phase IV. Instead of slugging forward slowly as in the past, Fifth Army would smash the enemy with one fierce blow and crack him open. [7]

On May 1, General Keyes, commanding II Corps, issued the attack order. It only dealt with Phases I and II of the overall attack plan, with the latter phase divided into three phases itself. Since the 85th Infantry Division occupied further advanced positions along the sea, it would engage in only the last phase, while the 88th Division would battle through all three phases. The main effort of the Corps was thus entrusted to the 88th Division as the more experienced of the two units in the line at that time. [8] The main weight of the attack was to be exerted in the wedge of hills running north from Minturno to Mount dei Bracchi. If these hills could be secured, then the enemy positions in the lower Ausonia Valley would collapse. On the right flank II Corps was ordered to give aid to the FEC by opening up the hills on the south side of the Castelforte road.

While the 85th on the left drove for San Martino Hill and part of S Ridge in its zone, on the right the 88th was to take the rest of S Ridge, including Santa Maria Infante, while elements of the division also captured Hill 413 (Mount Cianelli) to aid the French. For Phase II while the 85th remained in position, aided by supporting fire from the 88th, the Blue Devils were to drive up to Mount dei Bracchi and swing its right flank west through I Cerri and Mount Rotondo, aiming at Spigno; this point, together with Mount La Civita, formed its objective in Phase III. In addition the 88th had the task in this third phase of assisting the 85th Division in taking Castellonorato, facilitating the advance of the French into the Petrella massif, and sending forces west toward Mount Saint Angelo. (See Map 6).

In the build-up for the attack, interdiction fires upon crossings of the River Garigliano hampered supply. To counteract enemy observation and fire, II Corps employed smoke generator units which concealed the three bridges and one ferry which led into the bridgehead itself. Supplies reaching here were mule-borne and hand-carried into the forward positions. [9]

For objectives in Phase I of the attack, while the 351st moved against Santa Maria Infante, the 350th received the objectives of Mount Damiano, Ventosa, and Mount Rotondo. The 349th remained generally in Division reserve. In Phase II the 350th Infantry was to press on against Mount Cerri and Mount Bracchi; and in Phase III, while the 351st moved against Mount Civita, the 350th was to move against Spigno. (See Map 7).

In addition to support from the 383th Engineer Battalion, 313th Medical Battalion, 88th Recon Troop, self-propelled artillery of the 760th Tank Battalion, 804th Tank Destroyer Batallion, and 753rd Tank Battalion, the 350th had attached a 220-mule detachment from the 67th Italian Infantry.[10]

In the disposition of the Regiment, the First Battalion held the right flank near the crest of Mount Damiano; the Second was immediately on the left and also near the crest; and the Third occupied the westward slopes of Mount Damiano and Mount Salvatito where it protected the floor of the Ausente River valley. Opposing the regiment, elements of the 194th and 211th German Infantry Regiments of the 71st Division barred the coming advance. These enemy positions were very well organized atop the double-crested Mount Damiano. The higher crest held by the Germans rose to 413 meters while further north and west arose a distinct feature, Hill 316, also well organized and defended by anti-tank mines and barbed wire hung with noise-making devices. No foliage covered the peaks but only rock and loose shale., Here on the higher crests were individual and gun positions prepared by piling up stones to form sangars, since it was impossible to dig foxholes in this terrain. It was extremely difficult to fire into these positions effectively.

Mount Rotondo, a hill of 342 meters and lightly defended, was devoid of the well-built sangars found on Mount Damiano. Mounts Ceracoili, Cerri, and Bracchi were well organized in the more conventional fashion. Here were found foxholes, large dugouts, and improvised pillboxes as well as occasional sangars on out-croppings of rock. Spigno, high on the cliffs west of the Ausente Valley, was garrisoned but not organized for effective defense.

Roads leading to and through the area included a two-way unpaved road from Castelforte to the Ausente Valley while trails flanked the Ausente River, and a good unimproved road net, partially blocked by anti-tank mines, existed on the floor of

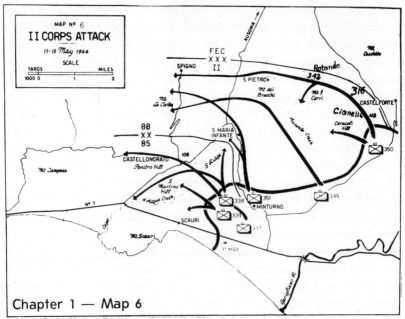

the western branch of the Ausente Valley. Although the river was bridged and also fordable at several points, the sparse trail net in the eastern branch of the valley restricted the number of wheeled transport which could be employed. Only one trail passable to mules broke the sheer cliff leading to Spigno.

In the first phase of the attack, Colonel Fry planned to in-

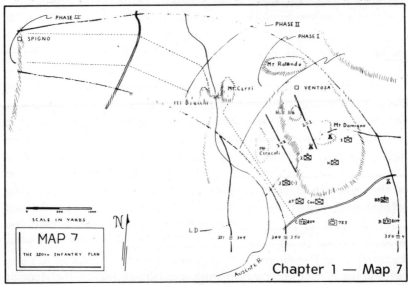

volve the First and Second Battalions in capturing Mount Damiano, Hill 316, and Ventosa, while the Third Battalion captured Mount Ceracoli and maintained contact with units on the left. While the 88th Recon protected the right flank, the Anti-Tank Company and supporting units of the 804th Tank Destroyer Batallion were to protect flanks against armored attack. Other units of engineers and medics were in general support. After securing the first objectives, the units best disposed were then to swing west to take Mount Cerri, Mount Bracchi, and Spigno.[11]

To mark boundaries between company and battalion boundaries, the Regiment employed the use of solid tracers drawing the line in the sky close above the heads of troops on Damiano - 40 mm for battalion boundaries and 50 cal. for company boundaries. To facilitate identification, each man was ordered to wear a white strip of clothing on the back of each arm between the shoulder and the elbow. Mules and Italian porters were allocated to each unit. [12]

On May 11 the day dawned ominously overcast. Some rain laid the dust. Commanders feared that the work of weeks in laying tracks and clearing mines would disappear once more in squelching Italian mud. By evening, however, the sky cleared and a mist started to rise in the river valleys. At 11 PM precisely 2000 guns opened the artillery programmes from Cassino to the sea. Operation Diadem had started. [13]

While the 88th attacked for Santa Maria Infante and Hill 413 (Damiano), the 36th Infantry Division was to be ready to pass through after the 88th had taken Spigno and Mount La Civita.[14] Before the artillery barrage at 2300 hours, May 11, the men of the 350th had noted the fields of scarlet poppies nodding and bobbing in the faint sea breeze. The smoke pots at the Minturno bridge drifted the acrid haze across the valley. Incoming shells punctured the stillness now and then with an incoming crash.[15] When the artillery barrage began at 2300 hours, a Bofors guns started sending its red tracers ricocheting up the mountain sides in the zone of the 350th to mark the boundary between the two assault battalions. Colonel Fry had been ordered to break German resistance on the right in the hills southwest of Castelforte.[16] Before daylight the attacking battalions had moved swiftly, the First on Hill 413 and the Second on Hill 316 to the northwest and had consolidated their conquests and so had secured the left flank of the French attack on Castelforte.

In the plans of attack the First was to capture and organize the defense of the crest of Mount Cianelli and then to advance on order. The Second, abreast along the western slope of the mountain, was to capture the final objective, Hill 316, on beyond Cianelli and part of the chain of hills running on toward the northeast. The Third for most part was in reserve except for one company which had the mission of capturing Mount Ceracoli, a minor hill in the Ausente Valley. For fear of enemy observation, the 350th had to occupy Mount Cianelli before daylight. Captain Floyd B. Haegstrom commanded the company responsible for that particular part of the attack.[17] (See Map 8.)

Along with the massive artillery pounding, the Air Force aided immeasurably in flying 1500 sorties and did a workmanlike job in knocking out enemy positions and battering the inadequate mountain communications routes over which he could move up reinforcements.[18] As a result of these attacks,

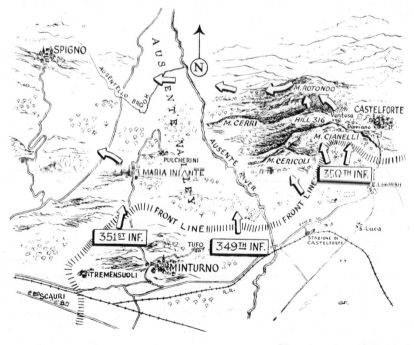

Chapter 1 — Map 8

by morning of May 12 both the enemy Tenth Army and Fourteenth Corps Headquarters had almost ceased to function. Both were minus their commanders, who were away on leave, and their deputies had to carry on against the massive Fifth and Eighth Army attacks. In the first days of the assault, however, Field Marshall Albert Kesselring realized that his fears of an airborne landing or a fresh invasion in his rear had no substance; thus he could order the movement and use of stratetic reserves into the battle zone.[19] However, he could not stem the tide of the advancing II Corps and the 350th Infantry.

The First Battalion of the 350th immediately scored a success in its attack. On the right the battalion sent two companies moving up through the olive groves on the terraced southern slopes of Hill 413, while the third rifle company maneuvered around the north side to strike the village of Ventosa. It was only forty-six minutes after the push-off that the height was taken from the 194th Grenadier Regiment in one fierce charge. Although the opposition was not as stiff as had been expected, the enemy yet resisted stubbornly from his concrete pillboxes and rock-lined foxholes until overrun and destroyed. During the night the battalion consolidate its possession. [20]

Very soon after the attack began, Company A became disorganized as the fighting progressed, having suffered severe casualties from enemy fire.[21] Previously the battalion had made considerable progress with A and B Companies advancing abreast, and company C still in reserve. After the disorganization of Company A, Company K now moved through Company A's ranks and attacked while the latter moved back to reorganize. Subsequently Companies B and K moved forward to their objectives, which they secured by daylight. At ths time Company C ran into heavy machine gun and mortar fire in its reserve position on the east side of Mt. Cianelli and could not advance until the French attacked on the right.

It was after the disorganization of Company A, following the feigned sudden illness of a company commander, that Colonel Fry ordered Colonel Coleman, Commanding Officer of the Third Battalion, to move up Company K. At this time also when a company commanding officer in Second Battalion became fearful, Lt. Richard Harwood, S-3, took command of the company.

In the First Battalion sector one platoon of Company K, now

attached under the command of Colonel Bare, attacked Ventosa and found it unoccupied. The Blue Devils captured an estimated fifty prisoners of war here and killed approximately the same number. The capture of Mt. Cianelli by the First Battalion gave the Regiment the dominating terrain in this part of the Fifth Army front. [22] Securing of this position aided the French immeasurably in their attack on Little Cassino, Castelforte, on the right.

The attacks of the First and Second Battalions on Mount Damiano can be described as almost a single entity of action. Almost immediately after the jump-off Company E encountered a minefield. It was here that Sergeant Shea would perform magnificiently, earning for himself the nation's highest award, the Congressional Medal of Honor. S-Sgt. Charles W. "Red" Shea of the Bronz, New York, a one-time peanut butcher at Yankee Stadium, went over the crest of Damiano shortly after dawn. By this time his platoon leader had been killed and the platoon sergeant wounded. While taking cover from enemy artillery, Sergeant Shea spotted two trip wires at his head and feet. He realized that he was in the middle of a minefield.

When Kraut machine gun fire opened up on his men, Shea did not hesitate but rose, started forward, and then turned just in time to see a German emerging from another machine gun position and pointing his machine pistol at him. Shea leveled his rifle, whereupon the Kraut surrendered. Four other Germans occupied the same position, but one refused to come out. Motioning with his rifle for the others to return to the rear, Shea then moved to deal with the other one in the gun position. As the last Kraut in the position rose to toss a grenade at an officer leading another platoon, Shea got him with one shot.

He then maneuvered to keep out of range of the enemy gunner, when suddenly he found himself directly beneath another machine gun next, "so close," he later related, "that I could have reached out and touched the barrel." Again one German refused to come out of this position after Sergeant Shea had captured two more Krauts with him. Suddenly this last remaining Kraut stood upright and fired eight shots from a P38 at Shea from less than 15 yards. Shea then pulled off eight rounds from his rifle and also missed, whereupon both now ducked for cover. Sergeant Shea now waited, another clip in his rifle. Spotting the German a few moments later, with blood streaming down one side of his face as he rose to toss a grenade, Shea fired. Dying, the Kraut heaved his potato-masher, but it was his last, futile gesture.[23]

In the Second Battalion positions, Company E held the portion of the battalion zone extending around Damiano and connecting with F Company in the rear, then in battalion reserve. Company G held the right portion of the battalion zone, extending to the right side of Mt. Damiano and joining with the First Battalion. In crossing its line of departure, Second Battalion had Companies E and G attacking abreast. After the crest of Mount Damiano had been secure, they were then to swing left to Hill 316, and Company F was to move from its rear position behind Company E and follow by bounds and protect the left flank of the battalion. A few minutes before time to cross the Line of Departure, the battalion commanding officer discovered that the commanding officer of Company E and his men had failed to reach the jump-off point.[24]

When a gap thus developed between Companies E and G, Lt. Col. Corbett Williamson, commanding the Second Battalion, committed Company F to close it.[25] About this time, around 2350 hours, the First Battalion, under Lt. Col. Walter E. Bare, announced it had taken the upper crest of Damiano. It was shortly thereafter that Company A encountered a minefield. The company had already suffered some casualties, perhaps from the fire of the 350th's own cannon company. Colonel Fry now attached Company K to the First Battalion and ordered Company L to Damiano to become the regimental reserve. By 0145, May 12, the Second Battalion reported Hill 316 secured. The First Battalion, meanwhile, pushed forward until daylight against increasing resistance, but by daylight elements of K Company had reached the town of Ventosa.[26]

In the Second Battalion sector, after the delay of Company E in moving forward, Company F now crossed on the left and G on the right. Under the capable leadership of Captain Roeder, Company G moved to the right to avoid mines and protective wire, while F moved straight forward, advancing very slowly through the minefield by infiltration. By 0430 at the beginning of light, the two assault companies had moved forward into the saddle between Hill 316 and Mount Damiano; they had bypassed many Germans but had eliminated the organized resistance in the area. Casualties had been heavy. The battalion had very little if any organized control. Company E, now under the leadership of one second lieutenant, had moved up and had joined Company F.

By 0600 hours, May 12, Colonel Williamson decided to hold what ground the Second Battalion had taken and to reorganize. Movement was extremely limited because of sniping from small groups of resistance still holding out on Hill 316. Exhibiting outstanding leadership, Colonel Williamson reorganized the battalion for the continuance of the attack on Hill 316.[27]

At dawn on May 12 the Third Battalion moved against Mount Ceracoli, west and at the base of Mount Cianelli and well forward in the Ausente Valley. Behind the attack of Lt. Col. Joe Felber's Company C, of 753 Tank Battalion, Captain Tom Cussans, Company I, led his company forward and promptly mopped up and occupied the position.[28]

For May 12 Colonel Bare of the First Battalion had the task of reorganizing the company that had failed in the initial night attack. He placed Company K in that company's former position on the left near the crest of Cianelli. Colonel Fry now planned for the Second Battalion to advance along the ridge to complete the capture of Hill 316 and for the First Battalion to swing through the town of Ventosa and pass on to capture Mount Rotondo.[29]

Despite the difficult terrain, plus enemy artillery, machine gun and mortar fire, the battalion held its objective and had dug in by daylight against an anticipted counterattack. When a strong German force struck the western slopes of the hill just before dawn, American artillery and mortars blasted the attacking Krauts while the Second Battalion covered the enemy with rifle and machine gun fire. The Germans were soon fleeing in confusion.

The 350th had now secured its initial objective from the Ausente around to Castelforte. The Blue Devils now waited until the French had cleared the north side of the Castelforte road (May 13). The Regiment would launch an attack on this day for its second objective, Mount Rotondo. With the acquisition of Rotondo, the Regiment would have completed the aid which had been requested by the FEC.[30]

At night time the wounded came back down the mountain.

The accomplishments that second night, May 12, were very limited. During the night Colonel Williamson gradually succeeded in easing Company F northward along Hill 316. To reach the next objective, Mount Rotondo, the Regiment would have to traverse a deep valley that separated this peak from the northernmost nose of Cianelli. The Germans now dropped back beyond this terrain to their second line of resistance. On the right of the line, Colonel Bare moved his battalion abreast of the French forces that had occupied the hills across the valley to the east. Daylight found the First and Second Battalions in this line.[31]

After little action during the daylight hours of May 13, primarily because of the difficulty of the 351st on the left and the slowness of the French to pull abreast on the right, the First and Second Battalions resumed the attack against the Krauts around 1700 hours. The First Battalion attacked with Companies B, L, and K abreast, K on the right and C Company in reserve. The Second Battalion supported this attack by fire, but E Company did advance to the western slopes of Rotondo and maintained contact with Company B.[32] It took only two hours and forty-five minutes for the two battalions to score a complete success. Company K secured the crest of Rotondo at 1945 hours on May 13. The First Battalion was then ordered to be prepared to move against Mounts Cerri and Bracchi, and the Regimental Command Post moved from Damiano to the valley floor south of Mount Ceracoli.

While this operation was in progress, the enemy had started a withdrawal; to cover the breach of their line, the Krauts began a counter-artillery fire pounding the 350th's lines to delay the advance. Colonel Fry acted upon a report to get fire on Rotondo, because the Krauts were running along the peak like rabbits and setting up machine guns. The replacement for Colonel Lively, Lt. Col. Rankin, directed fire against the enemy. The report from observers of this action read: "That's wonderful. We're killing plenty of Jerries. Keep it up. They're running like hell." At this time the first group of replacements began going forward on the afternoon of May 13.

Meanwhile a report from Major Mike Oreskovitch told of the French having advanced into the hills somewhere beyond Castelforte, but no one knew the extent of the advance. Under these circumstances, the Goums, the colorful African mountain fighters, were all set to advance up the Ausente Valley. Major Mike concluded the report: "Jerry is pulling out—they seem to be in full retreat everywhere."[33]

Although the 350th Infantry had made significant gains against the enemy on May 11 and 12, the Kraut commander of the 94th Division, General Steinmetz, issued an order of the day at dark on May 13 congratulating his troops on their success against the 88th and 85th Divisions' attacks. He said that "in spite of several enemy penetrations into our advanced positions, the main field of battle remains in our hands." Events on the French zone, however, had influenced greatly the withdrawal generally of the Germans from their defensive positions. In General Raapke's 71st Division sector the loss of Monte Faito and Castelforte on the first day seemed to have unsettled his defences. After the Kraut General Raapke had committed his immediate reserves early in the day, a single battalion of the 15th Panzer Grenadier Division was thrown in and decimated in the attempts to retake Monte Faito.

By evening, Raapke seemed to have appreciated the fact that his division was holding a long sector of the front against the might of the French Corps four division attack. Since the XIV Panzer Corps Commander, General Von Senger, was on leave to Germany, the less experienced deputy commander of the corps apparently decided that the withdrawal to a shorter line covering Ausonia was the only answer to Raapke's plea for reinforcements. As the Germans thus withdrew to establish themselves on a new line from San Giorgio on the Liri to Ausonia, thereby blocking the French axis of advance around the northern side of the Aurunci Mountains, they made no provision for the defence of tracks through the Auruncis as the area was deemed Impassable for all practical mililary purposes. At this time Steinmetz's 94th Division was generally continuing to block Keyes' II Corps axis around the southern side of the Auruncis;[34] but it was precisely through the Aurunci tracks that the Goums would pour to knife through the enemy defences.

Another factor in the success of the 350th's and II Corps' attack and the French Corps drive was the deception plan in Alexander's strategy. Kesselring had expected another Anzio-type landing in his rear and thus had weakened his front lines. In a cover plan for the mythical Civitavecchia landing beyond

Rome, the 36th Division had been sent back to Naples where its activities for amphibious training were well publicized. Further detachments of Canadian troops as cover were added, and allied aircraft repeatedly flew observation missions over the beaches of Civitavecchia. [35]

Although the belt of fortifications in front of II Corps had made the attack a slow-nibbling process, by dusk of May 13 II Corps had achieved important gains. The Spigno road junction was threatened, and the enemy had no substantial reinformcements. It was at this juncture that the French entered the Ausonia Valley. Before dawn the incessant attacks of II Corps and the French forced the enemy to withdraw from all his positions in accordance with an order from the German command to retreat to the Dora Line. [36] The French and Americans now pursued rapidly in order to attack the enemy's new line before he could get set. In the next day or two, II Corps and the French had broken the back of German resistance in the Ausonia Valley, wiping out the 71st Grenadier Division and battering the 94th Grenadier Division severely. From this time on the advancing Americans and French never ceased their powerful forward movement. [37]

The first week of Diadem, 11–18 May

Chapter 1 — Map 9

The line that the 350th and II Corps would now face, the Dora Line, was actually an extension of the Hitler line. In the northern section, the line blocked the Liri Valley and was fully fortified; the southern sector, called the Dora extension, actually entailed a staff planning line on which a few rudimentary defences had been started. The main points in the line ran from the village of Piedemonte on the slopes of Monte Cairo, north and east of Cassino, through Pontecorvo to Saint Olivia on the south side of the Liri River; it then continued through the Aurunci Mountains, in the 350th's area, to the coast. (See Map 9). [38]

With the withdrawal northwards of Raapke's exhausted troops of the 71st Division, a widening gap appeared in the center of XIV Panzer Corps' front - the very gap which the French commander, General Juin, had anticipated and for which he had organized the justly famous Mountain Corps (the Goums). With the fall of Castelforte on the evening of May 12, these Tabors moved silently through the ruins of the town and lay concealed along the hills to the west of the town throughout May 13 while the fighting had been going on to clear Monte Majo and the hills between Castelforte and the Ausonia road. On the night of May 13-14 the Goums received the orders for putting into effect the carefully prepared plan for breaking through the Aurunci chain. As the gap between the two German divisions, the 71st falling back north-eastwards on Ausonia and the 94th Division being pressed back by Keyes' Corps in a north-westerly direction along Route 7 and the coast, the conditions were perfect for the Goums to knife their way through the Aurunci escarpment, now almost undefended. [39]

In Keyes' II Corps sector, and the 350th's area, May 14 proved to be a turning point. General Steinmetz of the 94th Division realized that the withdrawal of Raapke's 71st troops on Ausonia had made his position untenable on the coast and that he would thus have to disengage and withdraw rapidly to the Senger Line if he was not to be surrounded and cut off on the coast. As he started his withdrawal on May 14, the 88th Division by nightfall approached Spigno at the foot of the Auruncis.

The horse-drawn artillery and transport made for slow withdrawal of the battered 94th Grenadier Division. Because of the success of the 88th Division particularly, General Clark, who had not expected to reach the Itri-Pico road with such ease and had envisaged shipping most of Keyes' Corps round to the Anzio beachhead as soon as it was clear that little further progress was likely along the coast or through mountains, now instituted significant changes in the attack because of the spectacular success of the French and II Corps. [40]

As the pursuit of the fleeing enemy began on May 14, the First and Second Battalions received the mission of moving directly west into the Ausente Valley. [41] Before daylight the First attacked toward the west and captured Monte Cerri; then Companies B and C joined Company A and attacked northwest, taking San Pietro on the north slope of Monte Bracchi. The battalion then moved to the east into an assembly position in the Ausente Valley and prepared to attack Spigno at daylight. This town lay at the beginning of the Ausente Valley, with Mount Cianelli on the right and Santa Maria Infante on the left. [42] The opposition encountered during the day was light artillery fire. Moving about six or seven miles across country on this day, the Second captured about twenty-five prisoners.

By early dawn the Second Battalion generally faced west along the slopes of Cianelli and Hill 316 and began moving cautiously toward the valley. The Third Battalion had the task of moving up the valley as a covering force while the other two battalions moved directly west into the Ausente. [43]

As the Third Battalion moved its rear command to Hill 100 and sent out a quartering party to Mount Cerri, they encountered a few mines but a number of well-dug German positions. Arriving on Mount Cerri, Companies K and L discovered the mountains had already been taken over by the 88th Reconnaissance Troops. After the troops had marched about two miles to Mount Cerri, they then dug in for the night. [44]

On this date the First Battalion secured San Pietro on the north slope of Mount Bracchi and then moved east to the assembly positions in the Ausente Valley in preparation to attack Spigno at daylight. From the vicinity of Ceracoli, the Second Battalion moved to join the Regimental Commander to the north up the Ausente Valley and bivouaced for the night in the vicinity also of Mount Cerri. [45] In these operations when a battle-weary company commander refused to take his company to lead the advance of the Third Battalion's move toward Cerri, Colonel Fry sent him back to the surgeon and then sent

Major Matthews, Regimental S-3, to assume commnd of the company. [46]

As the 350th on May 14 and the following morning drove across Mount Cerri toward Spigno (which the First would enter at 0730, May 15), POW reports and abundance of German bodies and equipment strewn across the hills witnessed to the almost complete destruction of the 71st Grenadier Division and also the extreme crippling of the 94th Grenadier Division. The pursuit could continue in earnest on May 16. As victory was definitely assured, trails and roads began to fill with streams of men, mule trains, trucks, tanks and tank destroyers moving west. By this time the corps artillery had occupied advance positions also. [47] As the 350th moved on, the men accepted with pride a report of a POW: "...those men...bearded, dirty, tired, angry, charging...with the blue cloverleaf insignia, fought like devils." [48]

By this period of the battle, the French Goums seemed to be everywhere-riding horses, wearing striped robes, calling for medics and tourniquets. [49] These knife-wielding troops swarmed over the hills, seizing in their brilliant daring advances such towns and mountains as Cerasola, San Giorgio, Mt. D'Oro, Ausonia, and Esperia. By May 16 the French Expeditionary Corps, attacking with the American II Corps, had thrust forward some ten miles along their left flank to Mount Revole while the remainder of their front slanted back somewhat to keep contact with the British Eighth Army. [50]

As the II Corps moved rapidly forward, the leading elements of the 88th Division and the 350th Infantry rode on tanks of the 753rd Tank Destroyer Battalion, and the Second Battalion followed close behind. Two columns moved along parallel to east-west dirt roads. When mines stopped a tank on the right road and an ambulance on the left, the troops continued to move on foot. After crossing the valley without opposition, the battalion climed the tortuous single trail to Spigno but found the town devoid of the enemy. At Spigno a patrol from the 351st Infantry moving up the main road from the south joined the First Battalion. At this time the French Goumiers were streaming up the mountains in pursuit on the right of the regiment. As the 351st continued its march forward, the 350th was ordered back into the valley as division reserve. For its superior coordination, conducted mainly by the 350th the 88th

Division was awarded the French Croix de Guerre. [51]

It was early in the morning of May 15, at 0400 hours, that the Regiment, less the Third Battalion, moved on Spigno, with the First Battalion and Company E riding on tanks. Since it was decided that the Infantry would have a hard time getting through, General Kendall had decided for tank support to make a clearing on the morning of the advance. [52] As the Blue Devils approached the town, Italians came out of basements and raced down the hillside screaming, "Tedeschi via." It was at this time that the Regiment now received instructions to move back down the hill and assemble in division reserve. [53]

The Regiment had two days of relative rest and regrouped its strength in the valley below Spigno. Meanwhile the 349th and 351st Infantry Regiments were moving directly across the mountain ranges toward the important road intersection in the village of Itri while the 85th Division cleared the road along the western coast beyond Scauri. Itri assumed increased significance at this juncture as the withdrawal of German equipment would have to pass through the area. On the afternoon of May 17, the Regiment received orders to move by trail and road to Marincia and thence across the mountains to join the task force under General Kendall. [54]

By this time Kesselring realized that if he did not block the French and II Corps advance round the southern side of the Hitler Line, the greater part of Tenth Army would be encircled. He accordingly ordered reserve units into action, the 26th Panzer Division to move from its blocking position in the Alban Hills to the Pico-Pontecorvo area. He also ordered the 305th and 334th Divisions over from the Adriatic Coast, so that by May 18 three of the five German mobile divisions were committed, but piecemeal. Too late Kesselring did not realize that the attack in this sector of the Gustav was no more than a holding attack. The 15th Panzer Grenadier Divison had been devoured first in small groups trying to bolster the defeated 71st and 94th Divisions; the 90th Panzer Grenadier Division had come next and had been sucked into the Liri cauldron. Now the 26th Panzer and 305th Divisions were drawn into the battle in the same way, while the 29th Panzer Grenadier and the Herman Goering Divisions sat coast-watching north of Rome, looking for an invasion force which never embarked.

It was after the capture of Spigno that Axis Sally of Berlin inadvertently named the 88th the "Blue Devils," a badge of honor accepted willingly by the valiant 88th All-Selective Service Division. She now changed her tone from one of mild derision to hysterical screaming. The 88th were now "a bunch of bloodthirsty cut-throats" and "did not fight like gentlemen." After a couple of expletives, she dubbed the clover-leaf division "those blue devils." [55]

Around 0900 hours on May 18, the Regiment had reached positions in the hills above Itri. Prior to this date the Regiment had moved across the mountains toward Itri. Trucks had been sent to take the men as far as Trivio, a small village north of Formia, where they then would begin their trek through the hills. There was only a cart track in this area, then a mere trail, used by mules and goats. Stragglers were everywhere who stopped the advance. As the men moved in single file through the ravines and hills, they stopped on the night of May 17 and slept in their positions, some going into the hut of a peasant. In the high mountains, the cold was unusually penetrating. [56]

In the action for May 19, the 350th supported the 351st in its attack on Mount Grande. As the 351st launched a final attack on this feature, the 350th Infantry supported the advance. The next day, the 351st would reach the Itri-Pico road, and the 349th would enter Itri. With these important areas, Itri and Mount Grande in control of the 88th, the Germans were forced to fall back on Fondi. [57]

Kesselring's deep concern over the penetration of II Corps and Juin's North Africans over the Pico-Formia lateral road during May 19 was deepened when his 15th Panzer Grenadier Division could do nothing to stop the Allied onrush. On the front in the central Pico-Pontecorvo area, the 26th Panzer Division had shown signs of stabilizing the front, but he could do nothing against the 88th and the French. He now reluctantly ordered von Mackensen to send the 29th Panzer Grenadier Division down from Civitivecchia to block II Corps' advance in the potentially strong defensive position along Route 7 between Fondi and Terracina, the last defile before Route 7 emerged into the flat Pontine marsh area, leading straight to the southern edge of the Anzio Beachhead. Because of disagreement between Kesselring and von Mackensen, the 29th moved slowly and when it did, it found Americans on the high ground above the defile which should have been the basis of its defensive position.[58]   The 350th had significantly aided in eliminating German effective resistance in these areas.

In fresh instructions on May 18 to II Corps, General Keyes called for the 88th to move in conjunction with the FEC and to drive across the hills northwest of Fondi toward Roccagorga. As the 349th moved out from Itri shortly after midnight of May 19 and rapidly led the 88th Division rush up the highway throughout the morning of May 20, the 350th Regiment came behind, and ahead the 91st Cavalry Reconnaissance Squadron ranged over the Fondi plain. By late afternoon of this day, when the 349th Infantry had taken Fondi, reinforcements streamed from Itri to Fondi along the road filled with trucks, armor and artillery. Both sides of the road were lined with marching men.[59]

While the 85th moved on Terracina, the 88th Division drove northwest across the mountains. The 350th came up from Fondi and broke through stiff resistance to occupy Mount Calvo on May 21, netting 110 prisoners in the attack. In this action eight Americans were killed, among whom was Captain Vick, 338th FA Battalion. The Second Battalion was now placed in division reserve near Fondi, with one company left to hold the hill until the 85th Division replaced them there. [60]

The following day, the 350th Infantry continued to push northwest toward Roccasecca. [61] For the next few days the Regiment would move rapidly to become the farthest advanced salient on the Fifth Army Front. The battles for Roccasecca and the San Biagio battle marked a second stage in the 350th action on the Road to Rome.

Before May 11, 1944, the south side of Mount Cianelli.

Lt. Charles W. Shea.
He won a Congressional Medal of Honor in the first few
hours of combat.

The rear of Mt. Cianelli, the first regimental objedtive, as seen from the regimental command post.

Another view of the first regimental objective.

Sketched at Fondi, Italy, May 27, 1944, by Pvt. G. Fagerholm.

U.S. Army Infantrymen wind their way across a small valley high in the mountains of Mt. St. Angelo, on the trail to Itri, May, 1944.

Sketch by Gus Fagerholm—Italian Theater, 1944 - 350th Infantry Reg't. from the collection of William Gardner Bell.

Members of M. Company, 350th Infantry Regiment, march on road past Spigno Road junction in Castellonarato, May, 1944.

Footnotes to Chapter I

[1] John P. Delaney, **The Blue Devils in Italy** (New York, 1947), 44.

[2] **Ibid.**, 46-58

[3] Lt. Col. Chester G. Starr (editor), **From Salerno to the Alps: A History of the Fifth Army, 1943-1945** (Washington, D.C., 1948), 176-177.

[4] **Fifth Army History**, V, 23.

[5] Starr, **From Salerno to the Alps**, 180-181.

[6] **Fifth Army History**, V, 27.

[7] Starr, **From Salerno to the Alps**, 182.

[8] **Fifth Army History**, V, 28.

[9] **Ibid.**, 8.

[10] **Historical Documents, WW II**, AGO Microfilming Job No. 200, AGO (TIS Library), Fort Benning Georgia, and Field Order No. 6.

[11] G-2 Summaries, 350th Infantry Regiment, May 10-15, 1944.

[12] 350th Infantry Regiment History, May, 1944.

[13] W.G.F. Jackson, The Battle for Italy (New York, 1967), 231.
[14] Starr, **From Salerno to the Alps**, 198.
[15] Delaney, **The Blue Devils in Italy**, 62.
[16] Starr, **From Salerno to the Alps**, 199.
[17] James C. Fry, **Combat Soldier** (Washington, D.C., 1968), 18.
[18] Mark W. Clark, **Calculated Risk** (New York, 1950) 347.
[19] Albert Kesselring, **A Soldier's Record** (New York, 1954), 241.
[20] **Fifth Army History**, V, 57.
[21] 350th Infantry Regiment History, May, 1944.
[22] First Battalion History, 350th Infantry Regiment, May, 1944.
[23] Delaney, **The Blue Devils in Italy**, 67.
[24] Major Richard Harwood, ''The Operations of the Second Battalion, 350th Infantry (88th Infantry Division) in the Supported Night Attack on the Gustav Line, East of Minturno, Italy, 11-13 May 1944,'' The Infantry School, Fort Benning, Georgia, Advanced Infantry Officers Course, Class No. 1, 1952-1953.
[25] 350th Infantry Regiment History, May, 1944.
[26] Ibid.
[27] Personal Knowledge, Captain Harwood, Lecture, Fort Benning, Georgia, 1952-1953.
[28] Fry, **Combat Soldier**, 30.
[29] Ibid., 32.
[30] **Fifth Army History**, V, 59.
[31] Fry, **Combat Soldier**, 33.
[32] Statement by Major Erwin B. Jone, then S-3 of Second Battalion, quoted by Major Milton A. Matthews, Lecture, TIS, Fort Benning, Georgia, ''Operations of the 350th Infantry (88th Infantry Division) in the Attack on Mount Damiano, West of Castelforte, Italy, and Subsequent Objectives, 11-15 May, 1944 (Rome-Arno Campaign).'' Personal Experiences of a Regimental S-2, 1949-1950.
[33] Fry, **Combat Soldier**, 34-36.
[34] W.G.F. Jackson, **The Battle for Rome** (New York, 1969), 110-111.
[35] Robert H. Adelman and Colonel George Walton, **Rome Fell Today** (Boston, 1968), 205.
[36] Starr, **From Salerno to the Alps**, 205.
[37] Clark, **Calculated Risk**, 349.
[38] Jackson, **The Battle for Italy**, 233.
[39] Jackson, **The Battle for Rome**, 143.
[40] Ibid.
[41] Fry, **Combat Soldier**, 40-41.
[42] First Battalion History, May, 1944.
[43] Fry, **Combat Soldier**, 40-41.
[44] Third Battalion History, May, 1944.
[45] 350th Infantry Regiment History, May, 1944.
[46] Fry, **Combat Soldier**, 41.
[47] Starr, **From Salerno to the Alps**, 207.
[48] Delaney, **The Blue Devils in Italy**, 73.
[49] Fry, **Combat Soldier**, 40.
[50] Clark, **Calculated Risk**, 348.
[51] Decision 843, **Cites to the Order of the Army by Charles DeGaulle**, June 21, 1945. Personal Posession of Major John E. Boothe, Fort Benning, Georgia, 1952.
[52] Fry, **Combat Soldier**, 45.
[53] 350th Infantry Regiment History, May, 1944.
[54] Jackson, **The Battle for Italy**, 237.
[55] Delaney, **The Blue Devils in Italy**, 79.
[56] Fry, **Combat Soldier**, 50-53.
[57] Starr, **From Salerno to the Alps**, 208-209.
[68] Jackson, **The Battle for Italy**, 239-240.
[69] Starr, **From Salerno to the Alps**, 217.
[60] 350th Infantry Regiment History, May, 1944.
[61] **Fifth Army History**, V, 83.

Chapter Two

The San Biagio - Roccasecca - Roccagorga Battles, May 20-26, 1944

After occupying Mount Calvo on the night of May 20, the Regiment moved out the next morning at 0500, the Second on the left and the First in the center. The First quickly reached its objective as it encountered no resistance, so it now became the lead battalion; the Second, however, ran into stiff resistance as it tried to enter the mountains. Here the Germans were defending the valley south of San Biagio from the hills on both sides. (See Map 1).

The major action, however, for the 88th as a unit during this period consisted in capturing an extnesive range of enemy positions from Monte Monsicardi all the way to Roccasecca dei Volsci, the farthest advanced position of the Fifth Army at that time. By May 22 the 88th had moved on to Monte Monsicardi. By its dash and aggressiveness the division had prevented the enemy from getting set in the Hitler Line in the region. Neither did Kesselring have time to bring up sufficient reinforcements to stem the tide. Having gained the mountain positions north and northwest of Fondi, the division protected the displacement forward of corps artillery. The 88th had drawn well ahead of the French left flank by this time. II Corps accordingly ordered the division to hold and improve its gains, while pushing an advanced guard northwest to Roccasecca dei Volsci, a point that the 350th reached on May 23[1]

The German view of the debacle about this time centers

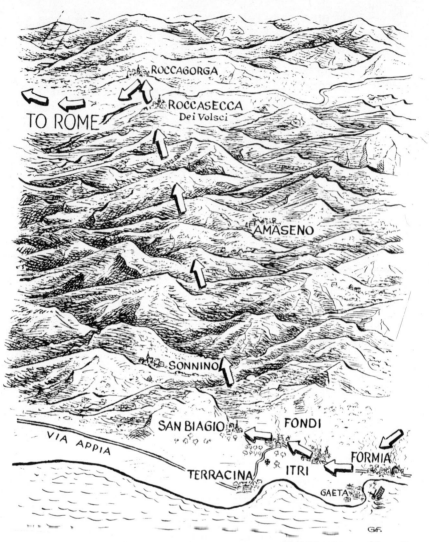

ROCCAGORGA

TO ROME

ROCCASECCA
Dei Volsci

AMASENO

SONNINO

SAN BIAGIO   FONDI

VIA APPIA   FORMIA

TERRACINA   ITRI

GAETA

G.F.

Chapter 2 — Map 1

about the inability to withdraw the divisions back into the
Senger barrier, running from Terracina through Fondi to
Pontecorvo, because the Krauts had to fight in front of the line
in order to preserve the junction with LI Mountain Corps,
fighting north of the Liri. Thus the divisions were thrown back
and never made a stand at the Senger barrier. (Indeed, the
Blue Devils were after the Krauts in a hurry.) Nevertheless,
the commander of the German XIV Panzer Corps moved his
divisions back in a northerly direction, offering occasional

Page 34

resistance, to an assembly point at Frosinone. He still had to maintain contact with the LI Corps on the left until all the troops fighting in the Liri Valley had again been put under unified control. While the 29th Panzer Grenadier Division engaged the French on a broad front, the XIV Corps generally withdrew northward with the main body of retreating troops, as the II American Corps generally pushed on westwards past XIV Corps.[2]

General Clark praises the exploits of the 88th Division on the southern front in this engagement:

> On May 22 the 88th Division on the southern front smashed northwestward across the mountains above the Fondi Plain to Mount Monsicardi and thus sealed the fate of the Hitler Line. While elements of the 85th Division were pushing across the Fondi Plain toward Terracina on the coast, the 350th Infantry of the 88th Division made a bold thrust from the center, deep behind the enemy positions toward the village of Roccasecca dei Volsci.[3]

In this push toward Fondi on Highway 7, men carried 50 millimeter mortars in baby carriages, and sometimes a bicycle supported a number of bandoleers of ammo. In pushing toward Roccasecca, the men passed through a road that bent sharply left in the town of Fondi; directly ahead and to the northwest lay the high mountain mass of Mount Calvo. Two valleys led upward into the mountain from the vicinity of Fondi, one from directly beyond the village, and one farther to the west, from the vicinity of San Biagio. The First Battalion had the orders to follow tentatively the large valley directly beyond Fondi while the Second covered the left and cleared the entrance to a small valley beyond San Biagio. The Third was to follow close column behind the First after the latter had moved out to get the mountains. Colonel Corbett Williamson of the Second was to move through San Biagio about a mile to the west. He then could follow Colonel Coleman's Third up the main valley or go up the valley beyond San Biagio if the route was not too difficult for passage.[4]

To implement the May 19 order from Fifth Army to cut the Sezze-Frosinone Road with maximum speed, the 88th Division was to drive across the hills northwest of Fondi toward Roccagorga while the 85th Division moved on its left flank toward Sezze. The area facing II Corps included a series of high mountains, deep gorges, river valleys, and flooded coastal plains. The sector varied in width from ten to twenty miles; from Itri to Sezze the distance across the mountains was thirty miles.[5] In implementing its orders of May 20, the 350th was to pass through Fondi and attack to northwest toward Roccasecca, while the 349th attacked on the right and the 351st took the mountain features along the Lenola-Vallecorsa Road and protected the division's right flank until the French caught up.[6] The First was to take Mount Casareccio, the Third Mount Latiglia, and the Second Mount Calvo. The First was to move directly from Fondi toward its objective, and then the Third was to move through the First to take Mount Latiglia, while the Second moved west along Highway 7 about 6000 yards and attacked Mount Calvo from the south. The Regiment would then move to Roccasecca, taking each mountain feature in turn. (See Map 2).

At dawn on May 21, the Regiment moved through Fondi.[7] The First, followed by the Third, moved toward San Magno and the Second moved west along Highway 7. The First went over

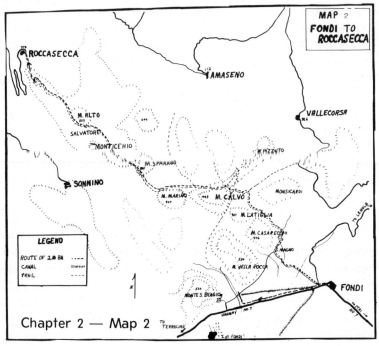

MAP 2
FONDI TO ROCCASECCA

LEGEND
ROUTE OF 2.ᴰ BN ....
CANAL ⊪⊪⊪⊪⊪
TRAIL ----

Chapter 2 — Map 2

Mount Casareccio without encountering any resistance and then proceeded to Mount Latiglia and Mount Calvo in turn. After spending the night on Mount Calvo, the First and Third Battalions moved out early on May 22 along a trail to northwest to Mount Alto, where they stopped for the night, the First on Mount Alto and the Third to the south on Salvatore. On May 23, the First Battalion moved into Roccasecca and the Third garrisoned the high ground overlooking the town. This point reached ten miles ahead of Fifth Army lines. These two battalions, led by the Regimental Commander, had slipped through the Hitler Line. [8]

After again paralleling the FEC at the beginning of the drive, the 88th now drew well ahead of the French left flank, which was driving toward Vallecorsa against heavy rear-guard action. The rest of II Corps now halted to hold its gains while the advance guard pushed northwest to Roccasecca dei Folsci on May 23. By May 24 the First Battalion had completely occupied Roccasecca while the Third garrisoned the high ground overlooking the town.

In the fighting to reach this position, the First Battalion under Lt. Colonel Walter E. Bare had moved through the valley without resistance and reported on the morning of the 21st that its advance guard would soon be on top of the first ridge, well on the way to Mount Calvo. At this point Lt. Colonel Williamson's Second Battalion engaged in a firefight near San Biagio, but Lt. Colonel Bare by this time had already led his battalion far past the position where the enemy were supposedly in front of the Second Battalion. In actuality, the enemy occupied all commanding heights around the Second with machine guns, so the action was scarcely a rear guard affair. [9]

After conferring in person with Lt. Colonel Williamson; the Executive Officer, Captain Ray M. Simpson; and the artillery Liaison Officer, Captain Mike Vick, Colonel Fry moved on forward on a tank and waved goodby to Captain Clifford M. Skalby, who was killed two hours later trying to help a wounded private. Colonel Fry's small group followed the trail by the K ration boxes left by the advancing Blue Devils. By evening he had come abreast of the First on the crest of Mount Calvo, where they spent the night. [10] The First had advanced approximately ten and one half miles during the day. [11] As the Third Battalion moved rapidly to join the rear of the First, Lt.

Colonel Avery Cochran, Executive Officer, changed the order of moving the Second into Division reserve, and thereby perhaps saved the rear of the First and Third Battalions.[12]

The march continued on May 22. Captain Borquist, S-3, and Colonel Bare became dubious of the assignment; the 349th, supposed to be on the right flank, was not in position. The First, nevertheless, was ordered to push along as rapidly as possible but to keep flank guards out. Colonel Fry hoped to get the high ground in front of Roccasecca that night. The Regiment, well in front of units on right and left, stretched along the mountain range, leading generally to northeast. Colonel Fry describes the march:

> Long plodding column of men moving steadily forward, their gray steel helmets, coveralls, and ammo bandoleers swung about their shoulders blending with the rocks and shrubbery. They would sit on their helmets when they stopped for rest. [13]

By evening the First and Third Battalions moved into a perimeter of defense about Roccasecca, with the hope that the Second would join the next day.[14] Since the Second had been stopped by the German force in between them and the First and Third Battalions, no food or ammunition could arrive from the rear until Colonel Williamson's Second had dislodged the Jerries in between the units. It was at this time that the four men of the radio team sacrificed their lives for their comrades.

In the 350th's thrust forward toward Roccasecca, four radio men led the advancing elements - Corporal Leonard Denlein, Northampton, Massachusetts; Pfc Walter Kaleka, Brooklyn, New York, Private Norman Fagan, Buffalo, New York, and Private Edward S. Wilbur, Detroit, Michigan, all of Headquarters Company, 350th Infantry.[14] They continued to report the action of the enemy from their road communications post ahead of the American front lines, although it meant death for three and capture for the fourth. They had volunteered to set up the important station and stayed at their posts, braving certain death, until they found themselves completely surrounded by enemy forces. The Silver Star was awarded posthumously to three of the gallant soldiers, who were killed May 23 in the vicinity of Roccasecca dei Volsci. Private Edward Wilber of Detroit was listed as "missing in action."

Private Fagan, the only regularly assigned radio operator in the party, was accompanied by the others who had volunteered for the task when they learned the necessity of establishing communications in the area at that time.

In their initial report, they stated that 20 Germans had been sighted at the foot of the hill; next, that the radio station was surrounded and that the enemy was approaching them on the three sides of the hill. There then followed a final message-a message that stated calmly that the gallant Blue Devils had abandoned their secondary position and were moving down the west slope of the hill. Carrying their heavy radio with them, they optimistically added that they "would check back in the nets" as soon as possible. Three of their bodies were found later by advancing troops who reached the scene of their final broadcasts.[15]

On the next day, May 23, Colonel Fry decided that the proper strategy would be to use machine gun and mortar fire to clock the road opposite the advanced position, inasmuch as going into the valley would invite annihilation. Captain James R. Ritts, commanding the machine gun company of the First Battalion, turned his weapons on German soldiers who were in the open washing their clothes in a street below the village. There were mortars on the enemy trucks on the roads that were shelled, and thus the highway was blocked for a Kraut retreat. Captain Ritts summed up his view of the situation:

> If we had had sufficient forces and artillery
> support in that spot, we could have ended the
> war in Italy right there. Up there we overlooked
> a valley in which was the conversion of all the
> major routes of escape for the retreating Ger-
> man Army. From this point we looked down on a
> network of roads leading to Littoria and Rome
> and Cassino. We sat up there watching the main
> strength of the German Army making its
> getaway and we couldn't do a thing about it. If
> we had had enough artillery support, we could
> have knocked out hundreds of vehicles. With
> enough support we could have ended the war in
> Italy. The biggest guns we had with us were 60
> mm mortars until a heavy-weapons company
> brought up an 81 mm mortar. We hit 'em with

everything we had but it just wasn't enough.[16]

One of the Third's supply trains was ambushed by the Jerries on this day. Planes dropped 81mm ammo, medical supplies, and dynamite, but the men were badly in need of rations. The Italian civilians hid their chickens and stock for fear of confiscation.[17]

As the First Battalion advanced to the northwest, one platoon of Company C occupied the town of Roccasecca dei Volsci. The rest of the battalion, less Company B, infiltrated into the town during the remainder of the day, under observation of the Germans in the valley below. SImilar to the capture of a Third Battalion supply train, a battalion mule train of the First, under Lt. White, was ambushed and this officer, along with Lt. Borkus and five enlisted men and several men from Anti-Tank Company, were taken prisoner.

As the battalion consolidated its positions in and around Roccasecca, Company B and part of the Third Battalion moved into town. From this area mortar and small arms fire was placed on enemy vehicles and personnel on the main roads in the valley below. Soon the enemy discovered the presence of the Blue Devils in the town and shelled it and the trail leading into the town, killing one and wounding several; but with the advantage of commanding positions, the Blue Devils inflicted an estimated twenty killed and several wounded on the small German force south of Priverno.[18]

At the dawn the next morning, May 24, the battalions on the slopes in front of the town waited the arrival of the Second. As two German cars were sighted, Sgt. George E. Ewel and Colonel Fry appropriated a light machine gun and fired at enemy vehicles below, Colonel Fry firing the weapon as Ewel fed the ammo.[19]

Late that afternoon Colonel Williamson's Second came up, and contact was made with the 349th on the right rear. Nothing significant happened on the night of May 24, and on the morning of May 25 Colonel Fry led his men into the valley. The next objective, the village of Roccagorga, lay about two miles to the north.[20]

Colonel Williamson's Second Battalion had had to battle for every position before joining the First and Third at Roccasecca. While the First and Third Battalions had moved toward and on to Roccasecca, the Second on May 21 moved west from Fondi along Highway 7 for about 6000 yards but made no contact with the enemy. In fact the Italian civilians reported that all Germans had gone. As the Battalion turned north off Highway 7 along a good road that would lead directly to the foot of the mountains and to a trail that led to their objective, Mount Calvo, the leading platoon of Company E reached the San Biagio-San Magno road, about 600 yards north of Highway 7. Here it was fired on from enemy positions north of the road by machine guns and rifles. Taking up positions along the road and to the left, with a creek and canal to the right and an orchard, to the left, the men found that they had very little cover in the orchard whereas the enemy occupied excellent positions on the side of a hill covering to the south and to the valley; they were well dug in and hard to locate.

Since the orchard was a poor place from which to launch an attack, the Battalion Commander decided that Company G would maneuver out in the valley to the left and hit the German positions with two platoons abreast and thus assault from the middle of the valley, while Company E aided from its position to the right of the north-south road just off Highway 7. The Artillery Liaison Officer called for artillery concentrations in the town of San Biagio, dominating the west side of the valley. Both compnies moved out in the assault and were on top of the dugouts before the Germans were aware of what had occurred. From a position gained some distance up the mountain, Company E fired down at the enemy; the 350th Infantry Regimental Commander directed tank fire on enemy machine gun positions. After the hill was reached, assault groups from ten or twelve places at one time kept moving as they located an enemy position. No mortar or artillery was employed by either side in the fight; the enemy used machine guns, rifles, and automatic pistols, and the Second Battalion hand grenades, rifles, and BARs.

After an intense fire fight of about another 45 minutes, the Regimental Commanding Officer ordered the Battalion to hold its gains, since he had just found out that the valley belonged to the 85th Division. Company E organized the former position of the Germans, higher up the hill. The Battalion had suffered 43 casualties, including seven officers and the Battalion Artillery Liaison Officer, who was killed. Company E later reported finding about 40 dead on the position. About 110 prisoners were taken. Then the Second was ordered back to Fondi into division reserve, an order that was changed soon thereafter (perhaps saving the First and Third Battalions).

Instead of reserve the Battalion was now informed to join the Regiment, which was nearly to Roccasecca. The 350th at this time had set up a rear command post at San Magno, and Colonel Fry had rejoined the First and Third Battalions to lead them up to Roccasecca. As the Second moved northwest along the road from Fondi to San Magno, a German artillery barrage zeroed in on them from the northwest. At the head of the column, around San Magno, the Regimental Adjutant, who had come out to meet the Battalion, was killed and several others wounded. The Battalion now moved into the mountains to join the other two, fully 20,000 yards to the northwest. The only trails leading through the mountains were mule trails.

In the movement forward, Company G led, followed by Companies E and F. They moved along the trails that went around the east side of Mount Cassareccio and to the east of Mount Latiglia. As Captain Roeder, Commanding Officer of Company G, led his group over the difficult terrain, which provided excellent cover among the many huge rocks, his lead squad was fired upon. Eventually locating a group of Germans running away and down the mountain less than 200 yards from them, the platoon opened fire, the enemy took cover among the rocks, and Captain Roeder, who could speak Pennsylvania Dutch, yelled down for them to surrender. Twenty-one of the enemy surrendered, whereupon the battalion then started moving again, and by nightfall it had reached Mount Calvo.

The next day, May 23, as the Battalion moved along the route toward Mount Marino, Company F was pinned down by fire from machine guns. The entire company was along the trail where the enemy could observe 600 to 700 yards of the company's positions. Company E, led by a commanding officer who had joined two days previously at Fondi, now sent a platoon around a hill toward the enemy's rear. A small German group, one of whom could speak English, persuaded the Americans that they were surrounded by a German platoon, whereupon the inexperienced platoon leader surrendered and told all the men to do likewise. With reinforcements now sent forward from Companies E, F, and G, the Germans returned the fire but then left the captured platoon and started running. In the meantime Company F had succeeded in overrunning the remaining Germans left as a covering force and began driving along the crest of the ridge toward the east.

Numerous prisoners were taken, and 30 of the enemy killed. Companies E and F had suffered 21 casualties. The Battalion then moved out again and crossed the north side of Mount Marino. It was on this peak that the radio relay station of four men had gone off the air earlier in the morning. Company F found three of the team's bodies, but the radio and other man were missing.

Adding to the complexities of battling its way through every enemy position, the Second now received a message that five companies of Germans were moving to Mount Marino from the southwest and also that the Second had the mission of protecting the regimental supply route as well as pushing to Roccasecca; further, that the battalion was moving too slowly. After Company F was ordered into positions on Mount Marino, it was learned that the information that five enemy companies were moving toward Mount Marino was false. Another message informed the battalion that Regiment was sending up a 90-mule train. Company F now remained on Mount Marino to protect the trail.

The rest of the Battalion then moved out on a trail running along the east slope of a long ridge that went up to Mount Sporago. After the 90-mule pack train had been ambushed, Company F came quickly to their aide and captured ten of the ambush party, who had been sent from Amaseno with the mission of occupying Mount Marino. A perimeter defense was now set up for the night. A message was received during the night that the Battalion was to contact the 85th Division coming up on the left.

The next day, May 24, the Battalion column moved over Mount Sporago and again was ambushed. The enemy's position in a saddle was well chosen. It took Captain Roeder's platoon of Company G over an hour to break through and capture 17 and kill two after his platoon had moved over the top of a hill where he could fire down on the enemy. The company was then ordered to leave one reinforced platoon on Mount Sporago to protect the trail and to contact Company F by patrols. After moving on toward Mount Alto, the Battalion, minus a platoon of Company E left on Monticehio, spent the night on Mount Alto.

Early on the morning of May 25, the Battalion moved out toward Roccasecca. A trail led down the hill to the town, and the Battalion column was now much shorter. It moved rapidly and soon contacted elements of the Third Battalion which garrisoned the high ground over-looking Roccasecca. In this engagement for May 21-25, the Battalion had nineteen killed and 69 casualties-seven of them officers. The Second had captured 198 Germans and actually counted 72 killed. In this engagement, the Battalion had moved with both flanks open, with no$_{21}$ artillery support and in daily contact with the enemy.

With the Regiment again operating as a unit, Colonel Fry now led his men into the valley toward the next objective, the village of Roccagorga, which lay about two miles to the north. The plans called for the First to lead the march down the hill, followed by the Third and the Second in that order. At the valley the Third had orders to swing to the right and reach a position abreast of the First. In this action toward Roccagorga, enemy infantry barred the advance.

Eventually Colonel Bare had his leading company of the First in what seemed to be a line that generally faced the enemy. The immediate goal, a road running perpendicular to the route of the advance, proved to be a rather difficult undertaking. After dawn Colonel Bare sent Company B forward to a hill, practically devoid of cover; yet the Battalion Commander was determined to take the position. After a heavy German artillery concentration, American artillery answered, hitting close to the rear of Company B. In this artillery exchange nine men were wounded, including Sergeant Hurshel Kidd and Lt. Kenneth Brown of Jamesport, Missouri.

By mid-afternoon of May 26, the Regiment worked slowly toward Roccagorga, with negligible resistance. Actually the Blue Devils were so close to the German lines that they could hear mortar shells being fired. Captain Jacob Zadik of Dallas, Texas, Artillery Liaison Officer, 338th Field Artillery, then in Priverno, directed artillery fire against the enemy, who slowly evacuated their command post.

The last hour of advance up the hill to Roccagorga was unopposed. The 350th now received the task of lending any possible assistance to elements of the French Corps coming up on the right, who would then take over the 350th's sector.

Colonel Fry ordered the men to move rapidly through Roccagorga; he had no desire to have the troops detained wining themselves as in Roccasecca.[22]

For the period May 26-29, the First continued to advance while meeting occasional machine gun, mortar, and artillery fire. For May 26 the direction of attack lay to the east of Priverno through a valley, but at 2100 hours the line of attack turned north across the valley toward Mount Castellone, where Company A ran into resistance. After being held up at 0200 hours by heavy machine gun fire along the highway, by 0600 hours the leading elements of the battalion had maneuvered to knock out the opposing machine guns after close-in fighting. Now the advance continued to the north and west, while the enemy tried to delay the march forward by artillery and mortar fire. The tired Blue Devils entrenched for the night on the north slopes of Mount San Angelo.

Prior to attaining this position, the Battalion had met friendly reconnaissance troops on the road from Sezze to Roccagorga. The next objective, Mount Castellone, was reached at daylight on May 28 where the Battalion remained in position throughout May 29. The next day the French forces pinched out the Battalion, which now pulled back to a bivouac area along the Roccagorga road with orders to move out on trucks in the morning. The next day, May 31, the First moved 62 miles on trucks and arrived in an assembly area east of Anzio at 1250 hours, passing enroute through the battle-scarred towns of Littoria and Nettuno.[23]

The line of action for the other two battalions followed generally the same course as that of the First. Attacking at dawn on May 26, the Third crossed the Amaseno River under enemy harassing fire; in this action, Captain Hotchkiss and Lt. Renfrow were wounded. Just before dark the Battalion moved northward from Priverno. Admist confusion about the route and objective, the Third came across a German Aid Station still intact with all of its equipment. After contacting approximately a company of Jerries in the mountains in the vicinity of Roccagorga and Mount Neri, the Battalion captured 17 and knocked out the German company and then placed security guards out in front. It then received word to remain in position. By this time the French were posed to pass through the unit. On the next day, may 31, the Battalion moved out in the morning and arrived in the vicinity of Velletri, after having passed through Anzio, where the terrain was marked with shell holes and foxholes, the evidence of excruciating battle.[24]

The fact that the 88th and 350th would be the first American units into Rome resulted from a number of rapid changes of command toward the end of May, 1944. After being ordered to clear the Amaseno River Line, the 88th quickly accomplished this task on May 28 and subsequently was attached to IV Corps. Shortly therafter the Division was pinched out by the French and the beachhead troops. It then prepared to move on May 31 into the II Corps sector in the vicinity of Anzio.[25]

After having relieved the 85th Division on the night of May 27-28 in the vicinity of Sezze, the 88th was already at the beachhead by the night of May 30. At this point II Corps turned over its zone and the 88th Division to IV Corps under General Crittenberger. Under IV Corps the 88 Division spent the next three days in mopping up the hills as far as Sermonetta while waiting for the FEC to advance sufficiently to relieve the division. After the 349th Infantry departed for the beachhead on May 29, the rest of the Division was on its way by May 31, after being relieved by the French; and IV Corps officially went out of the line on June 1.[26]

It would thus appear that for a time II Corps seemed to be out of the picture. After General Keyes had received orders to turn over his sector and troops to the fresh force, newly brought into being under General Crittenberger of the IV Corps, a coordination of plans for the march on Rome were formulated. Now VI Corps, the old beachhead force, was to push north on the side of the Alban Hills closest to the sea and into Rome, while IV Corps and the French and the British on the right would blot out any remaining German pockets in the area around Rome. Kesselring, however, changed this plan: he sent the Herman Goering Panzer Division to Valmontone where it blocked the Third Division and First Special Service Force, the VI Corps element attacking to the east. There were also other defensive forces and fragments of the Tenth and Fourteenth German Armies in this area, all of which fought a skillful rear guard action and thereby stalled the VI Corps attack.

In this situation Clark became disheartened; the IV Corps was going nowhere; on the right the French and British elements churned methodically forward toward Rome. Clark wanted to be first in Rome. Now at a meeting with Alexander, Clark decided to give the troops of IV Corps back to Keyes II Corps (even though he wanted Truscott of VI Corps to have the honor of capturing Rome) and now gave Keyes the green light to go into Rome. The result was to give the 85th and 88th Divisions the order to move north of Valmontone and thereby cut Highway 6. The plan called for securing the heights above Valmontone and then executing a wheel westward toward Rome over the Via Casilina. Now VI Corps would have to continue on its way west of the Alban Hills and get into the city whenever it could. [27] (See Map 3).

Chapter 2 — Map 3

It was the action of the 36th Division, lately sent to the beachhead when it had become apparent that the II Corps would not need its services, that actually paved the way for the 88th's move on Rome. As the VI Corps had faced formidable resistance and was obviously quite tired, the 36th Division received the task of attacking toward the strong point of Velletri. On May 30 the division discovered undefended high ground behind the town, the area of Monte Artemesio, and went through the seemingly impassable peak and also around it. This move effectively cut off the German garrison's retreat. When the Hermann Goering Division failed to unseat the 36th

Division, Clark now ordered attacks by both of his corps the next morning. The 85th, 88th, and 3rd were now directed to renew the attack around the northern side of the Alban Hills, cutting Route 6 and taking Valmontone on the way, while VI Corps advanced round the south-western side of the hills and the 36th Division drove through the center from its newly won position. [28] (See Map 4). The 88th and the 350th were poised for the quick dash toward Rome.

"MULESKINNER" IN SOUTHERN APENNINES

PVT. G.T. FAGERHOLM
ITALY, 1944

Supply by mule was normal in the mountains.

Chapter 2 — Map 4

Footnotes to Chapter II

[1] Starr, **From Salerno to the Alps,** 217.

[2] General Frido von Senger und Etterlin, **Neither Fear Nor Hope: The Wartime Memoirs of the German Defender of Cassino.** Trans. by George Malcom (New York, 1964), 248.

[3] Clark, **Calculated Risk,** 465.

[4] Fry, **Combat Soldier,** 63.

[5] **Fifth Army History,** V, 82.

[6] S-2 and S-3 Journal, 350th Infantry Regiment, May, 1944.

[7] Delaney, **The Blue Devils in Italy,** 83.

[8] Starr, **From Salerno to the Alps,** 217.

[9] Fry, **Combat Soldier,** 67.

[10] **Ibid.,** 72.

[11] First Battalion History, May, 1944.

[12] Fry, **Combat Soldier,** 71.

[13] **Ibid.,** 77-78.

[14] Delaney, **The Blue Devils in Italy,** 84.

[15] "Four 88th Division Men Hung on Until Bitter End," **Stars and Stripes,** 1944.

[16] Delaney, **The Blue Devils in Italy,** 85.

[17] Third Battalion History, May 1944.

[18] First Battalion History, May, 1944.

[19] **Ibid.**

[20] Fry, **Combat Soldier,** 90.

[21] Major Erwin B. Jones, "Operations of the 2nd Battalion, 350th Infantry (88th Division) in Clearning a Regimental Supply Route to Roccasecca, Italy, 21-25 May 1944," Personal Experiences of a Battalion S-3. Advanced Infantry Officers Course, 1949-1950, TIS, Fort Benning, Georgia.

Sketch by Gus Fagerholm—Italian Theater, 1944 - 350th Infantry Reg't. from the collection of William Gardner Bell.

[22] Fry, **Combat Soldier**, 90-103.
[23] First Battalion History, May, 1944.
[24] Third Battalion History, May, 1944.
[25] Delaney, **The Blue Devils in Italy**, 86.
[26] Starr, **From Salerno to the Alps**, 250-253.
[27] Adelman, **Rome Fell Today**, 236.
[28] Jackson, **The Battle for Italy**, 240-245.

Chapter Three

Rome-Pursuit-Rest, June 1944

After locating approximately eight miles north of Anzio on June 1, 1944, the Regiment for the perid of June 1-3 conducted operations on a piecemeal basis with the battalions moving mostly via trucks and organic vehicles. After traveling approximately 62 miles on May 31, the First Battalion arrived in an assembly area east of Anzio around noon time. The next day the Blue Devils again moved by truck 15 miles to an assembly area near Cisterna.[1] The Third Battalion during this period bivouaced in the Velletri area but departed there on May 31, passing through Anzio, on its way to the new bivouac area in the vicinity of Cori.[2]

The next day, June 1, the move of the Regiment was to the small village of Larinola. By June 3 the Regiment minus the First Battalion was concentrated in the vicinity of the village of Cesareo, where the First joined the other two battalions after having marched about 25 miles. It was here that a task force was formed of the First Battalion, one battery of the 338th Field Artillery, one company of 313th Engineers, one battery of six 105 MM self-propelled guns, and one company of medium tanks. Designated as a mobile pursuit force under Division congrol, the Task Force received orders at 0700 hours on June 4 to move on Rome and secure two bridges, Ponte Duca d'Aorta and Ponte Milvio, which crossed the Tiber on Highway 2, and to seize high ground on the outskirts of the city to the east of Highway 2. The Third and Second Battalions followed the Task

Force.[3]

The entry into Rome by the Task Force in the evening of June 4 was a culmination of various factors in the development of the battle for Rome on Corps and Army levels. Progress against German resistance on May 31 was slight, partly because of exhaustion and partly because the French had encountered strong resistance in attempting to reach Valmontone.[4] The Fifth Army forces, nevertheless, had moved forward from the collapsed southern front and had joined with the beachhead forces at Borgo Grappa on May 25. Because of the change in plans to place the II Corps again in the drive to Rome, on May 31 the 88th Division had come up to Anzio and in the evening moved to assembly areas near Rocca Massima. At 0500, June 1, II Corps began its final drive on Rome, with its first objectives Highway 6 and the Cave road. On the right of the 88th and 350th Infantry, the Third Division drove against enemy positions astride the Artena-Valmontone road to cut Highway 6 at Valmontone and then to drive on to the Palestrina-Cave road near Cave, thereby blocking off enemy forces to the east. At this time the 91st Calvary Recon Squadron continued to operate beyond the Third Division. In the sector of the II Corps, the 85th Division pushed northwest toward Mount Ceraso, the dominating height at the northeast corner of Colli Laziali, while the 88th Division, committed in the center of the line later, had the mission of taking the high ground at Gardella Hill just across Highway 6 and southwest of Palestrina.

Late on June 2 II Corps received the orders to govern its advance on Rome. In great wheeling movements from north to west, in the II Corps sector in the narrow corridor between Colli Laziali and the hills at Tivoli, the 85th pushed to the south; the 88th moved astride Highway 6; and the Third continued to the north. While one regimental combat team of the 88th Division helped to guard the long right flank of II Corps along the Cave-Palestrina line and since the Third Division now guarded the right flank until the French came up, the main attack toward Rome in the Corps zone now fell to the 85th and 88th Divisions, with the latter spearheaded by Task Force Howze on Highway 6.[5]

As all troops of Fifth Army moved forward by late afternoon of June 3, new orders went out to the troops. Since the fall of Rome appeared imminent, the important point now was to secure bridging sites in order that Fifth Army might continue the pursuit. The primary responsibility for securing these crossings fell to II Corps-which now sent the First Special Service Force and a battalion each of the 351st, 350th and 338th Infantry toward the assigned bridges. The situation on June 4 called for the employment of speedy forces heavy in fire power but with the minimum number of troops, the latter being for the purpose of avoiding congestion on the narrow streets of the city and for retaining maximum flexibility. The result of this reasoning was the formations of a number of flying columns from the various divisions of tanks, tank destroyers, engineers, and infantry, usually based on a battalion or less of infantry and a company of tanks. It was such a spearheading force that Lt. Col. Bare of the First Battalion, 350th Infantry, commanded.

The infantry became motorized. From the regimental service companies or from division quartermaster companies, and in other cases mounting decks of tanks, the infantry began moving until opposition was met. Columns of infantry advanced by foot and motor right to the suburbs of Rome but did not press into the city proper until the Tiber bridges had been secured.[6] Everyone wanted to be the first in Rome; thus spearheads veered from one road to another and crossed one another's paths in the frantic jostling for securing the goal.

Jammed bumper to bumper, all the rear echelon units from as far back as Naples followed. In the front line spearheads, the 350th had been directed to overtake the 351st, pass through it, and continue the attack, an order that obviously was resented by the 351st. When no word had been received of a junction between th e 350th and 351st Infantry, General Sloan early on the morning of June 4 ordered the 351st to push forward at once with one motorized battalion along Highway 101, enter Rome, and seize important bridges over the Tiber River.[7] Word was then later received that the third platoon of the 88th Reconnaissance Troop had entered Rome at 0715 hours, June 4, on Highway 6.

Meanwhile the motorized battalion of the 350th with other units, all under the command of Lt. Col. Walter E. Bare, Jr., battered through Nazi rear guards and crossed the city limits on the Via Palestrina shortly before 1730 hours. Joined by Italian partisans, the doughboys now cleaned out snipers from buildings along the route. Leading elements of the 88th Division had entered the Piazza Venezia in the center of Rome by 7:15 p.m., June 4, 1944.[8]

In this fight for Rome beginning on June 1 and 2, Mark Clark had thrown every man, tank and shell available into a typical American drive. Included in the force were eleven divisions, including the two British divisions on the coast, which had smashed forward against the tired German formations. It was the Hermann Goering and 344th Divisions that had given way first, letting II Corps through on Route 6. On the night of June 2-3, these divisions had retired to the Aniene River east of Rome, covered by rear guards provided by the 4th Parachute Division. The rest of the defeated Fourteenth Army conformed and pulled back over the Tiber west of Rome, destroying the bridges and ferries behind them.[9]

On that bright sunny morning of June 4 as the 350th moved down Route 6 toward Valmontone, Colonel Fry came upon the First Battalion and found Colonel Bare sitting under cover of a small knoll. As Colonel Bare rested and chewed on a straw, the smoke from a distant burning gasoline truck hid the sun from view.

"What the hell. Don't you want to see Rome?" Colonel Fry asked.

Colonel Bare replied: "There seem to be a lot of people wanting to go to Rome today. Right over the top of that hill there are a few individuals who don't seem to like sightseers. As far as I'm concerned, anyone who's in a hurry to get there can go ahead. They can have my place in line."[10]

During this day of triumph, the entry into Rome, advancing troops met only mobile rear guards, whose sole mission was to check them temporarily. Now and then snipers appeared at the rear of advance elements, or self-propelled guns and tanks fired a few rounds from good positions before withdrawing. Along Highway 6 and a road to its north, Via Prenestina, however, a real action occurred, holding up the First Special Service Force and 351st Infantry for approximately nine hours.

By early afternoon, the Americans had broken the last enemy resistance, however, and the First Special Service Force then drove northwest to a road junction on the Via Prenestina at the edge of the city proper by 1700 hours, where it was met by elements of Task Force Howze. By 2300 hours the bridges in the II Corps area had been secured. Behind these troops now came the First Battalion, 351st Infantry, and the First Battalion, 350th Infantry, both advancing through the city toward the northern most of these bridges. Shortly after midnight the 350th Infantry had reached the Ponte del Duca D'Aosta. [11]

On this historic Sunday the weary doughboys plodded through the crowd-jammed streets. With their rifles and helmets decked in flags and flowers, the Blue Devils found their greeting to be just a passing show. The weary business of war still ground on. On this night they slept on sidewalks and in doorways during short breaks, snatched what fun they could, and then secured their bridge and road objectives. New orders now commanded them to press over the river and up Highway 2 after an enemy that they were unable to catch or to make to stand and fight. [12]

As the 350th raced in hot pursuit of the enemy through Rome and beyond, it suffered a number of casualities. Meeting resistance on the northwestern outskirts of the city, the First Battalion suffered a casualty when Captain Borquist, S-3, was wounded. After wiping out the resistance with tank and ar- tillery fire, the battalion then advanced approximately six miles, capturing about 15 prisoners, and took up defensive positions for the night. The next morning the First attacked to the north, passing through the Second about noon, and captured Formello and continued the advance north. During this day the battalion moved approximately ten miles and entrenched south of Campagna di Roma. The next day the Blue Devils of the First moved north approximately five miles beyond the town, as it followed in reserve of the Second.

The Third Battalion during this period moved toward its new objective north of Rome, the high terrain at Torrevergara. With the objective taken by early evening, the Battalion CP housed at Ospedaletto while the companies, upon reaching their objectives, closed into the areas around the same time. The next day, after being held up by enemy fire in the vicinity south of Antanao, the battalion headed now northwest and after suffering a few casualties from enemy shelling, marched five miles to the bivouac area in Formello. On June 7 the battalion continued to march to reach the vicinity of Monterosi. By June 9 it prepared to move to the rest area. [14]

For the first few days of June, The Second Battalion moved rapidly from one assembly area to another, including Cori, Velletri-Artena, and San Caesaro. At this town the battalion followed the 351st through the town and then turned west along a power line that parralleled Highway 6 to the very outskirts of Rome. Entering Rome at approximately 2000 hours, June 4, the Blue Devils continued over the Tiber River bridge, which they crossed at 0800 hours, June 5. The G-I's then proceeded up Highway 2, where they met resistance just beyond the bridge. After losing five men killed and thirteen wounded, the unit continued five miles north on Highway 2 and then left the highway to move across country all night.

Resting only two hours that night, the Second reached Formello the next day. Along the way only sniper and slight machine gun fire delayed the movement, but at Formello the enemy shelled the objective. After remaining in this position overnight, Colonel Williamson's men reached Compagnano on June 7 and remained there until relieved on the following day.[15]

It was on the night of June 7 that the 351st Infantry passed through the 350th, whereupon the Regiment remained in bivouac in division reserve. In this position about five miles north of Campagnano di Roma, the regiment remained until June 13-a period of approximately a week's rest after the continuous combat beginning on May 11. While the regiment billeted in this area, the Replacement Company marched about 15 miles from south of Vergara on June 8 to a point about two miles north of Formello. On June 10 this company was disbanded after all the replacements had been attached to the various units. Beginning on June 12, all the battalions moved into the Albano area from the vicinity north of Formello. For the first time since the regiment had left the vicinity of Piedmonte on March 1, all the units billeted together in one locality.

In the period June 14-18 the men generally relaxed, received new supplies, and reorganized. Along with passes to Rome, there were also opportunities for some to visit Sorrento on three-day passes. The Excelsior Hotel on the Via Veneto, Rome's most fashionable **strassa,** became the officers' rest center. Along with rexation, however, the business of preparation continued; gas masks were issued; and the First Battalion kept alert for the division and guarded the beach during the period June 16-18.

For those men visiting Rome, there was the added attraction of attending the performance of Irving Berlin's **This is the Army**, playing at the Royal Opera House. The opportunity to laugh once more at the characters in a theatrical performance, which featured the great composer Irving Berlin himelf in a bit role, served as a tonic to the men's spirits.

After enjoying the relaxation, passes to Rome and Sorrento, and just generally the luxury of a peaceful, scenic area around Albano, on June 21 the Regimental Transportation Officer and Lt. Watson contacted the unit occupying the future zone of the regiment. All organizations would then close into this area in the early morning hours after daylight. [16] In this area north of Rome and approximately 75 miles from Albano, around Tarquinia, the men attended movies in the special service area, along with the usually prescribed training activities. [17] While undergoing training in preparation for the coming offensive in the Volterra area, the G-I's continued to visit the Spiritual Capital of the Western World, Rome. [18]

During the last days of June the entire regiment marched to the division area to witness a presentation of awards to

SKETCHED AT ROME, ITALY JUNE, 1944 By Pvt. G. FAGERHOLM

The artist, G. Fagerholm, states that he actually saw a wine-cheered infantryman strike this pose.

members of the division. Regular training included erection of three bunkers to be used as an assault target in future training; construction of wire entanglements; and range firing, including training in the use of M1s, carbines, bazooka, and anti-tank rifle grenades. In this month of June the records showed only 11 killed in action, with 48 being wounded and evacuated.[19]

Lt. Col Walter E. Bare, Jr., on the outskirts of Rome, June, 1944.

88th troops were first into Rome.

"Grazie, Liberatori!"

Tank sketched in Cori, Italy.

Footnotes to Chapter III

[1] First Battalion History, June, 1944.

[2] Third Battalion History, June, 1944.

[3] 350th Infantry Regiment History, June, 1944.

[4] Clark, **Calculated Risk**, 360.

[5] Starr, **From Salerno to the Alps**, 254-257.

[6] **Ibid.**, 263.

[7] Delaney, **The Blue Devils in Italy**, 91.

[8] **Ibid.**, 92-93.

[9] Jackson, **The Battle for Italy**, 246.

[10] Fry, **Combat Soldier**, 109.

[11] Starr, **From Salerno to the Alps**, 265.

[12] Delaney, **The Blue Devils in Italy**, 97.

[13] First Battalion History, June, 1944.

[14] Third Battalion History, June, 1944.

[15] Second Battalion History, June, 1944.

[16] 350th Infantry Regiment History, June, 1944.

[17] Third Battalion History, June, 1944.

[18] Second Battalion History, June, 1944.

[19] 350th Infantry Regiment History, June, 1944.

Page 60

Chapter Four

Chapter IV
From Volterra to the Arno, July-August, 1944

By the time the 350th re-entered the front lines after resting and training in the Tarquinia area, the Fifth Army had chased the enemy as far as Volterra. The Fifth Army by this time was less than halfway through its campaign, and the battles yet to come were to be severe. The 350th was a part of an important mission for the Fifth Army: To tie down enemy forces and prevent their withdrawal from the Italian peninsula and also to threaten Germany from yet another direction. To achieve this mission, Allied strategists had the following goals: Pursue the enemy to the Rimini-Pisa line, inflicting maximum losses and also to capture the Viterbo airfields and Civitavecchia; then to move on to Leghorn and the Arno River, about 150 miles north of Rome. Since Fifth Army had been reduced in strength at this time (the FEC and three American Divisions would be withdrawn for the Southern France invasion), its zone had been reduced to about 45 miles wide along the Tyrrhenian coast.

Although the terrain over which the 350th would travel was generally described as hard to negotiate with vehicles, in midsummer the task was not too severe. The area that the 350th would occupy was one of two principal zones for the Fifth Army-one mass of undulating high ground running to the Arno, the mountains varying only in height and slope. The backbone of the mountains ran more or less in a northeast-northwesterly direction, with lesser ridges jumbled together at all angles with narrow valleys between. About twenty miles north of Grosseto, the steepest mountains began. It was rough country for another twenty miles, culminating in a general summit on an east-west line through Volterra, marked roughly by Highway 68; from this line northward the hills are less steep and slope toward the valley of the Arno.

The immediate aim of the enemy at this period of the war was to trade terrain for time. Although Jerry did not make any real stand south of the strong defensive belt, the Gothic Line, about 20-30 miles north of the Arno, he nevertheless fought a fierce delaying action, especially as the 350th experienced in driving the enemy from the area of Volterra. The 350th's tactical plan, as that of the Fifth Army, was necessarily to keep close contact with the enemy and slow his retreat in order to cut off large bodies of his troops. The terrain, as much as the enemy proved a foe, for the mountains proved ideal for delaying action and took their toll on the Blue Devils physically and on their vehicles mechanically. In this area the bridges and culverts, averaging generally more than one per mile, had been blown up by the retreating Krauts.

It was also in this area north of Rome that the attacking Fifth Army encountered anti-German guerrilla bands in large numbers for the first time. They identified themselves by red-white-green arm bands.

From its period of training the 88th Division relieved the 1st Armored Division on the right of Fifth Army sector on July 8, with the 91st Division taking over the center of IV Corps to the left of the 350th. As the 88th moved to take over from the left elements of the 1st Armored Division on July 8, it soon met considerable opposition that continued for a few days. To obviate attacking the high-lying town of Volterra, American artillery and chemical mortars smoked it, thus permitting the division to encircle the hill and forcing the enemy to withdraw.

After the 351st Infantry had attacked against strong resistance around Laiatico on July 11, capturing it by a double envelopment and netting approximately 400 prisoners, enemy resistance then slackened and the division reached the high ground overlooking the Arno on July 18. In this drive the Blue Devils found many mines and booby-traps along almost every trail, but by methodical sweeping the G-I's gained the Arno by July 23.[2] (See Map 1).

By now Kesselring was able to throw reserve forces and

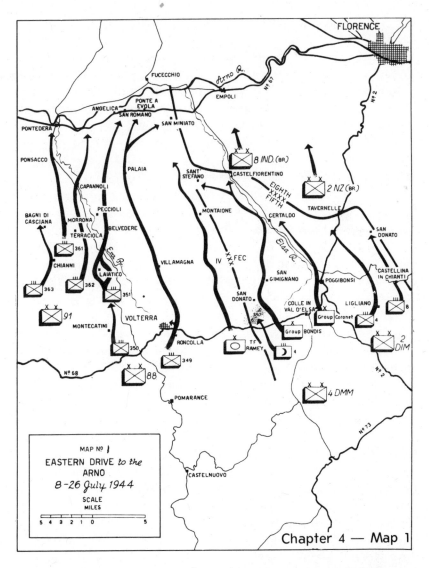

MAP N° 1
EASTERN DRIVE *to the* ARNO
8-26 *July* 1944
SCALE
MILES
5 4 3 2 1 0   5

Chapter 4 — Map 1

reinforcements into the battle and thus restored some semblance of organization; the last twenty miles to the Arno was studded with hard-fought engagements. With the men exhaused by over three months of action and with movement so rapid that they outran supplies, for the first time since May the G-I's assumed a defensive attitude and maintained only light screening forces along the river while resting and training units in rear areas for river crossing and assault on the Gothic Line. As IV Corps now took over the greater part of the Army front with a purely defensive mission, the bulk of II Corps held back in preparation for the next attack.

As the 350th underwent strenuous training in the area of Tarquinia in the first few days of July, it prepared to return into action against the enemy. Company B of 760th Tank Battalion joined the regiment in problems involving coordinated infantry-tank-artillery maneuvers. Along with training, the men enjoyed swimming in the Tyrrhenian Sea. On July 5, 1944, the division received orders to prepare for movement forward to relieve the 1st Armored Division. After regimental, battalion, and special unit commanders had made a reconnaissance of the new area, the regiment later moved under cover of darkness from Tarquinia to the new area north of Pomarance (approximately 75 miles) and completed the occupation of the sector on the morning of July 6. Although sporadic, long range enemy artillery fire disrupted movement during the day and continued into the night, no damage was sustained.

After regimental and battalion commanders made a reconnaissance of forward areas in preparation for impending action on July 7, the First Battalion received orders to attack on the left sector while the Third moved on the right with the Second remaining in regimental reserve. One company of tanks from the 760th Tank Battalion and one company of TD's from the 701st Tank Destroyers supported each battalion. [3]

In the movement forward from Tarquinia, the Blue Devils had traveled roads covered by at least six inches of powdery dust churned up by heavy supply and armored columns. The thick layers of dust covered everyone. It took six hours of slow travel to reach the destination on July 6, after which the battalions dispersed to different assembly areas. The front still lay five miles forward. The orders to attack immediately the next day were delayed, upon Colonel Fry's recommendation, because of lack of orientation of the area and the almost certain severe casualties that would be sustained with no advance first hand knowledge of the situation.

The hub of operations in this area, the little town of Saline, through which all roads leading north crisscrossed, lay in the valley on the 350th's side of the line. Plans called for the 349th to attack on the right of the town of Volterra with the 350th on the left. On the hub of Saline German artillery harassing shells continually dropped. [4]

The valley parallel to the front was to be the 350th's line of departure. The upward rolling hills immediately to the front were dotted with half-destroyed buildings, disabled tanks, and rotting cattle. Scarcely any cover for the advancing Blue Devils was provided here except the erosion-created depression in the ground. In the plans of attack, the First on the left and the Third on the right, the Second followed the First, with a gap between the Third and First to facilitate any needed maneuver. If the attack failed initially, the Second would probably take position in the line on the left of the First Battalion.

Before the attack a squad of the I & R Platoon miraculously escaped death as it moved forward to reconnoiter several houses for use as a battalion forward CP. Colonel Fry ordered two jeeps to move out at dusk on July 7 along a road to the left of the fortress hilltop town of Volterra. After moving about one-half mile north, the patrol found itself in the middle of anti-tank fire from the rear and to the front. Pushing the accelerators to the floor boards, the patrol quickly reached the crest of a hill where they found a German tank that had been knocked out. There was just enough room for the jeeps to squeeze between the tank and the hill, which blocked the view from the enemy. No enemy were found in the houses in the area.

About this time a foot patrol moving up advised the squad that there were mines across the road just beside the knocked-out German tank. The squad had run two jeeps over a field of German anti-tank mines and escaped without a scratch. The first jeep, driven by Private Clayton Eighmey of Erie, had rolled one mine over in a ditch, tipped up a second, one, and straddled a third. After completing its mission, the squad had returned over the route of its narrow escape before it was realized that the road had been mined. Accompanying Eighmey on this mission were Sergeant John Sohanachak, Camden, New Jersey; PFC Nicholas M. Draschill, Sebewaing, Michigan; and Private Lewis Alphine of Detroit. [5]

As the attacking units prepared to move out at 0200 hours on July 8, they found that the Germans had massed artillery of all types and were using it more extensively than at any other time. Enemy minefields practically overlapped one another. In addition, the Krauts had perfect observation from the hill-top perch of Volterra, dominating for about 11 miles in all directions.

The work of two G-I's from the 313th Engineers in clearing mines ahead of the infantry outposts aided immeasurably the advance of the Blue Devils. Cpl. Orval Sullivan of Ontario, California, and 1st Lt. John P. Tucei, Biloxi, Mississippi, cleared more than 400 yards of minefields, even though under direct fire of enemy 88's and SP's. They made the enemy shells work for them; immediately after the shell bursts around them, Sullivan and Tucei went back to their work, using the dust of exploding shells to shield them. They cleared the entire area. When a shell came in, they hit the dirt and immediately after the explosion, they went back to work, hiding in the dust clouds. Both won the Silver Star for their magnificent actions. [6]

As the attack moved off on schedule at 0230, July 8, the attacking First and Third Battalions reached the first phase line in one hour. Despite stiff enemy resistance, the Blue Devils reached their initial objectives before dark, well within the time allowed in the plans. Now the Second Battalion moved up to take over the Third's zone. The troops then rested on the initial objective and prepared to continue the attack the next morning. [7]

In this attack Companies B and C particularly suffered perhaps the severest casualties the battalion had experienced to that time. When tanks were brought up at daylight while the companies were being subjected to machine gun and sniper fire, the enemy responded with heavy mortar and artillery fire concentrations. The reserve company, Company A, caught in the barrage, engaged in a fire fight. Now as the companies, A and B, moved on from the first objective, enemy artillery and mortar fire grew less as the afternoon dwindled. After securing the second objective, the battalion then continued on to the third, one mile west of Fogliano. [8]

In the Third Battalion sector, the Blue Devils also came under heavy machine gun, artillery, and mortar fire, whereupon they dug in. However, the battalion took the first objective, the high ground west of Volterra, on time. In the process they captured 17 Jerries. Company K suffered numerous casualties. [9]

Viewed from the regimental command post, the First Battalion position could be seen on the long ridge which extended westward from Volterra. The means of access from the 350th Command Post was a dirt road that wound gradually up a steep hill toward the ridge. Several country homes could be spotted along this ridge, deserted by their owners, with dead cattle and sheep along the area. As Colonel Fry moved near the top of this ridge in the early morning hours of July 8, he spotted Captain Ritts and others from Colonel Bare's headquarters group. It was at this time that the Germans zeroed in with mortar shelling.

After having taken shelter in the unoccupied German foxholes, the Blue Devils continued their act of pillaging German weapons and other souvenirs hurriedly left behind by the retreating Krauts, the most coveted being the German P-38 pistol. Evidence of the intense fighting for this position was the row of bodies of nine men in a small vegetable patch, where enemy machine gun fire had caught them.[10]

The wounded were congregated in this area also. This was the extreme front line. In the previous battle Company C, on the left, had lost a platoon in the valley; and the commanding officer, Captain Throssel, was trying to get in touch with them. Company B, under Captain Haegstron, was at that time working forward on the right. The enemy was making his stand on a narrow ridge to the right, which extended toward the front, from some stone buildings, the only cover on the ridge.

While the First was experiencing these difficulties, the Third was holding its own. The Third found movement in daylight more costly, inasmuch as the men were nearest enemy observation from Volterra. The First, however, was in a better position to maneuver, and during this period the Second watched from the rear, ready to move in when needed. The tanks at this time moved up to help the attacking First, thus permitting the battalion to reduce enemy resistance in the immediate area.

Although the Third Battalion had been told to hold its own, the unit, under Colonel Coleman, hammered away at enemy positions within range and had had tanks moved forward to firing positions in the defilade just south of the ridge crest. The most formidable of enemy strongholds consisted of several buildings to the front, surrounded by a stone wall. From every crevice of these buildings, enemy weapons were used to best advantage. About this time Company I moved forward to help reduce the area. As one of the buildings the enemy was using as a fortress burst into flames, the German infantrymen spewed from doors like mice and waved white cloths. Company I then filtered forward. Ahead lay a deep valley. The enemy would have to withdraw beyond it to make his next stand.[11]

As night approached, Colonel Fry moved the regimental CP to the stone-walled enclosure surounding severl buildings, the objectives that Captain Haegstrom's Company B had captured after a severe battle that morning. Here Major Andrew Cheek, executive officer of the 760th Tank Battalion, joined the 350th Regiment to confer about support for the next day; also, Colonel Lively of the 338th Field Artillery as well as Captain Walter Fingerhut, commanding regimental cannon company, came to coordinate action for the next day. The last of the battalion commanders, Colonel Williamson of the Second, conferred with Colonel Fry about the resumption of the advance on the morrow toward the Arno River.[12]

Next day's action (July 9) consisted in moving to the Era River, crossing it, and advancing 2000 yards north. With the First and Second Battalions beginning the attack at 0400 hours and the Third in reserve, enemy resistance became stiffer as heavy artillery, mortar, and machine gun fire thickened. Although the Third Battalion started out in the morning as reserve, it again took up positions in the line to protect the right flank of the regiment, left open in the advance and thus subject to enemy fire from automatic weapons. The Third, to accomplish this mission, occupied the area overlooking the bridge over the Era River between Cipriano and Villamagna. As the intense fighting during the day caused a heavy expenditure of ammunition, it was necessary to make a temporary halt for re-supply.[13]

For the first time since the jump-off since May 11, the Germans employed the weapon, the "screaming meemies," in action against the Third Battalion.[14] In the First Battalion action, Company C was especially hard hit by mortar fire. The battalion moved on, however, to the high ground north of Villamagna where it encountered fire from several enemy machine guns. As the battalion dug in here, it continued to receive mortar and machine gun fire from the direction of Villamagna.[15]

As the Second Battalion advanced in the approach march on

July 9, several snipers and heavy artillery fire impeded their movement, whereupon the battalion sustained a number of casualties. On the next day, as the battalion was fully committed, enemy artillery became extremely active and inflicted a number of casualties. The Blue Devils of the Second Battalion took 64 of the enemy prisoner.[16]

It was in this action that Technical Sergeant Steven Kasmyna displayed exemplary gallantry in action. When the third platoon of Company E found itself in front of the rest of the company with its flank exposed, the enemy opened up with artillery and machine guns located on each flank and to the front, catching the platoon on barren ground. Sergeant Kasmyna crawled forward under an intense enemy barrage to carry a wounded man fifty yards to safety. After administering first aid amidst this heavy artillery barrage, he was unable to save his comrade's life. When he and one of his men then moved forward to the next objective, his comrade was instantly killed by fire from enemy machine pistols.

No longer with ammunition, Sergeant Kasmyna now attacked the two enemy soldiers there with his bare hands. He knocked one of the Krauts unconscious with a terrific blow of his fist and then pursued the second fleeing enemy when a machine gun opened up on his right flank. He then took cover and later returned to his platoon with one captured enemy.[17]

To counteract enemy activity, Captain Albert Standish, Artillery Liaison Officer and his radio operator, Sgt. Donald Fowler of Clay Center, Kansas, directed accurate artillery fire on enemy positions. This proved to be extremely beneficial to the advance, especially after Jerry had hit the regimental command post. After artillery fire had been directed on enemy mortar positions, the regiment continued to advance slowly.

It was amidst these actions on July 9 that Fortune smiled on Colonel Fry and his immediate entourage in saving their lives from Germans prepared to spring an ambush. As they came upon a building in the broad valley north of the Volterra Ridge, an Italian woman offered to prepare a chicken and wine dinner for them. A German patrol, above on high ground, waited for the group; over open ground, they would have run head on into the German ambush; however, there was also a route through a covered ravine toward the Second Battalion's positions.

While they were eating the lunch prepared by the Italian woman, the Germans decided that the American group had taken the path to the left and thus moved on.

After finishing eating, Colonel Fry and his men did move toward the First Battalion's position, along the route where the ambush had originally positioned itself. Moving forward, Colonel Fry's men encountered a German machine gun position in the process of dismantlement, including perhaps 11 of the enemy. After heroic action by Sgt. Clyde Pope (later Captain) and Staff Sergeant James Gaut, later lieutenant, the leader of Headquarters Reconnaissance Platoon, a number of the German delaying groups were killed and others taken prisoners.[18]

In this advance, Lieutenant Earl E. Danley, Company H, employed his machine guns calmly and efficiently. At this time there was a change in the Regimental Medical Section. Major Perrin, Regimental Surgeon, was relieved to be replaced by Captain Edward Stratman of Fort Thomas, Kentucky. Captain Lawrence Singmaster, formerly assistant surgeon of the Third, moved to take the vacated position of Captain Stratman.[19]

In the direction of advance toward the Arno River and Empoli, the immediate objective for the next day was a series of rolling hills. The advance ran through fields of vegetables, grapes, and grains that splotched the valleys and hillsides. Under each haycock generally appeared an enemy observation post, well camouflaged, with a profusion usually of automatic weapons. There was rolling, cultivated terrain all about this area. In these well-prepared delaying positions, the enemy gave ground only grudgingly. There was a great expenditure of blood each day to drive the enemy back. By this time with the 351st on the left and the 349th on the right of the 350th, the entire Blue Devil Division was committed to battle. The attacking regiment chalked up only a small advance on each seemingly endless day. Occasionally a battalion made a significant advance at night. Platoons took cover in ditches or any other cover available, getting whatever rest possible.

Generally for July 10-11, the regiment made gradual but steady progress, notwithstanding fierce artillery and mortar fire. Amidst stiffening enemy resistance on July 11, the Second Battalion, upon initiating a full scale attack in which the men were aided by a battalion of 4.2 chemical mortars, suffered a number of casualties-1st Lt. Buckner, the communications officer being wounded; and that night, Captain Ott (S-1) and 1st Lt. De Benedetto (S-4) together with three enlisted men, killed when their jeep ran over a Teller mine.[20] They had been traveling to join the Second Battalion, well beyond the front lines, when their jeep struck the mine. Staff Sergeant Albert C.P. Parker and PFC Winfred Arnett, along with Captain Ott, were killed instantly and Lt. Di Benedetto mortally wounded.[21]

A contributing factor to the deaths of these men was the inefficiency of a tank destroyer unit. The tank commander had ordered his men to turn back because he considered the mission too dangerous; in the meanwhile, Colonel Williamson of the Second Battalion had already moved his men onto the hill. When Colonel Fry moved to confer with Colonel Williamson at this time, he found the latter livid with anger; numerous American Blue Devils lay in death, dotting the area where they had attacked without proper tank support.

In this movement forward, The Second Battalion's Company F on July 11 completely routed a German counter-attack, when the company was aided by fire from five artillery battalions; its own heavy weapons company, along with that of the Third Battalion; cannon company; the 4.2. chemical mortars; and Corps artillery. The captured prisoners of war stated that the barrage was so intense that it was impossible for them to move in any direction. They were completely demoralized. Later over 125 German dead were removed from this area.[22]

The First Battalion on July 11 passed up the Second and took a ridge approximately 1 1/2 miles west of Villamagna. Since the enemy still controlled the high ground, he could direct accurate artillery and mortar fire on the troops and also the supporting tanks. Because of intense enemy tank fire, patrols from Company C were forced to abandon two houses that they had recently captured.[23]

In one company of the Third Battalion, Company K, casualties were counted as high as 50 percent. Among those killed was Captain Ortel. A litter squad of 50 POW's worked all night to carry out the WIA for evacuation to the rear. So numerous were the casualties that improvised litters of shelter-halves and blankets had to be used. Captain Stratman and Captain Singmaster performed magnificently in caring for the wounded. The next day, while still under constant artillery and nebelwefer fire and while still evacuating the wounded, the battalion received some replacements. They were not, however, properly equipped for combat. The platoon leaders had difficulty in controlling the raw replacements as they were brought up to the companies under intense enemy fire.

By July 13 enemy resistance weakened, and the advance was resumed. The Blue Devils on this day quickly captured their objectives and rapidly completed their missions. A number of personnel scheduled to return to the United States on rotation assembled near the personnel section to await further orders. On this day the First Battalion dug in about two miles west of Villamagna. The rifle companies then advanced to the high ground approximately two miles from Cadri. After securing the ridge west of Cadri, the battalion set up a defensive position and made plans to attack Chizzano on July 14.

The Second Battalion moved into Cedri on the morning of July 13, under cover od darkness. In the Third Battalion's atack at 0230, the GI's gained the high ground northwest of Villamagna, meeting little resistance. The men here regaled themselves with the huge supplies of vino, chickens, and rabbits, along with fresh plums and apples. They prepared then to move to another objective north of Cedri. Along with the long deserved and eagerly awaited rest came also fresh rations. [24]

On July 14 the Blue Devils continued the attack throughout the day. Meeting only sporadic opposition, the G-I's continued to advance. The First Battalion moved on Chizzano, but when a patrol from Company B reconnoitered the route and were fired on, they radioed for artillery fire and returned to the lines. After daybreak the battalion advanced toward Chizzano and found little resistance. They found the town abandoned, whereupon they continued on now toward Legoli approximately 2 1/4 miles north of Chizzano. [25]

The Second resumed the approach march early on July 14 and also encountered sudden heavy artillery fire at noon. By evening the battalion neared Tojano but suffered heavy casualties by intense small arms and large caliber artillery fire. During the night Company E took Sughera and Tonda with but two casualties, although they were subjected to bombing and strafing by a German plane during the attack. [26]

The Third Battalion received orders to move at 1800 hours to the vicinity of Tojano, after having had a day's rest. Before moving, however, the battalion commander received a message to occupy the high ground northwest of Castelfalfi, where the men arrived around 2200 hours and then posted security guards.[27]

Continuing the advance against strong opposition the next day, the First and Second Battalions led the attack while the Third Battalion followed and protected the right flank. On this day artillery struck the regimental command post and killed three enlisted men and slightly wounded Lt. Col. Cochran, the Executive Officer. Officer replacements joined the regiment during the day and went forward to join the units to which they had been assigned. After dark the Third Battalion relieved the Second, which then went into reserve. [28] For the next day's operation, the First and Third Battalions attacked with the First on the left. The close support provided by B Company, 760th Tank Battalion, enabled them to take their objectives rapidly against strong resistance, although enemy artillery fire proved less effective than in previous attacks.

After being held up by heavy enemy artillery and mortar fire in its attack beyond Legoli, the First Battalion ceased attacking and remained on a ridge approximately 1 ½ miles north of the town and made plans to continue forward on July 16. Since units on the left and right were far behind, the First Battalion attacking forces received fire from the flanks and rear. [29] The Blue Devils of the First Battalion were forced to remain on the ridge throughout July 16, approximately 200 yards beyond their positions of the previous day.

The same general outline of activities for the Third Battalion is similar to that of the First in this period, July 15-16, 1944. After receiving harassing artillery fire and encountering mines on all the roads, Company L moved out to take the next terrain feature but met with a Jerry counterattack and thus withdrew to their original positions. After replacements had been assigned, the battalion received a message to move out at 0200 hours on July 15 for the high ground near Tojano. When the attacking Blue Devils received enemy machine gun, artillery and mortar fire in the open terrain of attack, they were unable to progress during the day. [30]

As the regimental command post settled into a house in Chizzano, a few miles south of Legoli on July 16, Colonel Fry had to caution his men about the use of the gold-bordered china on government issue gasoline stoves. The mistress of the house had offerd abundant complaints. The grinding business of constant attack was somewhat alleviated, however, at this lovely home when Corporal Douglas Allanbrook afforded the men the pleasure of his talented performance on the splendid piano found in the house. It was shortly after this time that Captain Paul R. Carrigg and Lt. Luther Smith, both of Company B, 313th Engineer Battalion, were killed when an artillery shell landed on the regimental CP. The next day, the regiment received a visit from Eve Curie and other French officers of the **Volontaires Francaises.**[31]

The action of July 17 centered about the attack on Tojano, located on top of a sharp hill beyond a deep valley that ran north from Legoli. The Third Battalion had received orders to take the town on the night of July 16, while the First swung wide to the left to by-pass the high ground. Moving out in a night attack at 2300 hours, Colonel Bare's First moved smoothly to the attack. The Third registered no such success, and at the same time reports coming in by field radio about the Third's actions were not satisfactory. Unless the Third moved rapidly, the right flank of the First could be open to counterattack. When Colonel Fry hurried to the Third's command post early the next morning, Colonel Coleman, commanding, gave his reason for the lack of success: Captain Cussans had refused to attack, a charge which the captain readily admitted.

Obviously there was a conflict between personalities-Colonel Coleman apparently was more competent as a staff officer than a combat leader; then, too, combat weariness had taken its toll on Colonel Coleman. The attack at 2300 hours had been too slow, perhaps because of too much methodical planning. The orders to Captain Cussans to take his men in the attack around the face of a barren hill where his men could have been decimated came too late. Captain Cussans explained: "I simply would not attack and have my men killed on that open ground. I was perfectly willing to go forward at night, but we weren't allowed to do so. We know the Jerries are out there and they have had all night to prepare." Because the capable company commander of Company L had demonstrated valor and splendid leadership as a battle field commander in the past, Colonel Fry made the decision of relieving Colonel

Page 74

Coleman. 32

The action of the First Battalion for the remainder of the month of July centered about the town of Calconevisi. On July 17 as the battalion moved in a night attack, Company A on the left gained quickly the high ground to its front while C Company received some machine gun fire in its push forward. As dawn broke, Company A pushed rapidly to the northeast and by the time darkness fell, the battalion was attacking toward Calconevisi in two columns, with Company A as the right column, which soon outdistanced the remainder of the battalion by 200 yards.

As dawn broke, the other companies, in the order of B,C,D, and Hq. Company, moved to get parallel to Company A and reached Calconevisi simultaneously. As Company A halted to await for the left to catch up, it lost contact with the rest of the battalion for the night.

By 1200 hours the left column now bypassed a group of houses containing the enemy and had reached a point 3000 yards too far to the west; the men now halted and reorganized. The next day, July 18, the left column reached Calconevisi around 1200 hours, with the right column, Company A, arriving about an hour later; the latter company had run into a heavily mined field on the trail. As the battalion dug in around the town, the command post established its quarters in a luxurious apartment. Here in Calconevisi the G-I's enjoyed a variety of fresh fruits and vegetables.

By July 19 the battalion had taken up defensive positions in the area. The enemy shelling during the morning inflicted a few casualties. The battalion CP was set up about ¾ mile north of the town. The next day the battalion continued in the same positions. A prisoner of war who deserted to the First reported that the enemy had withdrawn to the Arno River, leaving behind as defense only mined trails and roads. They had had no time to mine the fields.

The next movement of the battalion consisted of patrols about 3000 yards northwest of Selvasan. There they encountered armed Italian partisans who gave considerable information about German dispositions. The following day, July 22, acting upon orders from regimental headquarters, the company commanders sent forward a platoon from each company to secure the positions captured previously by smaller patrols. After a forward movement of about two miles northeast of Calconevisi, the battalion now set up defensive positions in the vicinity of Colleferunacchi, where it would remain until relieved by elements of the 363rd Infantry, 91st Infantry Division. The men then moved by truck 12 miles to the new assembly area near San Vivaldo, Italy. [33]

The Second Battalion during this period operated part time with Task Force Ramey. As it moved to an assembly area near Montaione on July 17, one of the A-T trucks hit a mine, resulting in five minor casualties. After remaining in the area for two days, the battalion then moved on July 20 to San Stefano and later on the same day to Barbialla. As the battalion engaged in light patrol activity, it received scattered artillery fire. On this day the battalion was detached from the task force and returned to regimental control. It now advanced to Tojano and remained there until July 30 when it moved back to San Vivaldo for further training in river crossing operations. [34]

The greatest obstacle to the advance of the Third Battalion was primarily the heavy mine fields. On July 17 as the battalion advanced beginning at 2130 hours, it soon came under machine gun fire and also found it had walked into a mine field. A number of men suffered injuries, including Lt. Wirth and Lt. Shackleford. It was on this day also that Lt. Lee was killed in action. Early next morning, at 0730 the G-I's were ordered back to the original positions while engineers and tanks cleared out the mine fields. When the battalion pushed on again at 1230, the only opposition received was harassing artillery fire. When the men closed in for the night at Castel Barbialla, they found a piano, and the music thus proved a good morale booster,

For the period July 19 to 21 the battalion operated in the vicinity of Leccio and Collegali. On July 22 Captain Butsch became the acting battalion CO, thus relieving Colonel Cochran who now returned to regimental headquarters and re-assumed his duties as executive officer. Captain Cussans assumed the duties of S-3 of the battalion.

By July 24 the battalion occupied ground near the town of Canneto, still occupied by the enemy. Partisans continued to come through the lines with information on Jerry positions. After occupying defensive positions for a few days, the battalion moved out to a rest area in the vicinity of San Vivaldo. After walking about two miles after midnight on July 30, the men then moved by trucks to the rest area, arriving in the vicinity of San Vivaldo approximately an hour later.

Among the casualties from schu mines, Pvt. Marvin J. Niesel exemplified grim courage and fortitude when his foot was blown off by one of Jerry's cigar box size mines. As Colonel Fry, Rocky, and Niesel moved forward to reconnoiter for a CP position in Trojano, Rocky and Colonel Fry moved in front over the same ground where shortly after Niesel hit the schu mine. With the shattered bones of his lower leg protruding from the flesh in shreds, Niesel calmly took his own belt and used it for a tourniquet. A jeep came forward now and took him to the rear.

As replacement officers came forward during these trying times, almost all would plead that they had been trained for some type of duty other than combat. As Colonel Fry went with Captain Joseph Morey, the adjutant, to the rear to check on incoming replacements, only one of the group, Lt. Roule Mozingo, arose and volunteered for combat duty: "Colonel, I think I can command a platoon. I'd like to be with a rifle company."

By July 22 patrols from the regiment neared Empoli. Shortly thereafter the division was ordered withdrawn and directed to move to a rest area in the vicinity of San Vivaldo. [35]

In addition to the changes in officer command in the Third Battalion, other changes occurred. Major Oreskovich, Regimental S-4, was designated First Battalion Executive Officer, and Captain Houck was appointed S-4 in his place. For this phase of the campaign, the 350th Infantry's combat duty of active operations ended on July 24 when the Blue Devils were ordered to move to the bivouac area in the vicinity of San Vivaldo and California.

From the start of the July campaign of a little more than two weeks, the regiment fought more than fifteen miles across rugged, hill terrain in which the enemy frequently held the dominating observation features. The regiment traversed thick mine fields and relentlessly pushed the enemy from strongly held delaying positions. For the last few miles to the Arno, the Blue Devils continued the advance amidst heavy artillery and mortar fire. All these obstacles the valiant Blue Devils overcame as they proved once again that they could complete their mission on schedule. [36]

After the Volterra-Arno battles, the 350th bivouaced in an

area approximately two and one half miles northeast of the village of Villamagna, Italy. To mold the new replacements into the regimental structure, the regiment instituted a strenuous training program, especially in the tactics of river crossing. The fact that there were no streams, rivers, or lakes in the vicinity handicapped the training program.

In the bivouac area could be seen small villages amidst gently-rolling hills. The ridge lines, upon which were capped the small villages, contrasted with the numerous sharp gullies and small valleys. Although most of the ground was barren, here and there olive groves, vineyards, and small patches of trees followed the intermittent stream beds.

To implement instruction in river crossing training, attached units of the 313th Engineers, 19th Engineers, and II Corps troops augmented the training by regularly assigned 350th personnel. Also offering invaluable aid in this training were units from Artillery and Cannon Company, Tank, and T.D. liaison officers. As training began on August 2, 1944, Colonel Fry visited each battalion and summarized to the assembled officers the tactical situation and events known about river crossing operations. The training schedule especially emphasized the use of hand lines over fjords, foot bridges, and assault boats. The regimental communications platoon prepared for a wire team to practice river crossing with each battalion. On one night problem, the troops carried out the training over a steep valley, in lieu of an actual river site.

On Sunday morning, August 6, 1944, the regiment honored those who had displayed special courage in combat by the presentation of awards won on the field of battle. Brigadier General Kurtz represented the Division Commander. After Colonel Fry had given a resume of world events up to the present, he then introduced General Kurtz, who then presented the Legion of Merit and Silver Star to various individuals who had won the medals in combat. The First Sergeant of Company A, Olegardis Kiendanis, received the Legion of Merit and nineteen Silver Stars were awarded, including the following among others: Lt. Col. Walter E. Bare, Jr., Lt. Col. Corbett Williamson, T-Sgt. Hurshel Kidd, Sgt. Francis Gonsalves, Cpl. George Duffy, T-5 Herbert C. Salisbury, Pfc. Edward J. Gallant, Pfc. King Lee, Pfc. Clyde Manly, Pfc. George F. Purvis, Pvt. Joseph Annicchaiarico, and Pvt. Owen Sanderlin.

A number of men hospitalized at the time were also awarded the Silver Star: T-Sgt. Sam Mayo, T-Sgt. Richard J. Neely, and Pfc. Ralph P. Corbin; and one man on rotation leave, T-Sgt. Everett Sowden, was also a recipient of the award.

Those men who received the award posthumously included the following: T-Sgt. Harry E. Ricketts, S-Sgt. Raymond W. Grass, and Pfc. Ferdnand Rodrique. Of the 53 Silver Stars given throughout the 88th Division, the 350th Infantry received nineteen. The Regiment also awarded 43 Bronze Stars; the entire Division had received 83. Following the presentation, an extremely large number of Blue Devils attended religious services in their respective areas. [37]

By August 8 all battalion commanders concerned themselves with the use of pack animal transport for the coming mountain operations. These mule company sections were placed under the battalion S-4's for future operations. One day previous, reconnaissance squads visited a bivouac area site overloking the Arno River for future training. The regiment maintained close contact at this time with the New Zealand Division which occupied the sector. A number of men accompanied several New Zealand patrols to see their sector, the routes leading to the river, and the river site itself. Actual preparation for a coming attack was made at this time.

As a diversion from the regularly assigned combat training program, the Blue Devils especially enjoyed two stage shows currently in the area; one, the Fifth Army Special Service presentation, the "Stars and Gripes," proved to be especially amusing. The training for the period included cross country movement that emphasized maintaining direction and contact with adjacent units at night.

For the period August 15 to August 20, two variations in the regular schedule added interest and pleasure to the regular routine. The first was a contest among the companies in the firing of the rifle, machine gun, and pistol. Each man volunteered to contribute fifty cents to a fund to go to the winning organization; the prize amounted to $936.00. After tabulation of the final scores, Company B, commanded by Captain Floyd A. Haegstrom, took the prize, with a total score of 1006; following closely, Company L tallied 1005 for second place. As a reward for second place, Company L received one day free time and transportation to the beach for swimming.

The second point of interest with the variation from the usual routine was a series of parties held by officers from the various battalions in Castelfalfi. On August 17, it was the turn of the Second Battalion officers; and August 19, the First Battalion game the party at Castelfalfi.

By August 20 the regiment prepared for yet another move-this time to the Leghorn area. On August 19 in the evening a quartering party consisting of the regimental S-3, the battalion commanders, and a non-commissioned officer from each unit left for the vicinity of Leghorn to select new bivouac areas. It was at this time that Captain Morey assumed his new duties as regimental S-1. Throughout the day of Sunday, August 19, the men spent time at the beach in swimming and sun bathing.

The next morning, the combat team began the move over a dusty road for a distance of sixty miles. In this area the regiment operated as a combat team in Fifth Army Reserve, along with attached units. Known as Combat Team No. 2, the regiment ordered one battalion, motorized, to be held in

GIs watch Italian lady bake bread.

readiness for employment on two hours' notice. While in this area all troops received four hours training and four hours of swimming and supervised athletics daily.

Not only officers but also enlisted men had the privilege of club facilities in this area around Leghorn. The site of the clubs, the beach at Ardenza, a small suburb just south of Leghorn, immediately became popular as all Blue Devils regaled themselves with drinks and sandwiches and listened to various Italian orchestras employed for the occasion.

During the closing days of the month, the Blue Devils par-

Staff Sergeant James Gaut killed the machine gunners.

ticipated in competitive athletics, an activity that developed morale to its highest state. Each battalion appointed its own athletic officer who directed a rather extensive program. Along with sports, the men continued swimming and relaxation at the beach. By the close of the month, it could be reported that the health and morale of the troops had attained a very high level. All personnel looked forward to closing with the enemy and hastening the termination of the war in Europe.[38]

Commanding Officer of the 350th Infantry Regiment, Colonel James C. Fry.

SKETCHED AT THE ITALIAN FRONT By Pvt. G. FAGERHOLM

Clayton Eighmey

With the Fifth Army, Italy — Speeding along a narrow mountain road in Italy under fire from a Mark VI "Tiger" tank and skirting a sheer cliff, a squad of 88th Infantry Division soldiers recently ran two jeeps over a field of German anti-tank mines and escaped without a scratch.

The first jeep, driven by Private Clayton Eighmey of Erie, had rolled one mine over in a ditch, tipped up a second one and straddled a third.

The squad completed its mission, reconnoitering an abandoned German command post on the Fifth Army front, and returned over the route of its narrow escape before it was realized that the road had been mined. Five anti-tank mines, lightly covered with earth, were found.

Others on the mission were Sergeant John Sohanchak, Camden, New Jersey; PFC. Nicholas M. Draschill, Sebewaing, Michigan and Private Lewis Alpine, son of Mrs. Lillian Alpine, Detroit.

The accompanying drawing of Private Eighmey and his jeep, leading vehicle on the patrol, was drawn by Private G. Fagerholm, of the 88th Division.

• • •

Eighmey is the son of Mr. and Mrs. Delbert Eighmey of Erie. Before entering the Army December 9, 1942, at Ft. Custer he was employed by the Spicer Manufacturing Company in Toledo. He helped make axles for Army jeeps. He took his basic training at Camp Claiborne, Louisiana, where he was assigned to the 143rd "Cactus" Division. He arrived in North Africa with the 88th Division at the end of last year.

Private Marvin J. Niesel being taken to a jeep for evacuation.

GERMAN INFANTRYMAN, P.W.
AFTER CAPTURE AT VOLTERRA,
ITALY, JULY 10, 1944
SKETCHED BY PVT.
G. FAGERHOLM

A captured German command post made life more comfortable for Colonel Fry on occasion.

Typical terrain over which the Blue Devils fought in the July operation. German machine gun positions could usually be found camouflaged at the bottom of such hay stacks.

Taking the wounded into an aid station.

Mile after mile of rugged mountains lay between the Arno and Po Valleys.

Antitank ditch constructed by the Todt Organization to protect Futa Pass.

Sketch by Gus Fagerholm—Italian Theater, 1944 - 350th Infantry Reg't. from the collection of William Gardner Bell.

Footnotes to Chapter IV

Starr, **From Salerno to the Alps,** 269-275.

Ibid., 290-291.

350th Infantry Regiment History, July, 1944.

Fry, **Combat Soldier,** 127.

Personal Correspondence from Clayton Eighmey to the author, April 17, 1976; and Newspaper Clipping, Summer, 1944.

6 Delaney, **The Blue Devils in Italy,** 108.

7 350th Infantry Regiment History, July, 1944.

First Battalion History, July, 1944.

Third Battalion History, July, 1944.

10 Fry, **Combat Soldier,** 134.

11 **Ibid.,** 133-138.

12 **Ibid.,** 140.

13 350th Infantry Regiment History, July, 1944.

14 Third Battalion History, July, 1944.

15 First Battalion History, July, 1944.

16 Second Battalion History, July, 1944.

17 General Orders No. 82, Hq. 88th Infantry Division, 18 Sept 1944.

18 Fry, **Combat Soldier,** 142-147.

19 **Ibid.,** 147.

20 Second Battalion History, July 10-11, 1944.

21 Fry, **Combat Soldier,** 151.

22 Second Battalion History, July, 1944.

23 First Battalion History, July, 1944.

24 Third Battalion History, July, 1944.

25 First Battalion History, July, 1944.

26 Second Battalion History, July, 1944

27 Third Battalion History, July, 1944.

28 350th Infantry Regiment History, July, 1944.

29 First Battaion History, July, 1944.

30 Third Battalion History, July, 1944.

31 Fry, **Combat Soldier,** 152-153.

32 **Ibid.,** 155.

33 First Battalion History, July, 1944.

34 Second Battalion History, July, 1944.

35 Fry, **Combat Soldier,** 152-160.

36 350th Infantry Regiment History, July, 1944.

37 350th Infantry Regiment History, August, 1944.

38 **Ibid..**

Chapter Five

The 350th Infantry in the
Gothic Line Campaign:
The First Phase, September, 1944

Although the campaigns of the spring and summer of 1944 had proven the combat mettle, courage, and tenacity of the 350th Infantry Regiment, the battles of September-November, 1944, in the mountains just short of the Po Valley, would prove to be the most trying experiences yet endured by the regiment. One historian has described the Gothic Line campaign as an action wherein the German lines sagged and fell back but were still able to contain the Allied drive just short of the promised land-the Po Valley.

While the Eighth Army was beginning the attack against the German Gothic Line in the last days of August, the 350th Infantry was bivouaced approximately two and one-half miles east of Livorno, Italy, where it was pursuing a program of training with special emphasis on conduct of combat in mountainous terrain. Battalion, company, and special unit commanders received instruction in streamlining their battalions for the anticipated mountain operations. The Regiment was held in corps reserve at this time, with one battalion always on a twenty-four hour alert to be able to move for any emergency in two hours, to be followed by the remainder of the Regiment in eight hours. Along with training the men enjoyed themselves in their off hours in relaxation at the beach, including swimming and sun bathing.

Training included battalion combat problems with emphasis on entering the assembly area, advancing to the line of departure, and driving the enemy from the high ground in the vicinity of Volle Benedetto. The enemy detail was furnished by

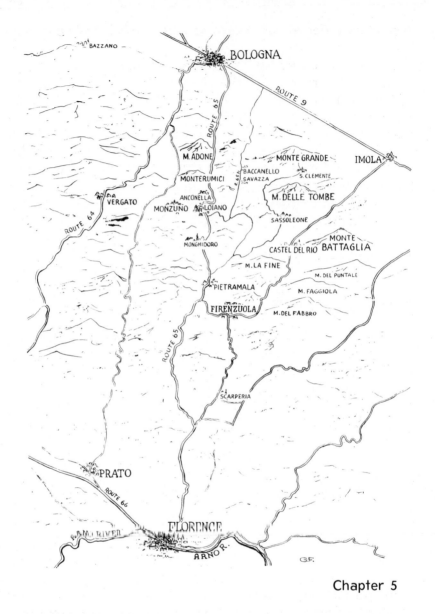

the Anti-Tank Company. Colonel Fry, Regimental Commanding Officer, was well pleased with the performance of the battalions. On the morning of September 5 General Paul Kendall, Division Commanding Officer, accompanied Colonel Fry to the site of the problems to observe the Third Battalion conduct their exercises. In the afternoon Colonel Fry presented awards to personnel of the First Battalion at 1300 hours; the

Second Battalion at 1400 hours; and the Third Battalion at 1500 hours.

Late the same evening Colonel Fry received a verbal order to move the Regiment just west of Galluzzo, Italy, to rejoin the division approximately three miles southwest of Florence. On September 6 the Third and Second Battalions began moving in the morning with Regimental Headquarters leaving at 1150 and arriving in the new area in a driving rain at 2030 hours. Special units and the First Battalion left the following day. (See Map I for route of movement). The weather was extremely bad, but the Regiment continued its movement in spite of the strong wind and driving rain and traveled a distance of approximately ninety-eight miles.[2]

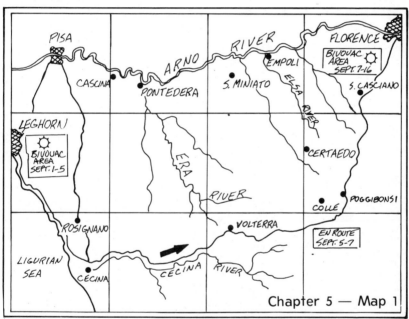

Chapter 5 — Map 1

After the Regiment had settled into the bivouac area, the men spent the next day in drying all blankets and equipment, cleaning weapons, and improving the bivouac site. During this process the Regiment was visited by General Kendall and General Ramey, the new Assistant Division Commander, both of whom were well pleased with the general orderliness and efficiency of the site even under the conditions of inclement weather and poor terrain for bivouac. At a meeting of battalion commanders, executive officers, and S-3's that afternoon,

Colonel Fry issued a memorandum which stressed the company and battalion's responsibilities in keeping their commands suitably organized, equipped, alerted, and enthusiastic in closing with the enemy. At religious services on Sunday, September 10, there was an increase in attendance, a trend which had occurred over the last six-months period.

Beginning on Monday, September 11, the Regiment continued its small unit training with the usual vigor and enthusiasm as everyone realized that the coming operations would test his ability, resourcefulness, stamina and courage to the utmost. In the mud-filled bivouac area, all personnel worked for improvement in general orderliness and cleanliness. Since only a one-way traffic network of roads led into and out of the area, special police from the I and R Platoon were created to aid in the operations of traffic control. On September 12 a reconnaissance party reported into the 91st Division CP for orders and instructions. Included in this group were Lt. Col. Cochran, the Regimental Executive Officer; Lt. Col. Bare; Major Oreskovitch; Captain Taylor; Captain Cussans; and Lt. Pope, the I and R Platoon leader. Increased emphasis was placed on the training of each individual unit for combat operations in the future.

In the highlight of the day, September 13, Colonel Fry spoke to Companies A and C, the purpose of which was to acquaint the men better with the Regimental Commander and his qualifications and experiences. Reconnaissance of the forward areas continued the next day, September 14, as Colonel Fry, Major Collier, Major Witter, Captain Ritts, Captain King, and Lt. Bryson moved to the 91st Division CP to obtain information of the area and to formulate plans for the future. Because the Regiment was bivouaced in the proximity of Florence, the men received passes to that city, where they could relax and enjoy a few days away from the general routine of military life. Training for the next day stressed individual cover and concealment, physical training, extended order drill, and squad problems. In the evening beginning at 2100 hours, the First Battalion engaged in problems relating to map work and compass reading.

On September 16 the Regiment was moving again. Returning from a trip to the Division CP, Colonel Fry issued a verbal order to move the Regiment to the vicinity of San Piero A.

Sieve, Italy. Another move closer to the line was anticipated as Division was expecting to commit the Regiment under control of the 85th Division. The first unit that made the move that day was Service Company, which traveled a distance of twenty-one miles late in the evening to settle into the new area at 2300 hours. Included in the combat team's movement of that day was the 338th Field Artillery, which closed into the area at 0345 hours the following morning.[3]

Although there was much activity around the Regimental Command Post with General Kendall present much of the day, Sabbath services were conducted with an outstanding number at attendance. Later that day Colonel Fry received a directive from Division, which read in part as follows:

> 350th CT will reconnoiter immediately an assembly area in rear of 337 or 339 Inf in 85 Div zone as far N of Sieve River as practicable and RCT will move under cover of darkness night of 17-18 Sept to area selected. Assembly areas will be cleared with CG 85 Div and this Hq. Be prepared to pass through elements of 337 and 339 Inf and launch atk prior to daylight of 19 Sept.

Following through with these instructions, a quartering party left immediately and selected a new area two and one half miles northwest of Borgo San Lorenzo with the Regimental Command Post in the village of Romanelli. Pressed for time, Major Melcher, Regimental S-3, issued a verbal order moving the Regiment to the new site with Cannon Company as the first unit to leave, crossing the IP at 1945. The Third Battalion had cleared the area by 2215, all foot soldiers marching to their areas a distance of eight and one-half miles. (See Map 2 for bivouac and assembly areas September 16-21, 1944.)

With the possibility of imminent commitment to combat, on September 18 four separate parties were dispatched to reconnoiter the road net behind the 337th and 339th Infantry Regiments: Lt. Pope, I and R Platoon leader, representing the Regiment; and reconnaissance parties each of engineers, medics, and artillery. To insure that the Regiment had full knowledge of the terrain as it moved into the lines, the Commanding Officer dispatched representatives to the two leading battalions of the 337th and 339th Infantry Regiments to serve as

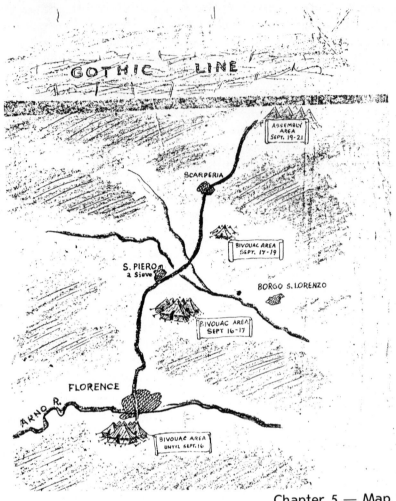

GOTHIC LINE

ASSEMBLY AREA SEPT. 19-21

SCARPERIA

BIVOUAC AREA SEPT. 17-19

S. PIERO a Sieve

BORGO S. LORENZO

BIVOUAC AREA SEPT 16-17

FLORENCE

ARNO R.

BIVOUAC AREA UNTIL SEPT. 16

Chapter 5 — Map 2

guides. The last unit of the Regiment to move into the new site was the Anti-Tank Company, which closed the Regiment's movement officially at 1400 hours. As the Regiment continued to await further movement orders on September 19, Colonel Fry held a meeting in the afternoon of all battalion and special unit commanders to issue the instructions that he had just received for movement. The Regiment's new assembly area was to be just north of Altuzzo Ridge, and instructions were given to the commanders to prepare to cross the line of departure at 0500 on September 21.

Captain Morey, Regimental S-3, immediately led the quartering party to the vicinity of Barco, Italy (in the Altuzzo area), to prepare for bivouac sites. At 1800 hours the Regiment crossed the line of departure in the order of Third, Second, and First Battalions. Two jeeps and two trailers were allotted to accompany each battalion to insure meals for the troops the following day. Service Company began preparing a new supply dump in the vicinity of the new area. The Regimental History concludes this period with the following summary:

> All organic transportation was ordered to move the following day. The Command Group of the Regiment moved to the forward C.P. (907987, Firenzuola map) in order to push the coming operations. The mule trains were ordered forward to the new area; all liaison officers were accepted from the attached units and all preparations were made for the coming jump-off. Field Order No. 9 was received which stated that Regiment would pass through the 337 Inf (at 946041, Palazzuolo map) and attack the following morning at 0500.[4]

In the initial campaign for the Gothic Line the 88th Infantry Division had been held in reserve, ready to exploit any breakthrough or to be able to continue the offensive against the retreating Germans. The crucial period for the 350th would come in the thrust toward Imola on the right flank of the II Corps, beginning on September 20, 1944, as the 88th moved into positions to relieve the 85th, one of the main American divisions that had originally pierced the formidable Gothic Line to the west along Highway 65 earlier in the month. The 88th was now to be given the task of punching through supposedly light enemy divisions to the right of the previous line of advance, the area along Route 65.

Several strategic and tactical considerations prompted the change in direction of attack from the main axis along Route 65, the closest route to Bologna in the Po Valley. There was still hope that a breakthrough in the mountains to the east, closer to the British XIII Corps boundary, could effect a pincer movement from the west in conjunction with a British spearhead from the east and thus effect the capture and-or annihilation of much of the German Tenth Army. The idea still persisted as a leftover from strategy around the Cassino-Anzio Front operations of May-June, 1944, when the Tenth Army had escaped such an encirclement; also the thrust toward Imola on Highway 9, the main communication artery in the Po Valley from the east leading to Bologna, could aid the hard-pressed British forces that had been unable to achieve the objectives in their drive, begun in August, 1944, by this period of September, 1944. These considerations thus prompted General Clark "to direct part of the U.S. II Corps across the mountains to Imola, twenty miles nearer to Eighth Army down Route 9 than Bologna, while his British XIII Corps continued to make its necessarily slow way across the exiguous roads toward Faenza, which was nearer still." [5] (See Map 3)

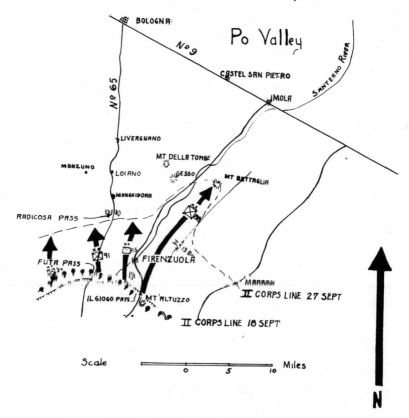

88ᵗʰ DIVISION DRIVE TOWARD IMOLA

Chapter 5 — Map 3

Instead of opposition by the "supposedly light enemy divisions" in the line of attack of the 350th, the Regiment would discover the most fanatically determined enemy in its path of advance. The Commanding Officer of the 350th, Colonel Fry, later wrote that the battles in the mountains just short of Bologna in September, and particularly Mt. Battaglia, was the story of 3500 American men, who fought, starved, froze, and died along the red line of battle. His memory retains the picture of "American and German bodies intermingled on the crest, a peak formed by three knifelike mountain ridges." [6] Describing the line of advance over which his "old-young men" would have to advance, he continued: "The rugged mountain terrain presented a picture so dismal my spirits sank. A forest of pines that averaged about ten inches in diameter had been cut down by our all-out artillery preparations. Shattered trees dangled at all angles. Water dripped from the shrubbery, and the mud made huge rolls on my shoes..." [7]

The preparation for the battles that would climax on Mt. Battaglia had begun on September 16, when Colonel Fry had issued verbal orders to move the Regiment from its area around Florence to the vicinity of San Piere A. Sieve, close to the front just north of Florence. The Second Battalion had been alerted for movement on September 16, 1944, equipment was streamlined, and preparations completed for mountain operations. The Battalion then traveled by truck column at night to the area around Vaglia, Italy, and on September 17 had closed into the vicinity of Borgo San Lorenzo. The following day the Battalion Executive Officer accompanied the Commanding Officer to reconnoiter the 337th Infantry positions, then in contact with the enemy. At 1800 hours that evening the Battalion moved approximately 15000 yards to the vicinity of Riberio, Italy, where it entered the Appenine chain of mountains there.[8] The Third Battalion had left the area south of Florence also on the same day, had driven 20 miles to a bivouac area, and on September 17 had moved 7 ½ miles further to the vicinity of Ferracciano, Italy, establishing its CP there on September 18. On September 19, the Battalion traveled approximately 13 miles on foot and began going up into the mountains as it started to rain.[9]

By September 19 the First Battalion had reached also the vicinity of Borgo San Lorenzo. The CO, Lt. Col. Walter Bare, and the S-2, Lt. May, went on a reconnaissance of forward areas, and by 1900 hours the Battalion had arrived in rear of the front line troops. [10]

After September 20 the 350th would engage in forty-four days of combat that would cost the entire 88th Division 6000 casualties. When the offensive was finally called off toward the last of October, the "Blue Devils" held the terrain farthest forward of the entire Allied line-they could look down into the valley of the Po, but few who originally formed part of the assault regiments were left to enjoy the sight. [11]

The assembly area for the Regiment before the jump-off on the morning of September 21 was approximately 2 ½ miles northwest of the village of Borgo San Lorenzo. [12] In this part of the battle front the Santerno River and Highway 6528 twist and turn through a narrow gorge flanked by high mountains for approximately half of the 30 mile distance separating Firenzuola, the key communication center for the continuance of the attack toward the Po Valley, from Imola astride Highway 9, the eastern communication artery in the British XIII Corps sector leading to Bologna. In these steep heights, broken only by narrow ravines, the supply routes up to the man in the foxhole would in general be over mere trails.

The terrain over which the 350th would advance was a high-peaked ridge forming the right boundary with XIII Corps. The area leading to the scene of the fiercest combat for the Regiment in September, Mt. Battaglia, stretched generally for a distance of approximately eleven miles, beginning with Roncaccio Hill, which paralleled the Santerno River; six miles further, Mount Puntale, from which a second ridge branched off to the north to Mount della Croce; and thence northeast for approximately three miles, passing through Mt. Acuto to Mt. Carnevale and thence two miles to Mt. Battaglia. These two peaks were to be the last major heights before the terrain begins sloping down through broadening valleys toward the plain. To control the river valley and the highway necessitated controlling the mountains on either side, and along these ridges supplies could be brought forward only with the greatest difficulty. This was the unprepossessing terrain over which the 350th would battle. [13]   (See Map 4).

The right boundary of the Division and hence the 350th Regimental zone would be the boundary between II and XIII

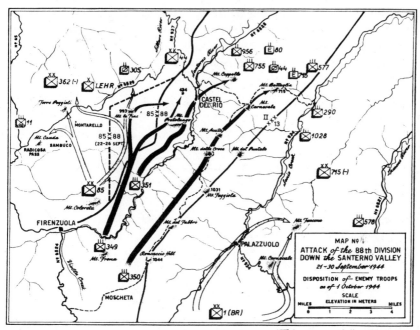

Corps, and the left would adjoin the 85th Infantry Division approximately 1 ½ miles west of and parallel to Highway 6528.[14] Moving out at 1800 hours, September 20, the Battalions entered the battle zone in order of Three, Two, and One. Order Number 9 called for the Regiment to pass through the 337th Infantry in the Palazzuolo map area and attack the following morning at 0500.[15]

As the Regiment jumped off to the attack at 0500, the actual fighting narrowed down to who occupied and controlled the network of roads, all of which in this area were inadequate for very effective communication and transportation. As the Regiment moved to the attack with the 66th Infantry Brigade of the 1st British Infantry on its right and the 349th Infantry as its supporting team on the left, the troops received sporadic but harassing artillery fire with the communication hub, Firenzuola, in the valley three miles to the west on the receiving end of concentrated artillery barrages. From the rear command post in the small town of Moscheta, Colonel Cochran, the Regimental Executive Officer, with experience in mountain warfare, was placed in command of all supply movements. He had the 12th Mule Pack Group attached to his command. While the light mist was falling after a previous hard rain, Colonel Cochran received the news of the occupation of M. Del Fabbro with very little resistance. [16] (See Map 5.)

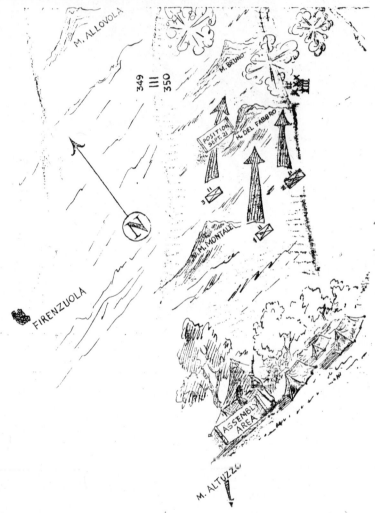

Chapter 5 — Map 5

Added to the difficulties of the 350th Infantry in addition to the terrain and poor supplies was the exposed right flank, since the Regiment and Division moved forward more rapidly than the British 1st Division on its right, the gap sometimes extending to as much as three miles. The First Battalion was assigned the responsibility in the first few days of guarding this flank, but when its services were demanded in the line, men from the 760th Tank Battalion were converted into Infantry and posted as flank guards.

The acute danger resulting from the gap between the Americans and the British was made clear on the night after the initial jump off. As the First Battalion set up its headquarters in a house below Mount del Fabbro, with B and C Companies moving into positions north and northeast of the house and Companies A and D pulling up later to the south and southeast, the inner left flank was left open. Advance elements of the 2nd Battalion, 132d Grenadier Regiment, blundered upon the house from the supposedly safe inner left flank. A fire fight developed, and the battle raged from room to room and floor to floor before approximately 23 officers and men were captured. The **Fifth Army History** gives the reason for the capture as the following: the dark night, American sounding machine guns used by the enemy, and several English speaking Germans, all of which confused the troops outposted about the area. [17] (See Map 6.)

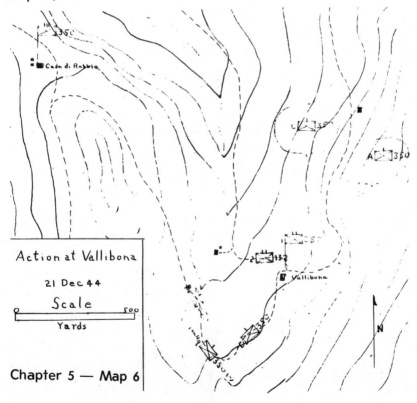

Action at Vallibona

21 Dec 44

Scale

500

Yards

Chapter 5 — Map 6

Accounts from Battalion histories, commanders, and personal narratives, along with those of captured enemy personnel, amplify these details. At the time of the capture of the First Battalion headquarters, the enemy was still putting up a stiff fight for the area around the key junction town of Firenzuola. As the 350th moved to the attack, the First Battalion, led by Lt. Col, Walter Bare, moved out in front. The reserve battalion, the Second, was stretched out almost in single file along a trail that wound through a narrow damp gorge. Late afternoon found the First Battalion on a ridge that formed the main avenue of advance, and on the right was Mt. del Fabbro. As Colonel Fry halted his advancing troops to allow the Third Battalion to pull abreast on the left, 20 captured Krauts marched by, an event that seemed to presage victory. Colonel Fry recalls that he said to Colonel Bare: "My CP group can go into that house" (by the name of Vallibona), pointing to some slopes on del Fabbro. "No, on second thought, you take it, Walter, and I will settle for this shack right in front of us. That will put me between you and Witter." (Third Battalion CO). [18] That decision was of crucial significance, inasmuch as the First Battalion headquarters would be captured by the strong German patrol that attacked around 2030 hours, approximately 30 minutes after the battalion command post had been established and some of the rifle troops had dug in.

Covering all trails with machine guns and hurling grenades into the house, the enemy patrol succeeded in capturing most of the battalion command post, including the CO, Lt. Col. Bare; the Executive Officer, Captain James Ritts; the S-3, Captain Sterling Borquist; Captain Murphy, the artillery liaison officer, Captain Romano, Company A CO; Lt. Ashcraft; Lt. McCabe; and some 20 enlisted men. The patrol had been bypassed in the fog and thus was well situated to spring its attack as night descended. One enlisted man was killed in the melee, and the Battalion S-2, Lt. May, barely effected his escape by jumping from a second story window. [19]

The interrogation report of a captured enemy soldier, P.W. Obergrenadier Klement, of the 8th Co., 2nd Bn., 132nd Regt., 44th Division, gave his version of the incident. He said that German Captain Knoll was leading his battalion, 200 men strong, to a new position. Sometimes around midnight they reached a building at 980060 and saw a dim light in the area.

Captain Knoll, Lt. Bauer, and Lt. Sellhorn, an English-speaking officer, and a spearhead of several men went forward to investigate. When shooting started as they approached the building, P.W. Klement dashed into the building, assuming that Partisans were trying to interfere with the Captain's advance. Instead he found American soldiers in the basement and top floor. They were firing in the direction of the hall.

As shooting increased inside the building, Captain Knoll went outside to order his men to take up a porcupine position, which would enable them to fire in all directions. Many hand grenades were thrown from and to the building, but none inside. After a firefight of approximately 30 minutes duration, the German officers and men brought a high-ranking American officer and several of lower ranks out of the building. The high-ranking officer was told to order his men to stop shooting and to surrender to the Germans. The English-speaking German, Lt. Sellhorn, called first upon the Americans in the woods to surrender to the 800 Germans unless they wanted their CO to be shot. Apparently this order was disregarded as the German P.W. heard a German-speaking American reply to this call.[20]

Details about this event recalled by two of the American prisoners fill in the narrative. As Colonel Bare moved toward the house at Vallibona, only a squad of men in front protected battalion headquarters. Colonel Bare gave orders for various rifle companies to take up positions around the headquarters.[21] Company A took positions in the northeast portion of the battalion area and Company C in the northwest portion, while Company D and Headquarters Company were to position in the vicinity of the command post. Company B occupied an area astride the trail to the south of the command post. Companies A and C quickly organized for the night and established local security. With the command post established on the first floor and the second floor designated as sleeping quarters for the command post personnel, one room on the floor and the outbuildings were to house the remainder of Headquarters Company, and Company B had not yet closed into the bivouac area. [22] The Regimental Command Post was located as Casa di Rabbio. (See Map.)

Colonel Bare gave orders for the Heavy Weapons Company Commander, who had just recently assumed that command, to come up to headquarters for instructions. His company was to take up positions to cover the extremely large draw then open to the enemy. Outside the building facing north, two men had been posted as immediate security.[23] As the two rifle companies proceeded past the headquarters, the commanding officer of Company A and his executive officer came into the house. Colonel Bare then gave orders for all men to turn off their radios to keep them from running the batteries down. Further orders stipulated that each commanding officer would send a runner to the battalion headquarters to relay any message.[24]

One reason for the delay of Company D into position in the movement toward Vallibona was the heavy equipment carried and the resulting slow progress over the steep mountain trails. About the time that the first men of the heavy weapons company arrived at battalion headquarters, a company of Germans attacked. A lone figure carrying a lantern approached the command post from the steps leading from the terraced area on which the command post building was located. After he had called in Italian to the two security guards at the command post entrance, the guards told him to put the light out, whereupon the German immediately fired a burst from a machine pistol, killing one of the guards and seriously wounding the other, who then ran to the upper part of the house through an open door. Immediately a large group of Germans dashed from the steps from which the first man had come and surrounded the command post building in a type of porcupine formation-two or three men with automatic weapons at each corner of the house firing in all directions away from the house.[25]

By this time the Germans had set up a machine gun down the path through which the Headquarters Company had proceeded and began firing. Some of the men from the head of the column ran into the basement of the house (which housed the animals), the part that faced the large draw. The rifle companies apparently realized only slowly that the headquarters was being attacked and thus did not react quickly enough to counteract the initial advantage of the attackers.[26]

A grenade thrown into the command post had caught the battalion commander and other personnel present completely by surprise. As they dashed up the steps to get their weapons on the second floor, the Germans thus entered the first floor.[27]

They pressed into the house, blowing the doors down with grenades, and came into the main room. For about an hour and a half following, a fight ensued between the Americans on the second floor and the Germans on the first. From a room on the second floor, Colonel Bare and Captain Borquist attempted to barricade themselves with mattresses. After about forty-five minutes the door to the small room at the south end of the second floor in which the battalion commander and the S-3 were isolated was blown from its hinges by grenades; both officers, wounded, now surrendered. Later the remainder of the command post personnel surrendered.

After the prisoners had been assembled in the command post, searched, and interrogated, the first platoon of Company D, having worked its way to a position up the hill from the command post, opened fire with its machine guns, firing into the command post and the upper floor of the building. Six Germans were wounded. It was at this time that the German commander informed Colonel Bare that he could fight his way out but could take no prisoners. He gave Colonel Bare two minutes to decide to order the battalion to cease fire. By this time Company A had also begun firing on the command post with rifles and 60 mm mortars. [28]

Colonel Bare considered all the alternatives; however, once he had made his dicision, he advised the German captain that he would do as requested. Bullets now came in through the side door. One of the Germans was hit in the calf of the leg.

As Colonel Bare started walking out, he began talking to his men and telling them that they had waited too long to give adequate help and thus requested them to cease fire. The Germans, he continued, would take the Americans down the mountains to their own line. The German commander then ordered the Americans to line up one behind the other with each placing his hand on the belt of the man in front so that they could proceed safely down the mountain. [29] The Germans now marched the prisoners down the same steps which were used in the attack on the command post. Just below the steps and at points on down to the bottom of the draw, the prisoners could see a column of Germans of the decimated 2d Battalion, 132d Regiment, 44th Division, with four mule-drawn close support howitzers. The German column which had had the mission of going into a defensive position in that area began to move back into the German lines.[30]

The trail that the men traversed was paralleled on either side by deep gulfs, so if any man lost his footing he would fall over the precipice. Eventually the prisoners came to a point where the ground leveled out and stopped for a break. For the next few days they scarecely received any rations at all.[31]

While the First Battalion was reorganizing after the capture of its leading officers, the other two battalions of the Regiment were making steady progress. There were two reasons primarily for the generally rapid advances of the 350th Infantry in the next three days after the initial jumpoff: the general disorganization of the enemy forces and the bulge formed by the attacking regiments of the 88th which widened the gap between the enemy 4th Parachute and 715th Grenadier Divisions.[32] By nightfall of the 21st the Third Battalion had reached Mount Bruno: the Second was on Mount Della Cistina one thousand yards to the southwest; and the First Battalion was protecting the supply lines by holding Mount del Fabbro and Hill 932.[33] On the morning of the 22nd, Major Mike Oreskovitch, the Executive Officer of the Second Battalion, and Captain Erwin Jones, the Assistant Regimental S-2 and S-3, were directed to take command of First Battalion. One day later Lieutenant Charles P. Lynch, Jr., assumed the duties as S-3.

By September 24 the enemy was offering fierce resistance to the advancing 350th. The Krauts now realized the threat coming from the 88th and rushed to head off the attempt to break through to Highway 9 toward Imola. Additional enemy units that fiercely contested each mountain peak included the 305th Fusilier Battalion, elements of the 132d Grenadier Regiment and of the 715th Greanadier Division, the Italian Bersaglieri, 1028th Grenadier Regiment, and the remainder of the 44th Grenadier Division that were moved into the line.[34]

By September 23 the 3rd Battalion appeared to be receiving the brunt of enemy resistance. By last light of day elements of the battalion had knifed forward to seize and hold formidable M. Della Croce, a rugged 712 foot mountain, "which resulted in the farthest advanced unit in the entire 5th Army."[35] The next day in its attempt to move forward from M. Della Croce toward M. Acuto, 1200 yards away, the Third encountered an enemy fighting with fanatical courage to block the advance. Both the

Second and the Third Battalions repulsed fierce counter-attacks and continued to move against stiff resistance. (See Map 7.)

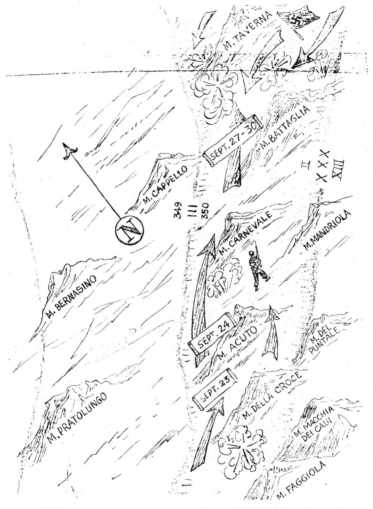

Chapter 5 — Map 7

In this attack Technical Sergeant Steven M. Kosmyna moved his platoon up M. Delle Croce, even before the other platoons of his company had moved forward. Having become separated from the remainder of the company because of a driving rain and poor visibility, Sgt. Kosmyna nevertheless led his platoon up the hill against intense enemy machine gun and small arms fire. Alone he braved the enemy fire to assault a machine gun position. After neutralizing the machine gun nest, he then ran toward an enemy-occupied sangar, was momentarily stunned by an enemy grenade (fortunately a dud) thrown into his face, parried a bayonet lunge, and then killed his opponent with a rifle bullet. With such inspiring leadership, Sgt. Kosmyna instilled in his men the offensive spirit necessary for driving the enemy from Mt. Delle Croce.

As the casualty rate was increasing by the hour, Colonel Fry moved forward to observe personally the conduct of the battle. Still the Division directives called for exerting every effort to advance "to capture the blue line in the zone," to protect the right flank, to maintain contact with British elements, to push patrols well forward on the Firenzuola-Imola road in the zone, and to protect the engineer parties holding the road. One battalion was to be held in reserve to be committed only with Division approval. By nightfall the Third was moving toward Acuto; the Second was on Il Castellaccio; and the First began to move to Mt. Macchia Dei Caui, to be in striking distance if called upon. [36]

On September 24 the First Battalion reported some movement to other positions; the Second advanced from Mt. Faggiola in the evening, reaching Roncozzola on the 25th with only light casualties and rested there until September 27, when at 0500, it would begin an advance through the Third to the summit of Mount Battaglia. At this period before the battle for Battaglia the Third Battalion, under Major Vincent M. Witter of Berlin, New Hampshire, suffered heavy casualties as it attempted to wipe out enemy positions in its drive to secure Mt. Acuto.

On the 25th as the Third moved to the attack, the enemy counterattacked from the front and rear. First Lt. Donald E. Muston of Company K and Detroit, Michigan, at this time moved his platoon forward and placed his men in a defensive position. When an enemy sniper opened fire from the right flank to harass his platoon, Lt. Muston unhesitatingly and singlehandedly stalked the sniper and killed him. As he then led his platoon in a fierce fight against the onrushing enemy, he personally accounted for four more of the enemy and aided in capturing five others. After forcing the enemy to flee, Lt. Muston then led his platoon in taking the battalion objective.

When the CO of Company L was seriously wounded and the

company disorganized after suffering heavy casualties, Captain Thomas S. Cussans, the Battalion S-3, of Flint Michigan, took command and saved the battalion as well. He then led the company to the next hill, going from man to man to encourage them.[37]

On this day the Second Battalion was just short of Mt. del Puntale, and the Third was on top of rocky and barren Mt. Delle Croce. The day before, Lt. George H. Carpenter, Company I CO from Malvern, Arkansas, had promised Colonel Fry that his troops would be on top of the hill the next morning; he kept his word, although he fell from a sniper's bullet on the 26th.[38] On the 24th Captain Edward J. Maher of Flushing, Long Island, CO of Company L, received a bullet through his chest but was saved by first aid.   [39]

By the 25th the Regiment was well ahead of the 351st Infantry Regiment in the valley on the left, south of Castel del Rio. Not only was the 350th suffering from heavy concentrations of artillery on the left and from the front, but also from the area of Palazzuolo, in front of the British slowly advancing troops on the right. The much-needed rest deserved by the valiant attacking Blue Devils would have to wait, however, as the message from Division Headquarters commanded: "Fifth Army plans require the capture of Carnevale and Battaglia. Take them as soon as possible."[40] (See Map 8.)

By this date the 88th was preparing to take the last commanding peaks in its zone-the aforementioned Carnevale and Battaglia in the 350th zone, with Mount Pratolungo on the left in the 349th zone. These heights were of paramount importance to the Germans, for "the loss of this chain of mountains, extending west to east through Castel del Rio, would deprive the Germans of the strongest defensive positions between Castel del Rio and the Po plains." The task of the 350th was to clear the ridge stretching from Mount Acuto to Mount Battaglia.[41]

The attack, set for 0600, September 26, began on schedule. During the first day of the attack the 2nd and 3rd Battalions reached positions north of Mount Acuto, and the 1st Battalion on the right seized Mount del Puntale. The advance, however, broadened the gap between the Regiment and the British 1st Division to as much as 8000 yards. More and more units from Army reserve were called up to man the long exposed flank to

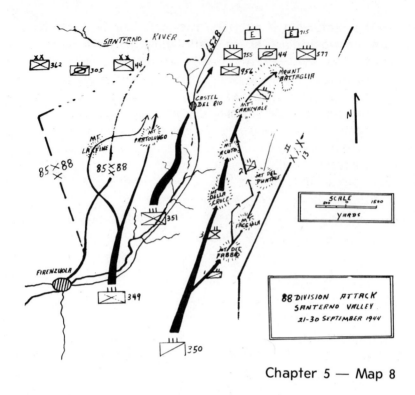

Chapter 5 — Map 8

assure the 350th Infantry that its supply lines would remain open.

Preparatory to the attack the 3rd was massed on M. Acuto just south of the village of Vallamaggiore, with the 1st approximately 500 yards west of M. del Puyntale, while the 2nd occupied the high ground in the vicinity of Roncozzola. Colonel Fry moved forward with the attacking battalions to personally observe the action on this difficult, barren, and open terrain, a factor which gave the enemy perfect observation. All casualties had to be moved back along the mule trails.[42] The 1st Battalion captured its objective, M. Del Puntale, in the early afternoon in spite of the tremendous mortar concentrations from outside the Regiment's zone on the right. The 3rd Battalion, still south of Vallamaggiore, met a determined enemy, while the 2nd moved forward on the right flank of the 3rd and captured Hill 669 just south of Vallamaggiore.

Colonel Fry leaves a vivid description of the 1st Battalion on Mount Del Puntale:

The picture my memory retains is of Major Mike moving across the battlefield with a heavy walking stick in his hand setting a proper example of courage, and the individual soldiers moving up the slopes of Puntale as if on parade. The sun was shining brightly on the red slopes and our heavy artillery support fire splashed about the crest of the hill and around a peasant's house on the east slope...Occasionally one of our soldiers fell but the line moved on steadily.[43]

At the end of the day, the 3rd was in position to move on Carnevale. Colonel Fry moved his CP to their positions to be near the approaching battle for Mount Battaglia. The 2nd Battalion, scheduled for the attack on Battaglia on the morrow, moved in with the 3rd at 2330, 26 September, to be ready to pass through the latter battalion. [44]

To prepare for reserves on Battaglia, Colonel Fry ordered Major Mike of the 1st Battalion to move to the vicinity of Battaglia and dispatched the 760th Tank Battalion, under Major Andrew R. Cheek, to guard the flank on the 27th.

It was on this day in the vicinity of Castel del Rio that PFC Herbert G. Goldman of Brooklyn, New York, paid the supreme sacrifice as he attacked alone an enemy-fortified house from which deadly machine gun and rifle fire held up the advance of his company. Even though wounded by a burst of machine gun fire, Goldman continued crawling toward the enemy and emptied his submachine gun into the strongpoint. As he rushed the house, he was wounded again but continued forward. As he finally arrived at the house, he placed his weapon in an opening and emptied his magazine, but at the same time he was mortally wounded by the enemy machine gun. Yet he continued in the attack. After rallying his waning strength, he crept to the window and threw several hand grenades, killing several of the enemy before he himself was mortally wounded by enemy machine gun fire. His gallant actions enabled his company to take the objective.

On this day of the beginning of perhaps the most trying battle fought by the 350th, the 1st Battalion, just north of M. Del Puntale, continued its advance, with the 2nd on Hill 669, moving through the village of Vallamaggiore and heading for Mt. Carnevale, while the 3rd was also moving forward in the attack.[45] The First, moving from Mt. Faggiola, met strong enemy positions around 1500 hours, notably Company C, and dug in and held gains amidst heavy enemy artillery and mortar fire. Beginning its attack at 0500, the 2nd advanced through the 3rd to reach the summit of Battaglia during the day.[46] After having captured Mount Carnevale and having sent 20 prisoners to the rear, the 2nd, before waiting for the 3rd to move up, moved on to Mount Battaglia, reaching the crest at 1535 hours.

In its drive toward Battaglia the 2nd drove the enemy, in its process of digging in, from Mt. Carnevale, whereupon the Jerries ran in retreat into the distance. The enemy then shelled the area with heavy artillery and mortar concentrations, inflicting heavy casualties. The 3rd moved out at 1300 and passed through previous I Company positions, the scene of a fierce counter attack the night before. Numerous German bodies and equipment dotted the area. Amidst rain the battalion set up its CP in the vicinity of Val Maffione.[47]

At 1535 Colonel Fry received word that his 2nd Battalion was on Mt. Battaglia, whereupon he ordered them to hold and consolidate their positions. A congratulatory message from Speedy 6 (Corps II Commander, Major General Geoffrey Keyes) cheered the leaders. (See Map 9).

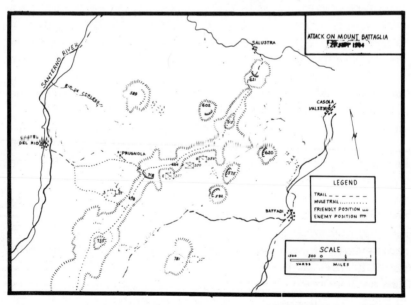

Chapter 5 — Map 9

By this time the 351st on the left had invested Castel Del Rio, but the British on the right flank were still from seven to eight thousand yards in the rear, enabling the enemy artillery to fire at an exceptional rate. As the 2nd moved on to Battaglia, Colonel Williamson, the CO, radioed: "Hell, Colonel, I can see the Po." Lt. Charles Lesnick, with Company G and from Seattle, Washington, stated that the enemy, apparently never suspecting the 350th that far forward into their territory, came forward in double column and were killed to the last man.[48]

After the first attack the Second Battalion formed a type of U-shaped defense. Before moving on to Battaglia, the commander of the Second Battalion, Colonel Williamson, had met General Ramey at the foot of the mountain. General Ramey told him to watch the flanks. Colonel Williamson then sent Captain Roeder's Company G out, with Company E on the left and Company F on the right. Companies G and E formed somewhat to the front, with Company F slightly in the rear to be used as reserve. Captain Roeder of Company G established the main defense. Immediately the Germans reacted with heavy mortar fire and small patrol attacks. There would then be attack after attack. Captain Roeder was all over the place exemplifying at all times superior leadership.

Captain Stoner of the Medics set up his aid station on the bottom floor of the castle atop Battaglia. He and his valiant medics would continue their treatment of the wounded for three days without sleep. At first the command post located on the third floor of the castle but later moved to the bottom floor with the medics.[49]

To this day there persists contrary views of the role played by the Italian partisans in the battle of Battaglia. Douglas Orgill, the author of **The Gothic Line,** states that the 36th Garibaldi Brigade, which had been engaged in local fighting around Bologna earlier in the month, guided the 2nd to the peak and later also claimed much of the credit for its successful defense. The Italian Resistance history describes the struggle as "the episode in which, more than in any other in the course of the Italian campaign, final victory was really a joint one, with equal sacrifice and will to fight."[50] Although armed with sten guns and German machine pistols, the partisans had not set up an organized defense. The orders from General Keyes to the battalion was to hold until the 351st came abreast on its left.

The road to Imola appeared open (and with it the possibility of trapping elements of the German 10th Army) as Mount Battaglia was the last important feature in the line of hills. [51]

Colonel Fry seriously questions the intent of an Italian partisan who voluntarily led him forward that evening. Fearing that he was purposely being led into enemy territory, Colonel Fry halted and began later to retrace his steps to make contact with the bulk of the attacking troops. As he halted for the night in a peasant's house, a German patrol attacked, killing two enlisted men. By this time the weapons were clogged with mud, the men were rain soaked, and Colonel Fry was caught with a single company far from his command post. A wounded man brought in at this time received first aid from the dedicated medic Owen L. Sanderlin, but because of a fault in the blood transfusion mechanism, the precious plasma flowed on to the ground with the result that the wounded man died. [52]

As all the battalions continued advancing, the supply situation increasingly grew extremely difficult. Rations had to be hauled by 2 ½ ton trucks as far forward as possible, then jeeped further before being loaded on to mule trains to the regiment, then located at Monduccio. The 1st Battalion reorganized for the attack on this day and moved out at 1800 hours, bivouacking near Mt. Faggiola at 1900 hours, approximately a two mile distance from the starting line. [53] For the 2nd Battalion, this would mark the beginning of almost incessant enemy counter attacks for the next five days as they grew in ferocity with each new encounter. The Battalion's reports read: "The enemy artillery fire was directed with great effect by well established OP's and was aided by extremely inclement weather, rain, and heavy fog, which hindered our own observations." [54]

Even before Companies E and F had taken position along the north-east spur on the day of the capture of Battaglia, elements of the 44th and 715th Grenadier Divisions launched a counterattack during a heavy rain in company strength. Company G courageously held on to its position, under the valiant leadership of its commanding officer, Captain Robert C. Roeder, of Summit Station, Pennsylvania. So critical was the situation that every man with a rifle in Headquarters Company of the 2nd Battalion "was sent up to defend the left flank, where they remained for three days." [55] In this large scale coordinated counterattack from the right left and left rear, the enemy, estimated at a regiment and a half, was thrown back down the hill only after fierce hand to hand combat.[56]

As the first day came to a close, the 1st Battalion occupied M. Carnevale and extended along the ridge to northeast and made contact with the 3rd which had two companies forward of La Carrovavaccia with one company occupying the hill in the area.[57]

For three days Company G of the 2nd Battalion, under the superb leadership of Captain Roeder for September 27 and 28, continued as the base company in the defense of Battaglia. (See Map 10). Before extending its positions to the peak of Battaglia, Company G had paved the way for its advance by first seizing Vallamaggiora, a subsidiary peak of Mt. Battaglia. For 72 hours thereafter Company G continued to carry out the brunt of the defense.[58]

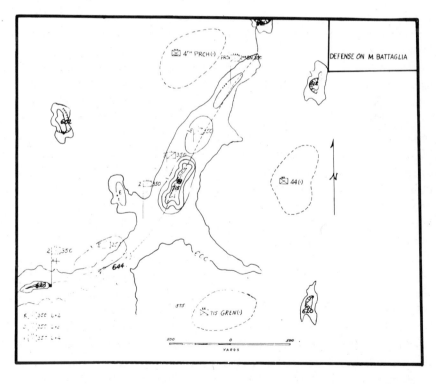

Chapter 5 — Map 10

On September 28 at dawn the enemy began his fanatical counterattacks again. Groups of 30 to 40 Germans tried to infiltrate unsuccessfully through the lines during the later morning. It was on this day that S-Sgt. Rocco "Rocky" Cotoia of New Canaan, Connecticut, made his way back through heavy shelling and obtained 19 men to lead them back to the virtually besieged castle-after he had lost all but four of his machine gun section. The machine guns began firing again upon his return.

When the last officer of his rifle company became a casualty, T-Sgt. Ralph N. Grippo of Union City, New Jersey, took command, led his men in the attack, and fired his BAR from the hip in order to get a better field of fire down the slope. He killed 24 with his BAR and two more with grenades.[59]

It was during one particularly heavy artillery barrage on the peak on September 28 that Captain Roeder was struck and instantly killed. The enemy artillery fire at this time was practically unopposed by American artillery support. In the heavy dense fogs and steady heavy rains of these days, the Battalion CP, a particular target of the enemy, sustained three direct hits in three days and suffered heavy casualties. From the few enemy prisoners captured, it was learned that the battalion was opposed by elements of five German divisions and at least one full enemy division of artillery, plus the heavy concentrations of mortar fire. It was to be only on the evening of September 28 that the first elements of one company from the 3rd Battalion and a portion of one mule train were able to get through in support. 60

Fifth Army History describes the battle at this stage as an attack beginning around 1700 of approximately four battalions from the 715th and 44th Grenadier Divisions, after a concentrated artillery and mortar shelling of the summit for approximately three hours previously. From the open right flank an estimated battalion attacked while the remainder struck at the Headquarters Company and Company G positions near the castle. The enemy, "carrying pole charges and flame throwers...fought their way almost to the summit before they were repulsed." [61] It was in this situation that Company K arrived at 1930 and immediately was committed along with Company G in the summit positions.

The next day of battle, September 29, found the Regiment in the process of consolidation, removing dead and wounded, and preparing for further counter attacks. As the 2nd Battalion continued to beat off counterattacks, all of the 350th's supporting artillery fired everything available during ths critical period. Extra litter bearers came forward as another counterattack caused heavy losses on both sides. Replacements, ammunition, and rations packed by mule arrived to the beleaguered units. By 2050 the 6th Armored Infantry Task Force had moved its last troops on to the ridge between Vallamaggiore and II Canovaccio, with the 14th Armored Task Force, under Major Cheek, protecting the right flank and the 6th Armored Task Force the supply lines. The Regiment then moved its entire force to hold M. Battaglia and the neighboring high ground. Word was then received that the Regiment was to hold its positions another day and a half until relieving forces of the British arrived. [62]

The 1st Battalion history accounts for the movement of the Battalion on this day from near Mt. Faggiola at approximately 0800 hours in a march of approximately six miles to a support position for the 2nd in the vicinity of Valsalva, arriving at 1700 hours with heavy weapons company taking a support position in rear of the 3rd Battalion. [63]

On this day as the 3rd moved out at 0630 along slippery trails, it was pinned down around 1100 on the trail in front of old positions of Company I. As it withdrew to the reverse slope of the hill for protection, other units of the battalion then proceeded in small groups down the trail, finally establishing a CP south of M. Battaglia. At 1600 it moved out again to the defense of the 2nd, which at that time spread along the reverse slope of the castle dominating the peak. All three Battalions were now together to hold Battaglia. Major Witter, commander of the 3rd, inspected the positions of the troops around the castle, speaking words of encouragement. [64]

Colonel Fry recalls vividly the events of this crucial day of the 29th when he was able to move all three of his battalions on to Battaglia. He describes the arrival of Major Mike Oreskovich, 1st Battalion CO, as he appeared in the opening of his tent, poking his head through a hole in his German poncho. He reported to Colonel Fry that the 1st would be there shortly. General Fry then invited Major Mike to sit down and have a cup of coffee. Then he said: "We're going forward to Battaglia. Orders are to hold that hill and from all I can gather I think

Williamson (2nd) is about chewed up. Witter (3rd) should be there by this time and we will get there before dark."[65]

To his commander's question about the number of men he had in the 1st, Major Mike responded: "Only about one hundred per company; we really caught hell on Puntale."

By that time, the wounded were coming down the mountain past Colonel Fry's outpost. A few days later when he returned along that trail, Colonel Fry observed that almost every rock was marked by blood. One of the wounded, Lt. Charles Lesnick, unabashedly weeping, reported that Captain Roeder had been killed. Major Mike placed his arm around Lt. Lesnick (who had not wanted to leave the area although wounded) and said something in Polish. Colonel Fry then remembers their moving on toward Battaglia, where he located his battle headquarters in a small, partially destroyed house 300 yards from the top. As Colonel Fry made his way to the partially-hid top of the pyramid-shaped hill, he was enshrouded in smoke, mist, and dust from mortar fire.

Near the crest Lt. Edmund B. Maher, of Providence, Rhode Island, met Colonel Fry, questioningly seeking an answer to the hours and days the battle would continue. With rifle, bazooka and bayonet, Lt. Maher had knocked out a mortar crew and then led a platoon in repelling an attack. In subsequent action he then dashed to the castle and bayoneted four Nazi paratroopers as they reached the doorway. All around German and American bodies lay one upon another. Inside the half-destroyed stone wall on the perimeter of the crest, the body of Captain Roeder lay where his men had carried him; even in death Captain Roeder seemed to continue to inspire his men just by his presence. As the mortar fire lifted, the muddy and disheveled but determined men rushed from cover of rocks and scrub bush to fire, and in the face of such determination the Germans had little heart to continue.

Throughout the night of September 29-30, the 350th men suffered through continuous mortar and artillery fire. At daybreak the enemy counterattacked again, this time with flame throwers, and drove the 350th troops from the castle; but immediately the determined "Battle Mountain" warriors reorganized and started driving the Krauts right back out again. Close hand to hand fighting proved the equal determination of the enemy and the Blue Devils to hold the ground.

As urgent calls for grenades and flame throwers went out; replacements began to arrive along with grenades, blankets, and dry socks and more ammo. A welcome message from General Ramey to Colonel Fry informed the Regiment that a British unit now on the right flank would relieve the 350th the next night in their present positions. Upon relief the 350th was to move to the M. Acuto area in reserve and for rest. [66]

It was in this attack in the morning hours that an officer came into Colonel Fry's headquarters yelling that the castle had been taken. After issuing orders and then moving onto the crest, Colonel Fry met Lt. Walter Scott, a bloody bayonet-tipped rifle in his hand. "We've got it back," said Lieutenant Scott, stepping over a dead German body. In all there were six stalwart German paratroopers lying dead there. The enemy replacements repeatedly had been brought from miles to the rear to attack. Colonel Fry thought that they had either been doped or were drunk.

With the Germans now realizing that their attack had failed, they laid down a mortar and artillery barrage on top of the hill to cover the retreat of the survivors. After going forward to check with the artillery observer, Lt. Nicolas Vergot, Colonel Fry came back down the hill where he encountered Lt. Scott and ordered him to relieve G Company. Lt. Scott then undertook to place his men in battle order. It was at this time that Colonel Fry was wounded in the arm from a mortar shell burst.

The next day when the Germans attacked, the lines held easily. New German bodies were lying outside around the command post. It was during this attack that Colonel Fry paid tribute to a valiant sergeant:

> Sergeant Manuel Mendoza earned the Distinguished Service Cross by taking his defiant stand on the enemy side of the castle where, with a machine gun cradled in his arm, he mowed down an enemy force that was following their barrage up the hill. [67]

Sergeant Mendoza became a legendary figure. Colonel Fry related the story told him by Lt. Scott about the sergeant when he was leading his troops to beat the Germans to the crest after an artillery barrage. Mendoza told a replacement to follow him. The frightened boy replied: "I can't, I'm just a replacement," to which Sgt. Mendoza replied: "I know you can't shoot, but come on and watch me."

The exploits of Captain Dick Hardwood, originally from Gulfport, Mississippi, deserve recounting. As a whole line of fleeing men came down from an attic during an artillery attack and stampeded over the ground floor where wounded were lying, Captain Harwood charged them like a football player and thus protected the wounded man, John Breen, from being trampled underfoot. Another bizarre exploit of Captain Harwood's concerned the capture of an escaping German, who had deserted his company. While he was walking around the front of the CP unnoticed after having been given a cigarette by Colonel Fry's trusted companion, Rocky, Captain Harwood recognized the Jerry by his helmet and potato masher grenades. Again he made a tackle, catapulting the surprised captive into the room. Such was the situation, sometimes half-comical, on Battaglia.

On September 30 B Company moved from positions near Mt. Carnevale at approximately 0800 hours to take over positions of G Company, the latter company then reverting to temporary 1st Battalion control. On the two mile march of Company B to these new positions, it was constantly shelled by heavy artillery and mortar fire concentrations. The relief was accomplished at approximately 1500 hours, with other companies occupying reserve positions in the immediate front. [68] At this critical juncture Company G had been reduced to approximately 50 men. [69]

The 3rd Battalion command post during this day remained in the same locality south of the castle. Fierce Kraut counterattacks were beaten off with hand grenades and machine gun fire. After the castle had been re-occupied, Captain Cussans personally directed the defense on this day. He moved forward through murderous enemy small arms, machine gun, and mortar and artillery fire to lead in the defense of the castle. Captain Cussans at one time ordered 60-mm mortar fire only 25 to 30 yards ahead of his own troops, but it effectively broke up one of the counterattacks. [70]

Major Witter personally made inspections throughout the day and gave words of encouragement. For this day, the Third Battalion history concludes: "Still raining, foxholes full of mud; the only officer left in L Company is Lt. Hebel, WIA, and SGt. Grippo has now taken over command. Lt. Smith has been transferred from M Company and made CO of L Company." [71]

After September 30 the defense of Battaglia became easier as units on the right and left flanks moved abreast of the 350th. With the capture by the 351st Infantry of Mount Cappello and the arrival of British units on the right, the enemy could no longer attack from the flanks. [72]

October 1 was the fifth consecutive day for the Regiment on Battaglia. As the gray blanket-like fog hid the shattered castle from view, the enemy counterattacked again at dawn against the weary but determined defenders. Following the usual artillery barrage, the Jerries, carrying flame throwers in the attack, were again repulsed by accurate rifle fire and grenades.

By 0700 the next day word was received that the enemy apparently would discontinue the attack but would continue with mortar and artillery concentrations. Security patrols were posted out 1000 yards to the northwest to Mt. Cappello as 59 men came up to haul back the wounded at 0945. Approximately 30-40 prisoners were taken. On this day American planes strafed enemy positions. An officer from the 1st Grenadier Brigade of the Welch Guards arrived at 1230 and was taken forward by the S—3 of the 1st Battalion, Lt. Lynch. [73] The morale of the troops was much better that day as the clear skies permitted the use of Allied planes against the enemy.

Even when it was about to be relieved on October 2, the 2nd Battalion still had to fight off another enemy attack. After seven days of continuous action, the 2nd left the mountain, relinquishing its position to the 13th Corps. [74] As relief was being effected, German artillery and mortar fire continually searched all areas of the trails and routes of approach to the battle area. After dark the British moved forward and relieved Companies C,D,I,K,G, and 1st Battalion Headquarters, completing the operation at 2040 hours. There was light enemy artillery fire throughout the night. [75]

Companies I and K were relieved by Companies A and B, and the former, along with the rest of the companies mentioned above, dug in near Valsalva, after a march of approximately six miles from the front, closing into the area early the next morning. Companies A and B and two platoons of Company D were still on front lines attached to the 3rd Battalion. [76]

While the 3rd Battalion maintained defense on Battaglia on

October 2, Sergeant Lee H. Beddow of Company L and Detroit, Michigan, protected the regimental headquarters from assaults by German paratroopers. As the enemy launched a vicious counterattack in an effort to regain the strategically important Mt. Battaglia, Sergeant Beddow directed his squad's fire and continuously fired his submachine gun at the attacking enemy, killing and wounding several. When he observed enemy paratroopers to enter the castle housing the regimental command post, he ignored the heavy mortar and artillery fire to move toward the building and engaged the krauts at close range, killing every German who had entered the castle. He then took his position at the doorway, where he killed every German who attempted to enter. He courageously held his positions against German machine pistols and grenades until he was seriously wounded and blinded by a mortar shell burst.

On October 3, Colonel Fry, at the castle on Battaglia, requested all available air OP's to be in the air if there was a sign of counterattack, but when the enemy did not choose to try to drive the defenders back, the evacuation of the wounded was begun. Blankets, codine, blood plasma and many litter bearers were dispatched to the forward aid station to care for the great number of casualties. At 2030, after another counterattack and after an urgent call for hand grenades and 60 mm mortar ammo, everything was again under control at the close of the day.[77]

In this attack Company B, entrenched on Battaglia and attached to the 3rd Battalion, aided in repulsing the enemy.[78] At this time men from the defending companies stood up on the crest of the hill, firing their rifles and throwing grenades. Most of the automatic weapons clogged and thus were of little use in repulsing the attack. Mortar fire was also used to good effect, sometimes only 25 yards in front of the embattled defenders. The 3rd Battalion historian reports that one man stood on the crest of the mountain and fired his automatic rifle from the hip in order to get a better field of fire.

October 4 found the relief of the Regiment continuing, with Companies E, F, parts of M, and H leaving by 0245. By first light only a portion of the Regiment was still on Battaglia, but because of enemy fire, movement was held to a virtual standstill during the day. The remainder of the Regiment later moved to the vicinity of the village of Valsalva to bivouac for a short time, where it reorganized, re-clothed, and received hot meals. The constant rains turned the bivouac area into a sea of mud. [79]

On October 5 the Regimental CO, Staff, and the remainder of Headquarters Company finally left Battaglia and closed into the new bivouac area. Companies A and B and two platoons of Company D arrived and bivouaced in the assembly area near Valsalva at 0300 hours after marching 12 miles from the front line positions. [80] For the 3rd Battalion Protestant Church Services were held in the Battalion CP, and the companies received some badly needed replacements. The presence of Red Cross girls giving out coffee and doughnuts, plus the PX and beer ration, raised the morale of the troops even further. [81]

During the September battles and particularly on Battaglia, the Medical Detachment performed magnificently. Since advances by the Regiment were rapid at first, the Medical Detachment encountered great difficulty in evacuation and supplying needed medicines and materials for treatment, especially since elements of the Regiment were at times 8,000 air line yards from the nearest passable jeep trail. To provide the maximum in treatment of the wounded, the Regimental Medical Section set up aid stations and evacuation systems over a broad area which moved in the rear of the battalions.

The treatment and evacuation of wounded had never before been so tedious and difficult as on this occasion. The almost impossible obstacles to overcome included steep terrain everywhere and continuous rain and mud throughout the entire operation. The aid stations on Battaglia cared for an extreme load of wounded, in particular from the 2nd Battalion, but the stations functioned smoothly and admirably even though under heavy shellfire almost continuously.

Most of the evacuation from Valsalva to Vallamaggiore had to be done at night, but the drivers of the medical jeeps performed tirelessly and courageously to evacuate the wounded over the slippery, muddy trails. No patients were injured, although the trip was perilous even in daytime. Four medical men were killed in action during this phase: Pfc Rook; Pvt. Fernandez; Pvt. Shreve; and Pvt. Bartosk. A total of 19 medical enlisted men were evacuated ruing the two week combat period for wounds from enemy fire. During the battle from September 20 to October 5, the number of patients evacuated included the following: Wounded, 503; Injured, 98; Disease, 262. [82]

There was no dearth of heroism among all the ranks in the Battle for Battaglia. For years to come children and grandchildren will be telling about the exploits of their fathers, grandfathers, and relatives in the struggle for "Battle Mountain," the meaning of the word **Battaglia**. In the recounting of after action sessions and reports, the men might confuse the time element involved, especially since each day and night merged into the next 24 hour period with hardly any perceptible division of time. A true account of these awe-inspiring and glory-filled days would not be complete without recounting the feats of these courageous Blue Devils-exploits that really appear incredible when one reads about them in the comfort of peaceful surroundings today; but nevertheless they are the true record of the brave Americans who fought and died on the crags of the Appenines north of Florence.

The account must include the action of 1st Lt. Edmund D. Maher of Providence, Rhode Island, who knocked out a mortar crew, led a platoon in repelling an attack, and then dashed to the castle and bayoneted four Nazi paratroopers coming to the doorway. The sacrifice of Pfc. Felix B. Mestas of Laveta, Colorado, for his buddies in giving them time to re-form and beat off an attack reflects credit on the valor of courageous American men who have served in the military. Pfc. Mestas manned a position on the forward slope of Battaglia for three days with his BAR, mowing the enemy down like grass as they vainly tried to get past him. After killing 24 of the enemy before they overran his position, Pfc. Mestas gave his buddies the time needed to re-form before he himself was killed.

T-Sgt. Beni Mazzarella of Woonsocket, Rhode Island, seeing the castle overwhelmed by the strongest Kraut attack, picked up a handful of grenades and charged the castle, killing six and wounding more. He then used a machine gun, charging alone at the remaining Krauts who broke and ran as he came out of the fog. The actions of S-Sgt. Lewis R. Hamm of Olney, Texas, demonstrate great perserverance of one continuing to close with enemy, although burned by a flame-thrower and wounded by a bullet in the hand. He killed the flamethrower operator and three more Krauts before he finally was evacuated.

At times rocks became the only weapons avilable. Pfc. Cleo Peek of Center, Colorado, an assistant gunner on a BAR, held off the enemy with his M1 when the BAR jammed; when the M1 jammed he threw grenades until they ran out and then hurled rocks at the enemy less than 25 yards from his position. The exploits of Pfc Jose D Sandoval of Santa Fe, New Mexico, are similar. After his BAR heated and jammed, he secured the machine gun of a dead crew, fired it from the hip, and killed an unestimated number of the enemy. Sgt. Alfred E. Cassidy of Cincinnati, Ohio, used his rifle like a mortar, pumping out rifle grenades like he was operating a mortar.

S-Sgt. Raymond O. Gregory of Kings Mountain, North Carolina, savagely played "King of the Mountain" as he rolled huge boulders down the hill into confused enemy ranks. The unselfish heroism of T-Sgt. Manuel V. Mendoza, a legend in his time, exemplified the indomitable will of the Blue Devils to hold their position on Battaglia. The account of his exploits is a vividly told tale of indomitable will and courage:

> During one counterattack, Mendoza opened up with a tommy gun on 200 Jerries charging up the forward slope. Ten of them died where they fell, others lay wounded, but the rest came on. Mendoza, now using a carbine, emptied his entire ammo supply of five clips into their ranks. A flamethrower licked out at him but he killed the operator with a pistol shot. Jumping into a machine-gun pit and pushing aside the dead gunner, Mendoza sprayed the surviving at-tackers until the gun jammed, then pitched hand grenades until the Krauts withdrew. Severely wounded himself by now, he nevertheless ran down the forward slope, retrieved enemy weapons lying there, captured a wounded Kraut and returned to consolidate his platoon positions.

The medics performed diligently and courageously under the most trying conditions. Sgt. John J. Regan of Waterbury, Connecticut, and B Company, 313th Medics, although wounded from a mortar barrage, treated five of the doughboys and patched up two members of his litter squad. Removing the wounded to a building, Regan then started back to get help from his collecting stations, a journey of fifteen hours, but he made it. Then he collapsed. The 2d Battalion surgeon, Captain Williard Stonner of Chagrin Falls, Ohio, never ceased from treating the wounded, although his aid station was reduced to a single room by enemy shelling. T-4 Joseph E. Silva saved countless lives as he worked tirelessly, shifting his patients from room to room as Kraut shells burst through the walls.

Two GIs, T-Sgt. Roscoe A. Webb of Columbus, Ohio, and Pfc. George O. Porter of Boston, Massachusetts, sweated out rifle grenades, flamethrowers and even pole charges as they consistently picked off enemy attackers in one bitter brawl. Major Erwin B. Jones of Brighton, Alabama, directed artillery fire on the attackers at one battalion point when Kraut artillery had wounded all the members and cut them off from the main unit. He personally killed 19 Jerries before relief came up.

On September 30 when T-Sgt. Ralph N. Grippo of Union City, New Jersey, took command of his company, two of his men, Pvt. Russell P. Glass of Akron, Ohio, and Sgt. John McKenzie of Lowell, Massachusetts, paused in the heat of battle to replace a firing pin in their machine gun, McKenzie covering with a tommy gun while Glass performed the repair job. [83]

These accounts of a few individuals' heroism attest to the courage, valor, perseverance, and intrepidity of the "Battle Mountain Regiment," as the 350th was now named. Thousands of unrecounted individual acts of valor do not alter the supreme effort and sacrifice of the Blue Devils of the 350th Infantry Regiment. Having been a member of that valiant team on Battaglia is a badge of praise to each individual soldier. The fact that their roles in this gigantic undertaking have not been retold does not detract at all from the glory due them.

Recommendations for award were started through channels for the gallant men of the 350th. On Battaglia they had stood off the enemy from September 28-October 5, although "exposed on three sides, denied air and ground observation, under terrific artillery and mortar barrages, and hampered by bad weather which made supply nearly impossible."[84] A number of officers and men received the awards of the Distinguished Service Cross, the Silver Star, and the Bronze Star medals; but the courageous action beyond the call of duty of Captain Robert E. Roeder, killed in action, deserved the Congressional of Medal of Honor, awarded to him posthumously. For its stand there, the Battalion under which he served, the 2d, was awarded the Distinguished Unit Citation. The citation to Captain Roeder praises the unselfish devotion to duty of an officer in the Army of the United States:

Captain ROBERT E. ROEDER, 01285307, Infantry, Army of the United States. For conspicuous gallantry and intrepidity at the risk of his life above and beyond the call of duty on 27 and 28 September 1944 on Mt. Battaglia, Italy. Captain ROEDER commanded his company in defense of the strategic Mt. Battaglia. Shortly after the company had occupied the hill, the Germans launched the first of a series of determined counterattacks to regain this dominating height. Completely exposed to ceaseless enemy artillery and small-arms fire, Captain Roeder constantly circulated among his men, encouraging them and directing their defense against the persistent enemy. During the sixth counterattack, the enemy using flame throwers and taking advantage of the fog, succeeded in overrunning the position. Captain ROEDER led his men in a fierce battle at close quarters to repulse the attack with heavy losses to the Germans. The following morning, while the company was engaged in repulsing an enemy counterattack in force, Captain ROEDER was seriously wounded and renderd unconscious by shell fragments. He was carried to the company command post where he regained consciousness. Refusing medical treatment, he insisted on rejoining his men. Although in a weakened condition, Captain ROEDER dragged himself to the door of the command post and, picking up a rifle, braced himself in a sitting position. He began firing his weapon, shouted words of encourgement, and issued orders to his men. He personally killed two Germans before he was killed instantly by an exploding shell. Through Captain ROEDER's able and intrepid leadership his men held Mt. Battaglia against the aggressive and fanatical enemy attempts to retake this important and strategic height. His valorous performance is exemplary of the fighting spirit of the Army of the United States. [85]

During the drive of the 88th beginning on September 21 and extending to October 3, 1944, the Division as a whole had suffered 2,105 battle casualties.[86] The 350th alone suffered 1420 casualties during this campaign, the bulk of them being sustained on Battaglia. The casualties resulted in 235 men killed in action, 277 missing, and 908 wounded. [87] Paying tribute to the Division (and by inference to the 350th particularly), the Fifth Army historian states: ''The drive of the 88th Division toward Imola, and in particular the defense of Mount Battaglia, came close to equaling the total casualties of II Corps during the 6-day period of the breaching of the Gothic Line.'' [88]

Sketch by Gus Fagerholm—Italian Theater, 1944 - 350th Infantry Reg't. from the collection of William Gardner Bell.

Monte Battaglia and adjacent mountains.

American dead in the castle ruins on Monte Battaglia.

Tiger turret commanding part of the Futa Pass.

Monte Battaglia (Battle Mountain) near Castle Del Rio.

Castle atop Mt. Battaglia.

Captain Robert G. Roeder, awarded Congressional Medal of Honor posthumously for action on Monte Battaglia, September, 1944.

Engineers prepare to remove a trestle bridge which has been undermined

Footnotes to Chapter V

[1] Walter P. Hall and William S. Davis, **The Course of Europe Since Waterloo** (New York, 1947), 1977.

[2] 350th Infantry Regiment History, September, 1944.

[3] **Ibid.**, September, 1944.

[4] **Ibid.**

[5] Douglas Orgill, **The Gothic Line: The Italian Campaign, Autumn, 1944** (New York, 1967), 183-184.

[6] Colonel J.C. Fry, U.S.A., "One Week in Hell," **Saturday Evening Post** (June 25, 1949), 36.

[7] **Ibid.**

[8] Second Battalion History, September, 1944.

[9] Third Battalion History, September, 1944.

[10] First Battalion History, September , 1944.

[11] John P. Delaney, **The Blue Devils in Italy** (New York, 1947), 128.

[12] 350th Infantry Regiment History, September, 1944.

[13] **Fifth Army History, The Gothic Line,** Part VII, 91.

[14] **Ibid.**

[15] **Fifth Army History,** Part VII, 91-92.

[16] Major General James C. Fry, Retired, **Combat Soldier** (Washington, D.C., 1969), 175.

[17] First Battalion History, September, 1944.

[18] "P.W. Interrogation Report," Headquarters 350th Infantry, September 24, 1944.

[19] Personal Account of Former Lieutenant C. Ashcraft to the author, August, 1976.

[20] Captain Roule C. Mozingo, "The Battlefield Commander Must at All Times Assure Himself that his Security is Adequate and Alert," Advanced Infantry Officers Class No. II, 1949-1950, TIS, Fort Benning, Georgia. Information concerning occurrences in the command post obtained from Lt. Col. James Ritts, then Executive Officer of the First Battalion, 350th Infantry.

[21] Lt. Ashcraft remembers only one guard; Lt. Col. Ritts gives the number as two,

one of whom was killed in the original encounter with the enemy.

[22] Personal Account, lt. Ashcraft.
[23] Lecture, Captain Mozingo, Fort Benning, Georgia.
[24] **Ibid.**
[25] Personal Account, Lt. Ashcraft.
[26] Lecture, Captain Mozingo, Fort Benning, Georgia.
[27] Personal Account, Lt. Ashcraft.
[28] **Fifth Army History,** Part VII, 92.
[29] 350th Infantry Regiment History, September, 1944.
[30] **Fifth Army History,** Part VII, 93.
[31] **Ibid.**
[32] 350th Infantry Regiment History, September, 1944.
[33] Third Battalion History, September, 1944.
[34] **Ibid.**
[35] Fry, **Combat Soldier,** 189.
[36] 350th Infantry Regiment, History, September, 1944.
[37] **Fifth Army History,** Part VII, 93.
[38] 350th Infantry Regiment History, September, 1944.
[39] Second Battalion History, September, 1944.
[40] Third Battalion History, September, 1944.
[41] Fry, **Combat Soldier,** 181.
[42] Personal Interview with Lt. Col. Corbett Williamson, Ret., October, 1976.
[43] Roberto Battaglia, **Storia della Resistenze italiana** (Turin, Italy, 1953), 406, as reported in Orgill, **The Gothic Line.**
[44] **Fifth Army History,** Part VII, 94.
[45] Fry, "One Week in Hell," 121.
[46] First Battalion History, September, 1944.
[47] Second Battalion History, September, 1944.
[48] Private Gerald S. Root, "Mt. Battaglia Battle Was 350th's Race," **The Stars and Stripes,** November 3, 1944.
[49] **Fifth Army History,** Part VII, 95.
[50] 350th Infantry Regiment History, September, 1944.
[51] Second Battalion History, September, 1944.
[52] Root, "Mt. Battaglia Race Was 350th's Race," November 3, 1944.
[53] Second Battalion History, September, 1944.
[54] **Fifth Army History,** Part VII, 95.
[55] 350th Infantry Regiment History, September, 1944.
[56] First Battalion History, September, 1944.
[57] Third Battalion History, September, 1944.
[58] Fry, **Combat Soldier,** 184.
[59] 350th Infantry Regiment History, September, 1944.
[60] Fry, **Combat Soldier,** 104.
[61] First Battalion History, September, 1944.
[62] Fifth Army History, Part VII, 96.
[63] Root, "Mt. Battaglia Battle Was 350th's Race," November 3, 1944.
[64] Third Battalion History, September, 1944.
[65] **Fifth Army History,** Part VII, 96.
[66] 350th Infantry Regiment History, October, 1944.
[67] First Battalion History, October, 1944.
[68] 350th Infantry Regiment History, October, 1944.
[69] First Battalion History, October, 1944.
[70] Third Battalion History, October, 1944.
[71] 350th Infantry, Medical Detachment History, September, 1944.
[72] Delaney, **The Blue Devils in Italy,** 139-144.
[73] **Ibid.,** 145.
[74] General Orders No. 31, War Department, 17 April 1945.
[75] **Fifth Army History,** Part VII, 97.
[76] Fry, **Combat Soldier,** 192.
[77] **Fifth Army History,** Part VII, 97.

Chapter Six

**The 350th Infantry Regiment in the
Gothic Line Campaign:
The Second Phase, October, 1944**

After the valiant defense of Mt. Battaglia, the 350th would be given only a short breathing space before re-entering the lines farther west in October, 1944. At the beginning of October, the entire division had been given a new sector which changed the direction of attack from northeast to north.[1] (See Map 1.) With only one day off the line the 2nd Battalion was ordered to relieve the 2nd Battalion, 349th Infantry, on Hill 548 in the vicinity of Pezzola. On October 10 Lt. Col. Williamson thus established his command post in this village. In this holding position the 2nd followed the 349th Infantry until the relief was completed at approximately fifteen hundred yards north of this position.

Before moving into position for battle again and while awaiting the anticipated orders for the entire Regiment to re-enter battle, the men endured hard rains throughout October 6 and on the following day, the 7th, the entire area was drenched by downpours. Nevertheless, the Regiment accomplished reorganization as soon as possible, but all the personnel had great difficulty in drying out clothes, blankets, shoes, and other equipment. The next day, October 8, orders from above commanded the Regiment to move to an assembly area in the vicinity of Sassoleone, a small village close behind the front lines of the 349th Infantry and to be prepared to continue the attack to the north.[2]

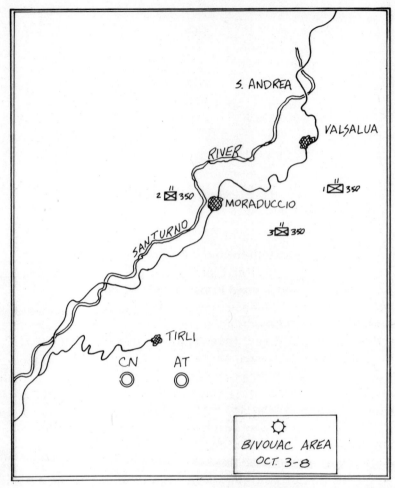

On October 9 a directive from 88th Division Headquarters announced the order for a coordinated attack with the 88th on the right and the 85th, 91st, and 34th in that order extending the attack zone to the left. The orders for the 350th were to make the main effort on the left, passing through the 349th Infantry, attacking at 0600 on the 10th, and capturing objectives to the north; and also to assist the advance of the 85th and to maintain contact with that division while at the same time preparing to continue the advance to the northeast while protecting the Division left. Jumping off to the attack at 0500 and passing through the 349th, the 3rd Battalion on the left and the 1st

Battalion on the right with the 2nd Battalion now back in reserve, the Regiment made determined drives to reach their objectives in spite of concentrated mortar and artillery fire, and as the 1st Battalion progressed toward Monte delle Tombe, its objective, it encountered small arms and automatic fire just 500 yards south of this mountain. Summarizing the day's action, the leading Battalions, the 1st and 3rd, reached their objectives with the 1st receiving the brunt of enemy counter fire. The 2nd Battalion was still in a reserve position.[3] (See Map 2.)

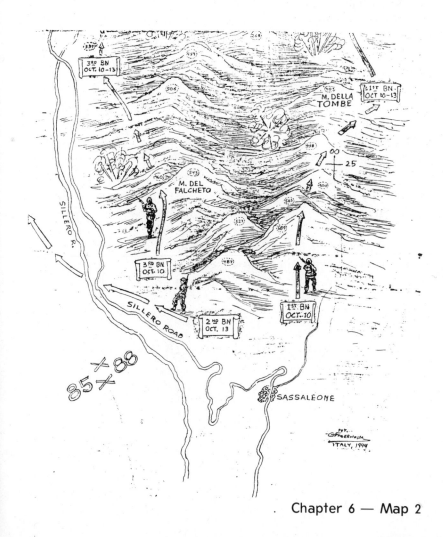

Chapter 6 — Map 2

For the 3rd Battalion the attacking companies, I, K, and L, moved through heavy sniper, mortar, and machine gun fire. After digging in for the evening at 1930, Companies K and L were harassed by artillery fire which was answered by American artillery. The Battalion awaited the arrival of the mule train at this time.[4]   The 1st Battalion also dug in on the front lines, holding defensive positions with the battalion flanked on the immediate right by the 351st Regiment and on the left by the 337th Infantry of the 85th Division.[5]

At this point a recapitulation of the action on the II Corps front along Highway 65, to which the offensive had moved after the failure to break through to Imola by way of Battaglia, is necessary to place in perspective the action of the 350th. By October 5 when the 350th was relieved on Battaglia, the rate of advance on the other fronts averaged approximately one mile per day. Although Ameican losses were high, still it could be anticipated on the basis of the past four days (to the 5th October) that II Corps would yet reach the Po Valley before the October rains turned to snow, although it was unlikely that the Corps would achieve a swift breakthrough. Yet the increasing bad weather, which aided the Germans by reducing the effectiveness of offensive weapons, coupled with the ability of the enemy to shift the 16th SS Panzer Grenadier and the whole of the 65th Grenadier Divisions to aid the 98th, 362nd Grenadier, and 44th Grenadier Divisions, the latter three being unable to withdraw, augured ill for the success of the II Corps drive.[6] (See map 3 for disposition of American and German troops.)

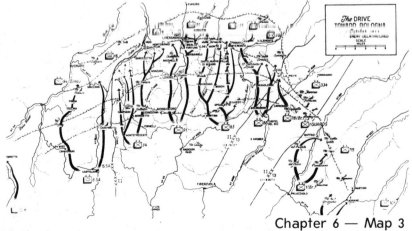

Chapter 6 — Map 3

In the third phase of the attack, from October 10-15, II Corps was faced with an enemy delaying line which was stronger in natural defenses than either of the two which had just been broken. From west to east these formidable defensive positions faced II Corps: Monterumici hill mass; Livergnano escarpment; Mt. Delle Formiche and the Monterenzio hill mass; and Mt. delle Tombe and the Gesso ridge facing the 88th Division. At this time, the 88th was to clear the east side of the Sillaro Valley to provide flank support.

For the third phase attack, the 88th Division first had to catch up with the 85th Division which had outsripped the Blue Devils in advance. The Blue Devils were now to aid in the assault on the Monterenzio Hill mass as well as possibly to drive to the northeast toward Castel San Pietro in the Po Plain. The 350th had the mission of bringing up the Division's left flank, near to the 85th lines.[7] It was in this situation that the 350th pushed off to the attack on the October 10, previously described.

Colonel Fry had returned from the hospital in time for this attack. Discussing the situation with General Kendall in Castel del Rio, the latter mentioned casually that the 88th would have the job of capturing Mt. Grande, the largest mountain and last major barrier before the Po Valley.[8] The combat zone at this time for the 88th was generally the area from the small town of Sassoleone up to the bastion of Mt. Grande. Following the path of advance from Castel del Rio, the road branches directly north, passing through Sassoleone and leading on to the Sillaro River Valley. The 349th was at that time of the battle engaged in the struggle for Monte delle Tombe, to the right of the road. The 350th moved forward in this second phase of the October offensive and dug into the mountain mass just above Sassoleone. The direction of the army attack was now almost due north. To concentrate the maximum force for this attack, II Corps was assigned a more constricted area of attack as the 78th British Division shifted westward in the new boundary zone. This division was now immediately to the right rear of the 350th. (See Map 4.)

Long to be remembered by men of the 350th, Monte delle Tombe rose up at the toe of a terrain horseshoe: the right side angled northeast toward Imola with the left ridge north toward St. Clemente, disappearing then into the valley before regaining stature in the formidable mass of Mt. Grande.

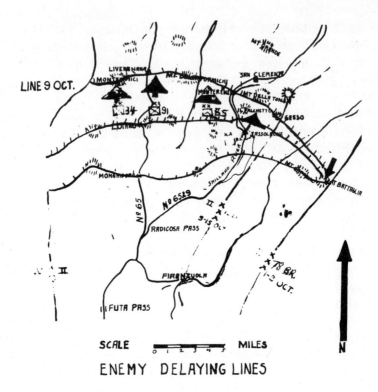

ENEMY DELAYING LINES

Chapter 6 — Map 4

Scarcely was there any artillery support or aid of liaison planes at this time as the rain, drifting fog, and clouds characterized weather conditions. In these rugged shrub-covered hills, the fog and drifting clouds at times augmented the security of the troops, because on either side of these barren walls rising from the Sillaro River were well concealed sniper positions. Colonel Fry's digressions from the narrative of the 350th compares favorably with the British analysis (and General Clark's) about the possible shortening of the war if only more men and support had been given to the American Infantry at that time:

> I think it is an excusable digression from the story to comment that the Air Corps fighter aircraft rarely assisted us in those bitter days. I have always felt that this lack of coordination coupled with the lethargy of the British, prevented the Fifth Army from reaching the Po Valley, the results of which will never be known, but might well have ended the war.[9]

Another Fifth Army historian has commented: "If Fifth Army had had only one of the divisions which it had lost in the summer, not to mention all the troops that had gone to France, our drive through the Appenines would have progressed much more rapidly." [10]

In the struggle for Mt. Delle Tombe on the 10th, the 1st Battalion had succeeded in gaining its objective and dug in, only to be pushed off the next day by a strong enemy force; the 1st then immediately made plans again to attack and capture the strategic height. It was supported by artillery concentrations in a continuous pounding of enemy mortar positions and kept enemy movement at a minimum by accurate harassing fires. As a result of anti-tank company's fire, in conjunction with firing of tanks of Company B, 76th Tank Battalion, thirty enemy prisoners came out of a white house and surrendered. They were from the 14th Company, 117th Grenadier Regiment. Both advancing battalions consolidated their positions and made plans to move off into the attack the following morning early, attacking to the northeast. A great morale booster to the fighting doughboys at this time came with the announcement that the Air Force was to make a major effort the following day with twelve hundred planes attacking all available targets in the Po Valley.

On this day, October 11, the 1st Battalion launched its attack at 0500 hours and occupied the ground at the base of Mt. Delle Tombe, 3200 yards north of the town of Curiolo. By 2330 hours, the battalion was continuing its advance northward. In the 3rd Battalion zone of attack stiff enemy resistance, including heavy machine gun and sniper fire, inflicted a few casualties. The 2nd Battalion CO arrived at the 3rd Battalion CP to make preparations for his battalion to pass through the 3rd at 1245, October 12. Amidst heavy mortar fire, replacements and supplies arrived at the front, including a reinforced platoon of the 349th in I Company's positions. Late at night, between 2300 and 2345, the enemy sent over a heavy concentration of artillery fire on the 3rd's position.

As the 1st Battalion continued its advance on October 12, it captured Mt. Delle Tombe, with C Company leading the advance. The Battalion then consolidated its gains and took defensive positions and dug in. At this time the 1st suffered a grievance loss with the death of its intrepid leader, Major Mike

Oreskovich, who had become the Batalion CO after the capture of Colonel Bare at the beginning of the 88th's advance in September. While with Company A, Major Mike was seriously wounded and died approximately 45 minutes later at 1130 hours. Lt. Col. Cochran, the Regimental Executive Officer, moved forward to the Battalion CP with the new CO, Lt. Colonel Deshon.[11]

In these initial days of the advance north of Sassoleone, the 1st and 3rd made some slight headway and for two days hung tight against fanatical enemy resistance. On the day that Major Mike was mortally wounded, Colonel Fry made his usual visit to the leading elements, through the hell of German artillery and mortar fire. He was met on the southern slopes of Delle Tombe by Major Witter, 3rd Battalion CO, and Major Mike, the 1st Battalion CO. Major Mike was optimistic. He felt that on the following night the forward elements would succeed in pushing beyond the crest of Delle Tombe and would then be in position to look down on the Germans at the little village of St. Clemente. Major Witter also felt that the enemy was breaking somewhat. Colonel Fry planned at this time to use Colonel Williamson's 2nd Battalion the following night in a swift thrust down the valley of the Sillaro River toward St. Clemente.

The goal of the 1st Battalion in this push was a cluster of houses labeled Calanco. Captain Erwin Jones, the 1st Battalion Executive Officer, reported that Major Mike was standing in the door of the command post when he was hit by a shell fragment. The death of Major Mike delayed Williamson's 2nd Battalion attack for 24 hours.[12]

During the day the P47's strafed the enemy constantly from 1530 until 1645 hours. As I Company and K Company moved forward on this morning, Company I reached its objective by 0900 and then received shelling of phosphorous shells in the vicinity of the forward CP at 0930. Company K took eight prisoners in the morning and then five more later. For the period October 13 through October 15, the 3rd Battalion experienced heavy artillery fire sporadically but generally reported light casualties. On October 14 the main event was the movement of the 2nd Battalion around the 3rd at 0700, when the 2nd took 85 prisoners.[13]

For the 1st Battalion during this period, Companies A, B, and C continued their advance after holding defensive positions throughout 13 October - Company C still occupying Mt. Delle Tombe; Company A near a house named Ca Caprara; and Company B near the advance CP at Mezzomonto. After Company B had made an advance of a few hundred yards during the early morning hours of October 14, preparations for relief were in progress, and Companies A and D were relieved at 2300 hours and arrived in the assembly area in the early hours the following morning. After marching to the bivouac area near Fontancies, the 1st Battalion was relieved by the 1st Battalion of the 351st Infantry Regiment.

Although the 1st Battalion had failed in its initial attack to gain Mt. Delle Tombe on the 12th, the 2nd Battalion scored spectacular gains during this period as it crossed the Sillaro west of Hill 339 on the night of October 13-14 and found a gap in the enemy defenses. (See Map 5.) It had cut through by the 14th to Hill 373 and by dark of the 15th had advanced over a mile north of the Sillaro, abreast of the 85th Division. On the rest of the division front action was limited to the renewed efforts of the 351st Infantry to take the Gesso Ridge, which fell on the 12th.[14]

The 2nd Battalion suffered relatively light losses in the initial attack. By dawn Colonel Williamson, Battalion CO, had set up his CP in the basement of one of the houses at Calanco. There was a crying need for officers as replacements during this period that the 2nd Battalion held the most advanced position of the Division. Two new replacements, Lt. William G. Bell (now with the Military Department in Washington, D.C.) and Lt. George Fumich arrived to assume their duties during this attack. Lt. Bell, assigned to Company G, found it necessary to appoint a Pfc as a platoon sergeant.

Company G at this time was occupying Hill 12 under the command of Lt. Edmund D. Maher. Lt. Maher and S-Sgt. William H. Curow, caught by Kraut artillery fire, fell within ten yards of each other. Lt. Maher's death left only one officer, 2nd Lt. John J. Yeager, in Company G, and he had had only a couple days on the line. From Company E Lt. John D. Zerbe, Jr., transferred to take command of the company. After the deaths of Curow and Boysen, Lt. Bell moved to the 3rd platoon and appointed privates and pfcs to take over the work of the non-coms. They did an excellent job. Among these men assuming senior responsibility were Pfc. Anthony D.

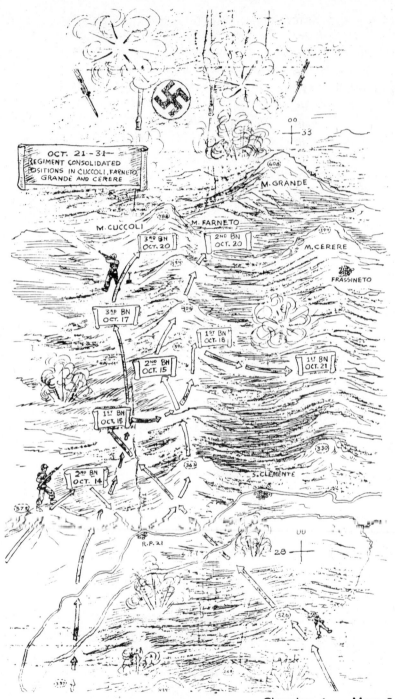

OCT. 21 - 31 —
REGIMENT CONSOLIDATED
POSITIONS IN CUCCOLI, FARNETO
GRANDE AND CERERE

M. GRANDE

M. CUCCOLI   M. FARNETO

3RD BN
OCT. 20   2ND BN
OCT. 20   M. CERERE

FRASSINETO

3RD BN
OCT. 17

1ST BN
OCT. 18   1ST BN
OCT. 21

2ND BN
OCT. 15

1ST BN
OCT. 15

S. CLEMENTE

2ND BN
OCT. 14

R.P. 21

Tomorazzo, later S-Sgt.; Pfc Cleo Peek, later S-Sgt; and Pfc Victor J. Petracco, later sergeant. Petracco's combat experience led him to give advice to a new platoon leader to keep his head down and not try to win any medals, but in vain; the new leader, in the vicinity of Monzuno, charged alone into a group of houses in Furcoli and was caught dead center by a Kraut burp gunner.

Enlisted men came up under cover of darkness as replacements during these hellish nights. Generals Clark and Gruenther made their appearances in the 350th's lines during this period and awarded the DSC to Colonel Fry. A number of sergeants received battle field promotions to the rank of second lieutenant in this campaign - Elmore Zibbel, Arthur B. Dodge, Harold B. Humphrey, James V. Woolover, Steven M. Kosmyna, Thomas H. Carmody, Charles F. Heady, and Clyde Pope.

Throughout these grueling battles for possession of one peak after another, Major Andy Cheek of the Tank Battalion daringly battled time and time again to get his tanks over the slippery advances toward Mt. Grande. He would finally receive an award, but perhaps his efforts really deserved the Congressional Medal of Honor. [15]

The attacks in which the 350th participated during the period October 10-15 were characterized by the heaviest fighting experienced by II Corps since the breach of the Gothic Line. Of nine infantry battalions in the 88th Division, by October 15 only four were commanded by lieutenant colonels. Obviously if the heavy casualties continued, the fighting efficiency of the attacking divisions would be diminished significantly. [16]

During this period, 10-15 October, the four attacking divisions suffered 2491 battle casualties, the 88th leading the number again with 872. The offensive progressively slowed down under the heavy attrition of casualties. The average of the corps advance during this period was between one and two miles, with the exception of the three-mile advance by the 350th which brought the left flank of the 88th abreast of the 85th. On the left flank, along the Monterumici hill mass, the II Corps front remained almost stationary. Even after having broken the strongest of the enemy's delaying lines, the forward troops were still 10 miles from Bologna. To slow the advance, Kesselring had succeeded in shifting elements of the 94th

Grenadier Division and of the 29th Panzer Division to bolster the defense of the 65th and 98th Grenadier Divisions. It was obvious that the enemy would soon have as many troops on the line as II Corps. 17 Other enemy formations facing II Corps included the 4th Parachute, 362nd Grenadier, 44th Grenadier, and 16th SS Panzer Grenadier. 18

Even with this formidable defense facing it, II Corps yet prepared for one final effort to break into the Po Valley amidst worsening weather conditions on the 15th. An early decision was imperative in view of increasing battle casualties, fatigue, lack of adequate replacements, an approaching reduction in artillery allotments, and the steady arrival of enemy rein-forcements.

In this final effort the plans called for the 34th to take Mt. Belmonte, move down the Idice River valley, and cut Highway 9; the 85th was to assist on its right and then turn east, as would the 88th on the right after taking Mt. Grande. The 91st and 1st Armored positioned astride Highway 65 with Mt. Adone their primary objective.

At the start of the offensive on October 16, units of the 88th spread over a wide area. Two battalions of the 350th were over one mile north of the Sillaro River, and to permit them to concentrate on Mt. Grande, XIII Corps took over the Gesso Ridge from the 351st and attacked north to seize Mount Spaduro. Thus by 2330 on October 16, the inter-corps boundary ran between Mount delle Tombe and Mount Spaduro and then skirted the south side of the Sillaro Valley, but until these peaks were taken General Kendall was forced to maintain part of his forces south of the river. The 350th had the task of continuing north to seize Mount Cuccoli, the high point to the west of Mount Grande. 19 (See Map 6.)

Although the 91st and 34th slowed down and the 85th made some gains in the high ground east of the Idice, the 88th Division by the 19th was drawing close to Mt. Grande and held Mt. Delle Tombe. The XIII Corps now shifted to the north, taking over Gesso Ridge and attacking for Mt. Spaduro, thus making a reduction in the 88th Division zone and consequently releasing additional forces for its attack. Because of the stiff resistance met by the 34th and 91st Divisions, the plan modification called for the 88th on the right flank to widen the flanks of the salient to reduce concentration of enemy forces.

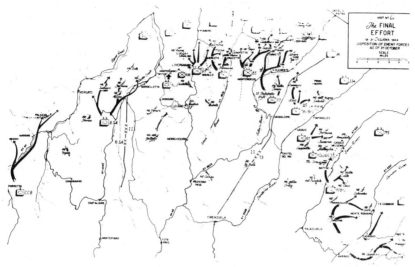

Chapter 6 — Map 6

The first step in this modification called for the 88th to take Mt. Grande and Mt. Cerere, the high point on a spur to the southeast of Mt. Grande. [20]

Big air attacks preceded the 88th's attack on the 19th, coupled with an artillery attack of 8100 rounds an hour between 1700-1800 October 19 in the area from Mt. Cuccoli east to Mt. Cerere, along with the aid of tanks and tank destroyers. Elements of the division had scaled Mt. Cerere and Mt. Grande by the 20th.

For this attack beginning on October 15 the 1st Battalion, after being relieved by the 351st, assembled in an area 3000 yards to the rear while the 2nd Battalion moved due east and southeast with Company E capturing the town of Mo Del Sillaro and then continuing the advance aided by Company F toward Hill 369. Plans now called for the 349th Regiment to be attached and moved into the assembly area in the large wadi, 1000 yards short of Calanco, and for the 1st Battalion to move 5000 yards due north to support the 2nd on call. The 3rd Battalion still constituted the holding force. As the 2nd Battalion moved from Hill 363 down the long ridge running due north to Hill 396, it was viciously counterattacked by a strong enemy force after enemy artillery had shrewdly smoked the entire ridge. Although Companies A and B were rushed to bolster the advance position, the 2nd Battalion had repulsed the counterattack after forty minutes of hard fighting. By night Companies E and F

Page 149

held Hill 396, Company G was on Hill 393, and Companies A and B of the 1st Battalion occupied the ridge between these two hills.[21]

As the 1st Battalion attacked on the night of October 15-16, it was disorganized by friendly artillery fire and thus made no progress toward Mount Cuccoli. The 349th, attached to the 350th, was driven back from the outskirts of St. Clemente by German tank and machine gun fire but succeeded by noon of the next day in re-entering the town. Before close of the 17th, the 349th had come abreast of the 350th. For the next few days action consisted in bringing up reserves and attacking up parallel spurs leading to the Mount Grande - Mount Cuccoli ridge.

By the 16th the 350th's left flank was protected by elements of the 339th Infantry, but units on the right flank were exposed to an extent of four or five thousand yards, a gap that made for extreme vulnerability. In the II Corps attack to reach "the green phase line" to push into the Po Valley, the 88th was to attack at 2000 with the mission of seizing Hill 454 and Mt. Cuccoli. As the Air Force flew missions against formidable Mt. Grande, the last enemy bulwark of defense before the Po, the innovation of searchlights at night to illuminate the Corps sector facilitated night work and marked direction of the front for night movement.[22]

With the 1st Battalion headquarters at Casa Catanco, enemy artillery fire zeroed in on the CP building. One officer and five enlisted men were wounded.[23] Companies of the 3rd Battalion moved forward in the afternoon to take up new positions formerly occupied by the 3rd, 349th Infantry, and were now to be ready on call.[24] After consolidation and reorganization, the Regiment again jumped off in the attack at 2200, led by the 1st Battalion, in the direction of Hill 454 and Mt. Cuccoli.

In the evening of the 17th, the 1st Battalion commander requested permission to begin his attack at 2000 instead of waiting five hours; Colonel Fry approved, and the 1st again opened its drive to advance down the ridge. Having reached its assembly area by this time, the 3rd prepared to launch an attack due north along a secondary road that followed a long draw for 2000 yards, leading to the high range of hills that joined M. Grande, 2500 yards to the northeast. A II Corps directive now ordered 3rd Battalion, 339th Infantry (on the

350th's left) to drive northeast from its advantageous positions towards M. Cuccoli, in an effort to take Mt. Grande as soon as possible. At the close of day both the 1st and 3rd Battalions reported progress toward their objectives, the 3rd's goal the village of Del Fabbio. [25]

For the period October 18-19 the regiment continued its attack to capture ridges controlling Mt. Grande, at this time occupied by the enemy. Of prime importance was the capture of Hill 454. A Corps G-3 report emphasized the resistance by the enemy with tanks and armored SP artillery and also anti-tank defenses. To meet this threat, the Regiment pushed well forward all TD and Tank units in close support of firing positions. On the Regiment's left the 339th Infantry moved parallel with the 350th units while the 349th Infantry on the right also met strong enemy resistance. Obviously the enemy intended to hold this dominating ridge controlled by Mt. Grande, and he signalled this determination by concentrations of SP and mortar fires on all parts of the sector, especially on an important supply and communication bridge and ridge occupied by the 2nd Battalion. In mid-afternoon a message was received that the 38th British Brigade was to move in on the Division's right on the 19th as flank protection. [26]

For the 18th the forward CP of the 3rd Battalion was located at Casetto with the rear CP at M. Melsillaro. [27] The 1st Battalion CP was at Casa Catanco and the rear CP at Casa Caprara. Early action on the 18th found the 3rd Battalion, with Company K in the lead, just 500 yards short of the important road junction on Hill 454, with the 1st Battalion capturing Ca Di Sesso after a slight fight.

On the 19th the 3rd Battalion continued its attack to capture the road junction on Hill 454. The 2nd Battalion moved through the 1st Battalion and proceeded down the ridge toward the village of Farneto. By early morning, 0530, the 2nd had managed to push 500 yards to Hill 454, and the 3rd was just 200 yards short of its objective. The projected relief of the 1st Battalion by the 351st was postponed. In its attack the 2nd Battalion suffered a counterattack against Company F, but it was repulsed with able assistance from the supporting artillery.

In the later evening the 3rd Battalion received news that the 339th Infantry had occupied Hill 454 and that another unit was to pass through it to a point 800 yards down the road. The 3rd Battalion was to precede that unit with the object of placing one company on the south ridge of M. Cuccoli and one company between that ridge and the village of Farneto. The orders for Lt. Col. Williamson were to leave the ridge, start cross country, hit the road just east of Farneto, and then to continue on to M. Grande.

Shortly after 2300, the 3rd Battalion had not moved, because it had not contacted the 339th Infantry. In continuing its attack, the 2nd Battalion encountered stubborn enemy resistance in the attempt to make its way around the ridge. [28] The 1st Battalion was finally relieved by the 3rd Battalion, 351st, and marched to the rear assembly area for 24 hours rest. [29]

The 3rd Battalion on this date suffered impuslive and deadly concentrations of artillery fire on the CP and other positions throughout the evening, which resulted in wounding seriously two men, who were given first aid and evacuated. In the heavy bombardment around 1830 the CP was hit, and a recon car, jeep and three-quarter ton wire jeep set on fire. The fire lasted from 2200 to 0300. [30]

By the end of the day, October 18, the 350th Infantry had all three of its battalions north of the Sillaro with some elements near the crest of the ridge leading up to Mount Cuccoli. Attacking at 0315, October 19, the 2nd Battalion had reached positions within 500 yards of Mount Cuccoli, the objective, before dawn. On the west 1000 yards away, the 3rd Battalion was within 200 yards of a trail along the crest of the ridge. Later in the day contact was made with the 3rd Battalion, 339th Infantry, attacking eastward along the trail. Before the close of the day the 339th, 350th, and 349th were ready to converge on Mount Grande. [31]

On the right of the 350th, the 349th attacked in a blinding rain, capturing Mount Cerere and 11 Germans. Before dawn of the 20th, the eastern slopes of Mt. Grande were in the hands of the 349th, and Company F then moved to the summit. A partial explanation for this victory resulted from the success of the 350th and 339th in action two days before from the ridge stretching from Grande into the zone of the 85th on the left. On the afternoon of the 20th, Company I, 350th Infantry, reached the summit of Cuccoli, the major height on the ridge. The 2nd Battalion secured the village of Farneto by dark, 200 yards to the east. The 337th now took a portion of the ridge lying west of Farneto, thus permitting the 350th Infantry to aid in consolidation of Mount Grande.[32]

Capture of these positions by the 2nd Battalion after Company I had occupied M. Cuccoli had been made imperative by the following message from the Commanding General to the Regiment at 1440: "We must get something on Farneto before dark; have unit move towards Grande to contact 349th Infantry; get tanks and TD's on M. Grande."[33]

On this date, October 20, elements of the 85th Division effected the relief of the 3rd Battalion. Major Witter, commanding, was replaced by Major Butch because of illness. The 3rd was then ordered to relieve the 2nd Battalion that night as the latter was ordered to spearhead in a further attack. Both Regimental and 3rd Battalion CP's were located in the same place in the vicinity of Parrdi Rignano. The 3rd Battalion S-3 was reassigned to the 2nd Battalion.[34]

After the 1st Battalion had bivouaced in a rear assembly area on this day, the personnel reorganized and cared for weapons and equipment. Shortly before noon, Company B with part of Heavy Weapons Company attached move out for the front, with the remainder of the battalion leaving the assembly area at 1800 hours and marching 6000 yards to take up defensive positions on high ground at Ca di Luccia, southwest of Mt. Grande.

Realizing the gravity of the situation at this stage, Captain Ray M. Simpson, ammunitions officers, made a special effort to move extra supplies to the front in order to have a substantial reserve, if needed. At 1845 enemy tanks were heard on the highway between Farneto and M. Grande, but apparently were withdrawing. Soon after the relief of the 3rd Battalion at 2200 by the 337th Infantry, a patrol of the 350th ran into an enemy half-track towing an AT gun. The vehicle was knocked out with the enemy personnel either being killed, captured, or wounded.[35]

The capture of Mt. Grande presented grave problems for the Krauts. Like Battaglia, its capture was a serious tactical loss. Elements of the 44th, 98th, and 90th Divisions, along with the remainder of the 90th from the 8th Army Front, assembled opposite the 350th and the 88th to head off this threat. To meet this mass of enemy troops, II Corps ordered all available air craft and division artillery to deliver extensive harassing fires to aid the valiant attackers.

Since the rest of II Corps front had remained virtually static during this final effort phase, General Clark now decided to abandon the second and third phases of II Corps plans of attack and to concentrate on expanding the bulge on Mt. Grande. The main effort fell to the 88th and 85th Divisions, to be assisted by XIII Corps.[36]

It was during these grueling attacks by the 350th after the 15th that Colonel Fry made the decision to relieve Lt. Col. Williamson. As the 2nd Battalion on one of those nights made an all-out attack to get a ridge line west of and leading to Mt. Grande and thus moved toward the cluster of houses known as Farneto, immediately north of St. Clemente, Colonel Fry contacted Colonel Williamson by phone to issue orders for the 2nd Battalion's attack. Detecting the awful strain endured by this courageous commander through the tears in his voice, Colonel Fry moved from his CP along a trail where the contours of twisted bodies, both American and German equally divided, lay in death. He made the decision of relieving Colonel Williamson and appointed Major Donald Yongue, who then came forward to command the 2nd until the end of the war.

The large number of green replacements in the line at this point illustrates the gravity of the fighting in these mountains short of the Po Valley. Over 1300 replacements had come up in the last few days. On the night of October 20, when Captain Cussans commanded the 2nd Battalion, Lt. Bell was sent with his platoon to make contact with the 349th on Mt. Grande. After a briefing with his sergeants, they struck out on a trial, with the men bunching up since they had had scarcely any combat experience, until they were scattered by their leaders. This patrol blew up a Kraut tank, and Lt. Yeager, observing the action, said he counted 14 dead, with the loss of two Americans killed and six wounded. [37]

After General Clark had made the decision to shift the main attack north of Mount Grande, verbal instructions were issued on October 22 for the attack in an area from the right flank, in the Mount Castelazzo area in the 88th zone, to the Ribano Hills in the 85th zone. These two heights, approximately three miles northeast of Mt. Grande and the same distance from Highway 9, represented the last possible defense line short of the Po

Page 154

Valley. After their capture II Corps would then be prepared to cut Highway 9, and troops were to be held in reserve for this purpose. To aid in this attack, XIII Corps was to mass at least four brigades north of the Santerno River and to make an immediate attack on the chain of hills south of the Sillaro River to aid II Corps in opening Highway 937 to Castel San Pietro. In the initial attack the 351st and elements of the 85th Division would lead the way.

The line of departure for a continuation of the drive centered about one mile north of Mt. Grande and then about 1 ½ miles to the east toward Vedriano, an equal distance from Castellazo. It was here that the 351st would lose Company G in an enemy encirclement, but renewed orders called for an attack at night on October 24-25. About three companies of the 351st Regiment were virtually destroyed by October 26. [38]

The other regiments were in no better condition. Plans of using the reserve 362nd Infantry Regiment were ended by the torrential rains on October 26, when a flash flood took out all the bridges across the Sillaro River and so prevented movement of the Regiment north of the stream. All transport was now tied up south of the river. Ammo and rations had to be hand carried over the swollen stream and then taken over washed out jeep trails to reach Mt. Grande. From there mules alone could reach the forward troops. It was in view of this situation that General Keyes on the afternoon of October 26 issued verbal orders to the 85th and 88th to pull back to defensible ground and dig in. [39]

The flooded streams and washed-out bridges were not the basic causes of the halted offensive. Its primary cause was under strength in all the regiments after more than six weeks of bitter fighting. Only the hope of crossing the last mountain separating them from the Po Valley had kept the brave men from halting earlier. Of the 15,716 battle casualties suffered by the attacking divisions since September 10, the 88th Division, "which spearheaded the last attack from Mt. Grande, alone had suffered 5,026 casualties. At the end of October it was understrength by 1243 officers and men." [40]

The history of the 350th during this last phase from October 21 on to the end of the month is told by phrases of "patrol action," "little activity throughout the Regimental sector with light harassing fires in a few locations throughout the area," "light activity all through the sector with patrols the main center of attraction," "lull in the fighting," and "extensive patrolling and consolidating...positions." 41

In the period 25-26 October, the 350th was ordered to extend its right of the line to cover a part of the area that had been occupied by the 351st Infantry on the northern edge of Mt. Grande. The job was given to the 1st Battalion. At that time Colonel Fry headquartered in Gasolina, a four room structure, with a haymow upstairs and a stable in the basement for animals. Lt. Colonel Cochran, ordered forward to monitor the 1st's conduct, reported that "the attack is coming against Charlie's company (Lynch). He's a real dynamo and they are killing plenty of Jerries. Nothing to worry about." 42

The front line of the 350th at this time anchored its left on a knob known as Mt. Calderaro, which protruded into the enmy position toward Vedriano. (See the attached sketch.) Opposing the 350th were the German elite paratroopers, perhaps the most disciplined and hardened of the enemy facing the Regiment, who fought with a tenacity and aggressiveness typical of their disciplined ranks. Every trip to Mt. Calderaro was made at extreme hazard, and along the trail could be seen dead Germans, bloated and saturated with rain.

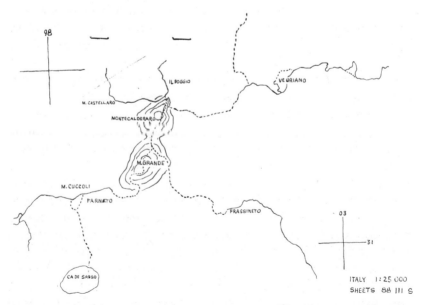

Chapter 6 — Map 7

The supply lines passed through the little town of St. Clemente, which quickly became a bottleneck. The enemy pounded the spot uninterruptedly. The quip, "I've had plenty of St. Clemente," expressed the attitude of every G-I passing through the area.

It was at this time in St. Clemente that Captain (Dr.) Reid saved the life of a small Italian girl strangling to death from a throat congestion. Captain Reid placed a breathing tube into the child's neck, enabling her to breathe and thus be saved from death. Ironically, Captain Reid's own child had died of a similar throat condition in the United States while the doctor was serving in Italy. [43]

On October 24 after the 351st Infantry had suffered a two-battalion counterattack at Vedriano, the 3rd Battalion of the 350th moved to its aid toward Mt. Grande. On October 27 word was received that the 2nd Battalion would replace the 3rd on Mt. Grande with the 3rd Battalion sending one company to Ca Di Sasso. By this time the Division MLR had been established with its left flank based on Montecalderaro, extending southeast for a distance of 2500 yards to its right flank position at Frassineto, which faced all the gradually sloping grond running northeast into the Po Valley. The RRL backed up this line with its left flank anchored on M. Grande extending fifteen hundred yards to the southeast to the right flank position of M. Cerere. Thus the reserve line was established roughly four to five hundred yards behind the MLR. Heavy, steady rains fell almost continuously during the previous three day period, hindering all operations and movement. [44]

During the period 28-29 October the 1st Battalion relieved one battalion of the 351st on Mt. Grande. Inclement weather hampered all patrol operations, both friend and enemy, during these two days. In the early morning hours, October 29, the 3rd Battalion completed its movement into the Ca Di Sassa area amidst increased enemy fire, perhaps signalling a change in enemy intentions. A patrol from the 1st Battalion just before midnight contacted enemy tanks with Krauts digging in around them; a fight ensued, with grenades being thrown; however, the patrol withdrew with important information. Screaming meemies fell on Mt. Grande shortly thereafter in the draw to the northeast of this strategic height and covered the trail joining Mt. Cuccoli with Mt. Grande.

The period October 30-31 would bring a change in the lull for the past seven or eight days. Two captured prisoners of war from the 98th Division explained to the 2nd Battalion that they had seen a battalion of their paratroopers the day before just eight hundred yards northeast of Mt. Grande in the large draw. Suddenly at 2115 the enemy quickly and fiercely couner-attacked Vezzoli from the east, whereupon the 1st Battalion requested reinforcements. Two platoons of the 2nd Battalion and Company I were sent to aid. After repulsing the attack, the 1st Battalion and its reinforcements again beat off an enemy attack beginning at 2225 and lasting for one hour before they were driven off with heavy losses. Again at 0103, October 31, the aggressive enemy attacked viciously Company C; these stubborn troops refused to give ground. Another attack at 0310 was again thrown back. Supporting artillery continued to aid the defending troops and except for a small counterattack at 1900, which was easily repulsed, the day drew to a close. The Regiment was once more proving its proud reputation as the "Battle Mountain" Regiment. [45]

MONTE LA FINE, APENNINES, ITALY, IN OCT. 1944 BY PVT. FAGERHOLM

After Battaglia the regiment was reorganizing in a muddy valley near Monte La Fine.

An 81mm mortar crew in the Mt. Grande area.

Exhausted doughboys going back for a rest.

Mt. Grande, North Appenines, town of Farneto in foreground.

A Fifth Army vehicle passes blasted and bombed buildings in Loiano, Italy.

Footnotes for Chapter VI.

[1] Narrative, 1-31 Octover 1944, Headquarters 88th Infantry Division, 26 November 1944.

[2] 350th Infantry Regiment History, October, 1944.

[3] **Ibid.**

[4] 3rd Battalion History, October, 1944.

[5] 1st Battalion History, October, 1944.

[6] **Fifth Army History, Part VII,** 122.

[7] Starr, **From Salerno to the Alps,** 350-351.

[8] Fry, **Combat Soldier,** 202.

[9] **Ibid.,** 204.

[10] Starr, **From Salerno to the Alps,** 353.

[11] 350th Infantry Regiment History, October, 1944.

[12] Fry, **Combat Soldier,** 208.

[13] Third Battalion History, October, 1944.

[14] Starr, **From Salerno to the Alps,** 352.

[15] Fry, **Combat Soldier,** 207-210.

[16] Starr, **From Salerno to the Alps,** 353.

[17] **Fifth Army History,** Part VII, 139-140.

[18] Starr, **From Salerno to the the Alps,** 356.

[19] **Fifth Army History,** Part VII, 155.

[20] Starr, **From Salerno to the ALps,** 358.

[21] 350th Infantry Regiment History, October, 1944.

[22] 350th Infantry Regiment History, October, 1944.

[23] 1st Battalion History, October, 1944.

[24] 3rd Battalion History, October, 1944.

[25] 350th Infantry Regiment History, October, 1944.

[26] 350th Infantry Regiment History, October, 1944.

[27] 3rd Battalion History, October, 1944.

[28] 350th Infantrry Regiment History, October, 1944.

[29] 1st Battalion History, October, 1944.

[30] Third Battalion History, October, 1944.

[31] **Fifth Army History,** Part VII, 156-157.

[32] **Ibid.,** 158.

[33] 350th Infantry Regiment History, October, 1944.

[34] Third Battalion History, October, 1944.

[35] 350th Infantry Regiment History, October, 1944.

[36] **Fifth Army History,** Part VII, 159.

[37] Fry, **Combat Soldier,** 210-211.

[38] Fifth Army History, Part VII, 160-162.

[39] Starr, **From Salerno to the Alps,** 359-360.

[40] **Ibid.**

[41] 350th Infantry Regiment History, October, 1944.

[42] Fry, **Combat Soldier,** 214.

[43] **Ibid.,** 215-216.

[44] 350th Infantry Regiment History, October, 1944.

[45] 350th Infantry Regiment History, October, 1944.

Page 162

Chapter Seven

The Second Winter in the Appenines:
November-December, 1944

Although II Corps would plan immediately for a new offensive to begin in December in an effort to push into the Po Valley, the positions south of Bologna occupied by the 350th Infantry at the beginning of November would generally remain the farthest advanced into the German lines protecting the valley. The month of November for the Regiment began with little enemy activity noted throughout the sector. Operational plans called for the relief of the Regiment by the Second Infantry Brigade of the First British Infantry Division, which was to relieve a battalion each night, beginning November 2, 1944, until the relief was completed. Because of the inclement weather and the terrible condition of the roads, the relief by the British proved to be extremely difficult.

In the early morning hours of November 1 enemy movement was reported at Casseta, a house located on the side of the large draw that formed an approach to Mt. Grande from the east. A number of rounds of artillery covered the area over a thirty minute period to harass any enemy grouping in that locality. Shortly thereafter the Third Battalion completed the relief of the First Battalion without incident. In the evening at 1800 hours elements of the British advance party arrived to make a reconnaissance of positions prior to the relief by the First British Division. [1]

For the battle-weary Blue Devils, Florence seemed a haven

of refuge from the hell of battle in the mountains. The four-day rest periods that began on November 2 raised the morale of officers and men as they enjoyed the comforts of the rest centers in the Renaissance city along the Arno, with its numerous artistic monuments and other attractions. Even amidst the hardships of war, the population of Floence seemed to retain its pride and sense of self-respect and decorum. It was also at the beginning of November that Lieutenant Shea of Company "F" received his second lieutenant's bar and the appointment to the officer grade. [2]

During the first few days of the month, the First Battalion held defensive positions at Montecalderaro at Mt. Grande in the vicinity of St. Clemente. The battalion's situation remained virtually unchanged through November 5 with enemy activity limited to sporadic artillery fire. The Third Battalion, in defensive positions also, reported light enemy activity until the afternoon when a concentration of mortar and artillery fire landed in the vicinity of the command post. The next day, November 2, an enemy barrage on the command post at 1500 injured two radio operators. As relief of the entire battalion was expected momentarily, a quartering party was sent to reconnoiter the new rest area. The Second Battalion also reported the departure of an advance party to the future rest center, Montecatini, to arrange for billeting of the battalion. Because of inclement weather and resultant bad roads, the relief of the battalion was delayed until November 5 when it would move approximately 90 miles to the rest center at Montecatini.

During the period November 2-4 concentrated enemy mortar and artillery fire broke the comparative inactivity at a time when engineers were laying anti-personnel mines in front of the Third Battalion sector. As a combat patrol of the regiment moved toward Casa II Vezzolo and discovered the enemy dug in around an abandoned U.S. tank, it was fired upon by a machine gun from underneath the tank and another one from the house beyond. Another patrol on a mission toward Casetta, a house one thousand yards east of Mt. Grande, also encountered an enemy ambush patrol just three hundred yards short of the objective and after a short fire fight withdrew.

Upon being relieved by the First Loyals, the Second Battalion withdrew to a reserve position in the valley in preparation for

the move by trucks to Montecatini.³ It would not be until November 6 that the Fist Battalion would be relieved from the defensive positions at Mt. Grande. It then moved to the rear assembly area near Casetta, where it went into a 24-hour reserve behind the relieving British Brigade unit, prior to movement to the rear.

While the First Battalion remained on the defense at Mount Grande during the first few days of November, the enemy launched an attack designed to throw the Blue Devils from their positions. It was during a counter-attack of November 3, 1944, that Private Mack C. Bootle of Charleston, South Carolina, won the Silver Star for gallantry in action. When an enemy soldier succeeded in setting up a machine gun in a position to rake the entire area with fire, Private Bootle left the safety of his foxhole and began to crawl toward the machine gun. He was met with a burst of fire that blew the rifle from his hands, but Private Bootle continued to crawl forward and killed the gunner with a well-placed grenade. When another enemy soldier passed the haystack where Bootle had killed the machine gunner, Bootle killed him with his last grenade. He then retrieved the enemy rifle and returned to his position and continued the fight.

As all units of the Regiment prepared for movement to the new rest area in Montecatini, patrols were active to ascertain enemy movement; likewise, the enemy continued mortar and artillery shelling to disrupt movement of the Regiment. After patrols from the Third Battalion met machine gun cross fire from a trail junction in their area, they moved back to their former positions. Enemy artillery shelled the First Battalion positions on Vezzola and also on Mt. Calderaro. To delay enemy movements, the Air Force the next day, November 5, flew sorties toward S. Martino, Varignano, Vedriano, and roads north and in the Il Poggio area. As the British moved to the relief at Mt. Grande on this day, they suffered one KIA and one WIA from medium artillery concentrations.⁵

During these first few days in November the men of the Regiment were eagerly awaiting the long-deserved rest after six weeks of steady combat. The Second Battalion closed into the rest area at Montecatini on November 6, followed by the Third on the next day and the First on November 8. For the first four days the men rested and relaxed in this seemingly war-

free town; in addition many others journeyed to nearby Florence on one-day passes.[6]

It was indeed a surprise to the Blue Devils that such a paradise as Montecatini could exist so close to the mud of the front lines that they had occupied since September. Not only were there showers and clean clothes for the men but also the indulgent luxury of sulphur and health baths for those who desired them. The relaxation that the spa afforded contrasted sharply with the recent trying combat experiences in the Appenines, where almost all survivors enjoying the comforts of Montecatini remembered the loss of a comrade only a few days before on those rain-drenched and mud-filled heights.

The favorite rallying point for the proud Blue Devils, the Trianon Theater, had just recently been converted into a huge night club. It included 189 tables on the main floor and a balcony upstairs. The Blue Devils paid a total of 30 cents for a shot of rum, whiskey, and cognac. In charge of the club was Lt. William Hearne, formerly of the 88th Division, but the Blue Devils could expect no favortism from him; all combat-weary men were treated alike at the Trianon.

The Red Cross girls, ever faithful to their duty whether in combat or rest areas, performed admirably in this relaxed atmosphere. In their "Tent Club" in the town, the queen of jitterbug, called by the G-I's "Mississippi," performed nightly. Actually "Alabama" would have been a more exact appelation for this lady, Ann Jenkins, who came from Mississippi's sister state.[7]

Although theaters in the town ran continuously, the highlight of all performances was the incomparable Miss Katherine Cornell playing the role of Elizabeth Barrett to Brian Aherene's Robert Browning in the production, **The Barretts of Wimpole Street**. At the last performance of the show, the 350th Infantry presented the cast with a huge bouquet of flowers in appreciation of their outstanding contribution in bringing to the doughboys experienced in combat this nostalgic drama of the power of true love. The uplift in morale and the relief for only a few hours from the thoughts of death and destruction by such talented performers were of incalculable value to the mental and spiritual outlook of the men. After the last performance the entire cast accepted the invitation of the Regimental Command Post to be their guests for a short but delightful evening dinner given by a small group of officers representing all units of the Regiment. [8]

On Monday, November 13, various units resumed regular training, including range firing, ordnance inspection of all weapons, squad and platoon problems, and leadership training. At a special ceremony various officers and enlisted men received awards of silver stars, oak leaf clusters to the Bronze star, and Legion of Merit decorations. The 350th boasted somewhat of receiving more awards than any other Regiment in the Division.

The two delightful weeks of rest and rehabilitation in the resort hotels of Montecatini soon passed, and the Regiment received a directive from Division headquarters stating that the 350th Infantry would relieve the 338th Infantry, 85th Infantry Division, by the night of November 21-22 and would assume command of the present 85th Division sector on November 22. [9] The Third Battalion, the first unit to leave, departed at 0700, November 18, for forward positions. The battalion traveled a distance of about 85 miles and then detrucked about two miles south of the village of Baccanello. By 0200 hours, November 19, the battalion had completed the relief without incident.

The Second Battalion moved at 0820 on November 19 for its destination in the vicinity of Savazza, Italy. By 2000 the relief of the Second Battalion, 338th Infantry, had been accomplished without incident and on schedule. The movement of the regiment followed Highway 6627 to Florence, turned on to Highway 65, and then right on to 6529. It then followed a trail marked by the military police over to Highway 6531 that led toward the front line positions. The 350th's front lines centered on strategic Mount Fano, the important high ground in this sector.

The process of rotation of battalions began at this time with the reserve battalion remaining for six days in positions near Bacanello, a small village situated on the main road and approximately twenty-five hundred yards behind the front lines. It would then relieve one of the forward battalions, which would then return to the rest area. Each battalion thus spent twelve days on the line and six days in rotation in the rest area. [10]

In this area into which the 350th settled after returning from Montecatini, the winter line extended north along Route 65 with

Monghidoro the rear line, extending then through Loiano, toward Pianoro, the front line position. All along this area, from the deep valleys protruded the outlines of artillery positions and ammunition dumps, along with aid stations, supply distribution points, motorparks and all the multitudes of impedimenta necessary to supply the army battle line.

The area occupied by the 350th at this time followed the valley east of Loiano, where the road leads toward Ozzano d'Emilia on Highway 9. The road followed the course of the meandering stream, the Idice, and when the 350th relieved the 85th here on November 19, 1944, it was really a new regiment of new replacements primarily; nevertheless these replacements, too, exhibited the bond of high morale and the espirit de corps of the older veterans of the 350th tried in combat.

Into that area filled with splotches of snow, the column of trucks had made its way over muddy roads, and by dusk the leading battalion had halted on November 18 to await the last lap forward under cover of darkness. From a cluster of houses around Savazza, an area that would be his headquarters for a rather extended period, Colonel Fry was never more than just a couple hundred yards off the road which led through Fiumetta and Baccanello toward Razzone. Along that main muddy supply road, a seemingly uncordinated mixture of telephone lines enmeshed in all directions. Because much of the valley was under constant enemy observation during the daylight hours, movement was largely restricted, but even with the greatest precautions almost every day some vehicle would be hit. [11]

By November 23, 1944, the battalions occupied the following areas: Third, in the vicinity of Mt. Fano; First, Fiumetto; and Second, C. Bacca. During this period a number of men were reported AWOL, and also Italian civilians were evacuated from forward areas, including fifteen brought to the 350th Regiment command post where the Allied Military Government took control of them [12]

These days of November consisted in patrol activity to probe enemy lines and capture prisoners for interrogation. Areas of patrol action included the vicinity of Pizzano, Orbega, and Castle Colombara.[13] For relief from the constant occupancy of the front lines, a number of officers and enlisted men continued to receive passes to the Florence Fifth Army Rest Center, with some also visiting the Rome rest center.[14]

Along the front line of the Regiment extending from the western side of the Idice River up and along the precipitous slopes of the line of hills to the east of the Regiment's supply route, Colonel Fry visited a front line commander every day and spoke with the battalion commanders directly or by telephone two or three times each day. Among other heart-rending eventualities that combat men frequently encountered was the sight along the road in November of the bodies of Lt. William G. Watson, a supply officer; his driver, Private Herman N. Collins; and S-Sgt James Eineker, whose jeep had received a direct hit. Men with tasks to perform and knowing they could do no more in such situations usually hurried by without displaying their subdued feelings of remorse.[15]

The inclement weather and untoward conditions of battle permitted respite at night and on foggy days to permit truck loads of men to rush a couple of miles down the road where there were field showers in large hospital units. There they would receive new outfits of fresh clothes after showering. In these November days both officers and men shared the same comforts and privations as they billeted together in command posts in peasants' buildings. Even company headquarters enjoyed such comforts, but for frontline platoons there was little to offer except dugouts on the reserve slopes of hills.

The front line of the 350th at this time ran across the extreme crest of Mt. Fano, the highest point in the area. In the ravines to the right and left German and American patrols matched wits in trying to out-maneuver one another during these nights. On sunny days the men who had to be on top of Mt. Fano at all times climbed the reverse side of the hill to re-read the few dog-eared magazines distributed to them; but on rainy days, all these front line troops could do was to huddle in trenches, wrapped in dirty OD blankets and covered with an olive drab shelter-half, with muzzles of rifles always visible along the corners of the shelter half. At first numerous German bodies lay plentifully in evidence, and the instructions to the front line troops to have them interred properly and the graves marked were generally ignored.

The Second Battalion experienced the dangers of daylight patrolling in November, 1944, when a unit asked permission to surprise a known enemy outpost. As the patrol advanced somewhat concealed through the drifting fog down the Idice valley, the rest of the company posted machine guns to aid in the withdrawal. Coming close to the enemy positions, the patrol met a German under the safety of a white flag from a nearby building. The leader of the American patrol forgot the frequently dastardly tricks of the enemy on such occasions and arose from the cover of the river. Immediately a second German appeared; the Americans were forced to drop their rifles and started toward the German-held house, when suddenly the Blue Devils whirled upon the Germans and for a moment made them their prisoners as they wrenched the enemies' rifles from their hands. As the patrol then began to retrace their journey towards the river bank, German fire opened from all directions; the American machine guns tried to help but to no avail. Only one badly wounded soldier returned; the rest were either killed or captured.

For supplying the 350th Regiment there was a 150 mule train stationed in Baccanello, under the leadership of Lt. John Remish. Divided into sections, these mule trains slogged forward in the night along slippery slopes to deliver ammunition and rations. After going as far forward as possible, the mule trains were met by carrying parties who took the supplies to the needed areas. The mules then brought the wounded and dead back along the trails.[16]

During the months of November and December, 1944, the 350th Infantry Regiment, along with the rest of II Corps, planned to resume the drive toward the Po Valley; the Eighth Army had already launched a limited offensive that resulted in achieving a better position in relation to the Fifth Army front. The Fifth Army had scheduled an attack a few days later.[17] At this time II Corps stood by on a seventy-two hours' notice. This operation, known by the code name **Pianoro**, had available the 34th, 85th, 88th, and 91st Infantry Divisions and the First Armored Division. The plan envisaged an attack along Highway 65 with Mt. Monterumici, Mt. Adone, and Mt. dei Frati, rugged features southwest of Pianoro, as the initial objectives. There would then be a drive north to capture Bologna.[18] For two months there was preparation for the offensive, but the weather deteriorated so rapidly that traffic was almost impossible and the whole Italian front settled down in the mud.[19]

The 350th men, along with others of II Corps, could look toward a winter campaign in higher and more rugged mountains under worse conditions of cold, rain, and snow than that experienced a year before by the Fifth Army south of Rome. [20]

All that miserable winter the Army sat down, and from the enemy strongholds facing them they were under constant fire. Now Italy had become the "Forgotten Front" back home, and the soldiers felt this slight bitterly. There was scarcely any mention of the 350th Infantry's exploits in the newspapers' back home, and thus the doughboys were deprived of the important morale builder of publicity. [21] (See attached sketch for positions during month of December).

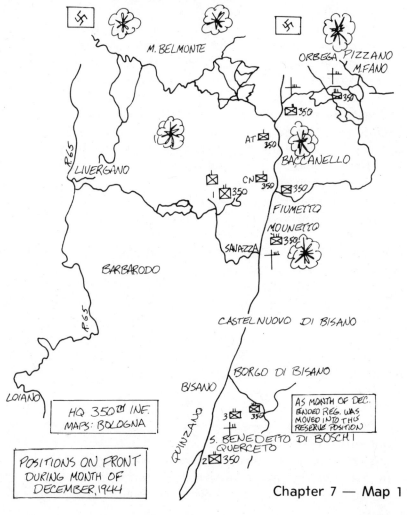

Chapter 7 — Map 1

During the months of November to December, the center sector, which included Highway 65, was occupied by the 34th Infantry Division to the left of the 88th Infantry Division, with the Blue Devils extending eastward to the XIII Corps boundary and thus covering the Idice River valley and the Mt. Belmonte front, the most northerly point reached by Fifth Army - a position where the troops atop Mount delle Formiche and Mount Belmonte could look down into the Po Valley. In this area Highway 9, at the foot of the mountains, could be seen from Mount Grande on the left of XIII Corps. At this point the Army had advanced slightly more than sixty miles from Florence. The elite troops of the enemy Fourteenth Army, the First Parachute Corps, opposed the left and center of II Corps front. In these positions the towns of Pianoro, three miles north of Livergnano on Highway 65, and Vergato, on Highway 64 to the west, became the nerve centers of the defensive system; between these two highways, the excellent observation post of high, rock-sloped Mount Adone afforded the enemy an excellent view of the activity behind Fifth Army lines.

Although Italy might be a forgotten front to the public back home, it was not viewed that way at all by the Germans. The fact that northern Italy was of great value to the German war effort was indicated by the retention of many first-class divisions and much equipment at a time when they were sorely needed both on the eastern and western European fronts.

By December 28, 1944, when Fifth Army announced postponement of the assault, the Fifth Army front lines were essentially the same as they had been for the preceding two months. The 88th Division extended its lines at this time when the 34th Division (less one combat team) went into reserve at Monghidoro. Amidst the cold and rain in the high Appenines, persistent and difficult diseases to combat took their toll on the effectives for combat, the most persistent being infectious hepatitis. By December 161 out of 1000 were afflicted with the disease.[22]

At the height of the hepatitis epidemic, on one of his visits to the front Colonel Fry found Captain Charles Lynch, commanding officer of Company C, wrapped in blankets near a fire in his command post. Although the captain's eyes shone as he talked a long time and shared reminiscences of his family life with Colonel Fry, his face was flushed with fever; he said, however, that he would be in top shape next morning and did not want to be moved. Reluctantly he had to give in to his bout with yellow jaundice and be evacuated for treatment.

About this time Colonel Fry had to deal with the incident of relieving a battalion commander. The officer came to talk to Colonel Fry, introduced by Sergeant Major Francis Costello. Sorrowfully the commander told Colonel Fry: "I don't believe in the battalion and I don't think they believe in me. I don't think they could fight their way out of a paper bag." Colonel Fry had to make the decision to relieve the distraught commander in the interest of the welfare of himself and the battalion. [23]

In this static period of patrol action, an incident of the incongruities of combat occurred in the exploits of First Lieutenant Frederick L. Griffiths of Shaker Heights, Ohio. On a patrol action he ran several times to the crest of a hill, hurled grenades into the Kraut trenches, and then ducked below the brow of the hill to escape the heavy return fire. After exhausting his supply of grenades, he was surprised to see sixteen Krauts coming up the hill with their hands above their heads. Later four others were found dead in their positions.

As freezing cold and snow covered the entire front by December, most reporters shied away from seeking new stories on the activities of the man in the snow-filled and frequently rain-drenched foxhole. The faithful Sid Feder, however, continued to share the trials of winter combat with the infantryman as he came up to cover the activities of the 88th Division for the Associated Press. [24] After the war he would pay tribute to the gallant Blue Devils in an article for the **Saturday Evening Post:**

> By New Year's Day, 1945, the Blue Devils had suffered 11,825 casualties in nine months, including 2137 killed. In March when they marked their first anniversary in action they had been in combat 280 of a possible 365 days and had destroyed or damaged a dozen enemy divisions. [25]

During the month of December, the 350th sector, dominated by the 557 meter high Mt. Fano, generally remained static. Two battalions now covered a three thousand yard front with a reserve battalion 2500 yards to the rear in a rest area (which received heavy fire on numerous occasions although technically in reserve). From these so-called static positions the regimental team continued its particularly aggressive, well-planned, and superbly-led patrols for the purpose of probing enemy positions, sometimes to fight and take prisoners, sometimes to obtain a complete knowledge of the terrain to the front in event of a future attack, and sometimes to seek new enemy positions. 26

From December 1-7 the First Battalion occupied defensive front line positions on Mt. Fano near Casa Vagae, Italy, southeast of Pianoro. Some of the information gained and events reported give an interesting index on the experiences of the men engaged in these patrols. Noting a herd of cattle on the right side of Mt. Fano, one patrol safely observed that no mines were in that area. On another occasion a patrol from Company C, assigned the mission to reconnoiter the route to Collina, returned to report the route impractical as they had had to wade water waist deep. Company A reconnoitered to Ca Colombara and beyond to ascertain the strength of the enemy and capture a prisoner if possible. The patrol gained a working knowledge of the terrain and reported no casualties, although the enemy zeroed in on them with mortars as they followed the return trail back to their unit.

On December 3, 1944, a patrol from Company B, intent on capturing prisoners, returned after running into heavy mortar fire and observing five of the enemy near a house at Pizzano and two machine guns on high ground in position for effective grazing fire. The next night a Company A patrol of one officer and twelve enlisted men went on a mission whose object was to ambush a supply train. A strategically placed BAR team aided the patrol to return, although two enlisted men were reported missing. Experiencing an intense mortar fire concentration, the BAR team sought shelter in an abandoned enemy dugout. The two enlisted men who were missing later made their way back, but the BAR team waited until early dawn to return to insure not being fired on by friendly troops. One of the enemy walked into Company A command post shortly after the fire fight and was immediately made a prisoner.

From December 2 and for six days following the Second Battalion billeted in the area of Fiumetto after being relieved on December 1 by the Third Battalion. Training included range firing by all companies and lecture and demonstrations by the battalion A and P Platoon on the subject of enemy and American mines.

The Third Battalion, located at C. Rocca on December in the previous position of the Second Battalion, picked up two Italian civilians for questioning and sent them under guard to the Regimental Headquarters for further questioning. On the next day, enemy artillery fire zeroed in on the town of Baccanello, the supply hub, killing five Italian mule skinners and wounding nineteen others. Fear of Italian spies caused the Third Battalion to be on the alert for any suspicious personnel. On December 4 the battalion apprehended another six Italian civilians for questioning. The news that six men had been chosen from the battalion to return home on TDY and rotation proved to be an uplift in the morale of the men. It was also at this time that Major James G. Holland transferred from the battalion to regimental headquarters.

The battalion history for the period December 5-7 reported the routine experiences of men in defensive winter positions: heavy artillery landing around the command post; news of the officers eligible for rotation; patrols encountering scarcely any resistance; arrival of rations; and tanks bogging down in an attempt to move to forward positions. On the third anniversary of Pearl Harbor, the enemy coverd the area between the battalion and Regiment with a tremendous barrage of artillery in the morning and afternoon, thereby starting numerous fires. A number of men were wounded; but throughout all these vicissitudes the morale remained good.

From December 8 until December 15 the First Battalion occupied defensive reserve positions at Fiumetto, Italy, after having been relieved by the Second Battalion during the late evening of December 8. On December 10, 1944, Major Holland assumed command of the battaion as per VOCO. On December 11 Major Holland and Major Jones, the Executive Officer, accompanied Colonel Fry to Company C positions to present a medal to an enlisted man. Generally the battalion followed the schedule of light training, taking showers, and digging in. Sporadically the enemy unleashed heavy artillery barrages, scoring a hit and inflicting casualties in one such barrage on

Company B.

At this time a part of Company B, billeted in dilapidated buildings in an area between Savazza and Fiumetto, was struck by a single round of heavy artillery that killed eight men who were sleeping in the area. Even before Colonel Fry could visit the area, Sylvia Simmons, Rosamond Myers, Frances Beatty, and Virginia Crawford, the ever-faithful Red Cross girls, were there dealing out coffee and doughnuts in the shambles of a barn in their efforts to keep morale high. [27]

The Second Battalion moved into the vicinity of C. Vaglie to relieve the First Battalion on December 8, after having marched cross country for three and one-half miles over mountainous terrain. On this same day the battalion sufferd the loss of its S-4, 1st Lt. Watson, when an enemy shell made a direct hit on his jeep, killing his driver and the supply sergeant also. To replace Lt. watson, Lt. Price, the Battalion A and P Officer, assumed the duties of S-4. From these positions the Second Battalion sent out numerous patrols until relieved on December 21 by the Third Battalion, whereupon the Second Battalion returned to regimental reserve in Fiumetto. [28]

For the period 8-15 December the Third Battalion reported the usual patrolling activity and sporadic heavy enemy barrages. Heavy rains and washed out bridges made supplying very difficult at times during this period. Especially was the town and area of Baccanello a favorite target for artillery concentrations. To break the monotony of constant patrolling and defensive warfare, the Regiment continued to provide leave for officers and men to the rest center in Florence. While in this area Major Witter, the Battaion Commanding Officer, received the promotion to Lieutenant Colonel.

From December 15-24 the First Battalion occupied front line positions at Casa Rocca, Italy. Continued patrolling in the area of Ca di Razzone revealed enemy machine gun positions and mortar firing positions that later were shelled by Division artillery. The battalion officers, Major Holland, Major Jones, and Lt. Boatner, S-3, frequently stayed overnight at the forward company positions to observe the activities of the patrols and to gather information on enemy activity. At Pizzano on December 22 a patrol from Company A spread out and proceeded to clear the north end of the town, flushing out three of the enemy in the encounter. Another patrol followed a road toward enemy lines amidst mortar fire; then proceeded to a footbridge; crossed the stream knee deep; found a way up the bank 100 yards from the bridge; and continued down the road to a destroyed bridge. On Christmas Day the battalion prepared for relief by the Second Battalion and by 2255 hours had bivouaced for the night in the Fiumetto area.

From December 21 until Christmas day, the Second Battalion remained in regimental reserve in Fiumetto. Travel was extremely difficult because of the hazardous mountain trails and deep mud. After remaining in this reserve area for only four days, the battalion had its Christmas dinner served on December 24, and Chaplain Faber conducted services at midnight, followed by another service on Christmas morning. By 2130 on December 25 the battalion again closed into the area at C. Rocca, relieving the First Battalion. No casualties or accidents occurred on the two mile road march from Fiumetto.

From December 16-21, the Third Battalion remained in the reserve area at Fiumetto. On December 21 the Battalion made preparations to relieve the Second Battalion and moved into these positions around C. Vaglie, Italy, amidst a heavy fog which limited observation. It would be the first Christmas day for this battalion in the front lines. Relative quiet prevailed until the end of the year. On December 29 the 349th Infantry Regiment relieved the battalion. In the reserve area at Fiumetto the men had to wait until December 31 for their Christmas dinner. Yet it was a white Christmas even for the men on the front lines, with snow covering the mountain peaks in all directions. A quota of men began leaving at this time for the Montecatini Rest Center.

For the period 26-30 December the First Battalion again relaxed and recuperated in Montecatini. On December 31 it again traveled back to the front lines, a distance of 85 miles, and then marched two miles from the detrucking area to Fiumetto, arriving at 1745 hours and going into reserve behind the 349th Infantry Regiment.

As the men and officers took their turn at the front, they carried only what they could on their backs. On one such occasion just before Christmas, Colonel Fry talked to Major Witter, who had driven from Fiumetto to Savazza to see Colonel

Fry just before the Third Battalion left for the front. When Colonel Fry asked Major Witter what he was carrying in his musette bag, the Major replied: "Nothing. I hope to get a bedding roll up tomorrow on a mule, but I'll probably be carrying two or three rifles before we get to the top of those hills tonight." Colonel Fry then gave him his eider sleeping bag that he had salvaged from a dead German paratrooper. Among these troops on the march was a young lad carrying with him an artificial Christmas tree he had just received from home. He said to Colonel Fry: "If I have to drop the rifle or the tree, it will be the rifle." Incidents of this nature demonstrate the longing for the old Christmas spirit among the men.

Then there was the incident of medics saving a shoe pac from an amputated stump. The two scarce items in the early winter that every GI needed were the heavy-lined white parka for operations in the snow and the high rubber shoes known as shoe pacs. As the wounded left for treatment in the rear, they were always requested to leave their parkas and shoe pacs in the aid stations when they departed. As Captain Stoner, Regimental Surgeon, amputated the mangled leg of a young soldier who had just been hit by a shell fragment, he and Captain Peter Griffo, the Regimental Dentist, wrapped the good leg in blankets and removed the shoe pac to save for someone else. They then looked at the shoe pac on the amputated leg. When Captain Stoner staid, "I guess we should save it," there was no one left in the aid station to aid him but Captain Griffo.

It was a Godsend for the morale of the men to have the talented musician in Regimental Headquarters, Sgt. Douglas P. Allanbrook. He lent his talents to bringing cheer at Christmas as he played medleys of old Christmas favorites on the piano and Sgt. Bongiovi led the men in singing the old favorite carols.

As Christmas approached, the various companies and headquarters along the shell-ridden roads imaginatively improvised on the old Burma Shave signs motif as they placed the greetings of "Merry Christmas" along the thoroughfares at different intervals. There was a fear that the Jerries on Christmas would attempt an attack, but on Christmas the G-I's heard the strains of "Silent Night" in German as the Jerries sang in their celebration, too. For fear, though, that the Krauts might think the 350th had relaxed too much, the artillery sections threw a few rounds around the spot just to remind them that the 350th was alert. One Red Cross girl, Frances Beatty, did not take advantage of the Christmas season to remain in a rear area but cheerfully moved among the front lines dispensing doughnuts and coffee.

The folks back home in the United States received thousands of greetings from the Blue Devils at Christmas in the form of a V-mail letter in lieu of Christmas cards. It read: "Christmas Greetings from a Member of the Fighting 350th Inf." In the center appeared a representation of a Christmas wreath with an Infantryman in the center, underneath which was an emblem and the words "Fidelity and Service." (See attached illustration).

The Blue Devils spent their first Christmas in the lines in Italy in the high Appenines, just short of Bologna.

Officers of the 350th Infantry Regiment, Italy, Winter, 1944-1945.

TO:

FROM

(CENSOR'S STAMP)

SEE INSTRUCTION NO. 2

(Sender's complete address above)

Christmas Greetings
From

Fidelity and Service

A Member
of the
Fighting 350th Inf.

HAVE YOU FILLED IN COMPLETE
ADDRESS AT TOP?

REPLY BY
V---MAIL

HAVE YOU FILLED IN COMPLETE
ADDRESS AT TOP?

☆ U. S. GOVERNMENT PRINTING OFFICE : 1943 16—28143-5

SKETCHED BY G. FAGERHOLM
AT THE ITALIAN FRONT, FEBRUARY, 1945

Sergeant Owen L. Sanderlin.

A typical 88th Division Medical Corps soldier, who repeatedly risked his life to aid the wounded on the battlefield.

Sketch by Gus Fagerholm—Italian Theater, 1944 - 350th Infantry Reg't. from the collection of William Gardner Bell.

Mud-clogged roads contributed to the slowing down of the
II Corps drive

Jeep fails to ford the Sieve River during late October
floods.

Combat troops relax in a Montecatini square.

Footnotes to Chapter VII

[1] 350th Infantry Regiment History, November, 1944.

[2] S-1 Journal, 350th Infantry Regiment, November, 1944.

[3] 350th Infantry Regiment History, November, 1944.

[4] News Clipping, Hometown Newspaper, November, 1944.

[5] S-2, S-3 Journal, 350th Infantry Regiment, November, 1944.

[6] 350th Infantry Regiment History, November, 1944.

[7] Delaney, **The Blue Devils in Italy,** 165-171.

[8] 350th Infantry Regiment History, November, 1944.

[9] **Ibid.**

[10] **Ibid.**

[11] Fry, **Combat Soldier,** 217-219.

[12] S-1 Journal, 350th Infantry Regiment, November, 1944.

[13] S-2, S-3 Journal, 350th Infantry Regiment, November, 1944.

[14] S-1, Journal 350th Infantry Regiment, November, 1944.

[15] Fry, **Combat Soldier,** 220.

[16] **Ibid.,** 222-225.

[17] Clark, **Calculated Risk,** 406.

[18] Truscott, **Command Missions,** 453.

[19] Clark, **Calculated Risk,** 406.

[20] Truscott, **Command Missions,** 459.

[21] Sid Feder, "The Blue Devils Stumped the Experts," **Saturday Evening Post,** CCXIX (September 7, 1946), 25.

[22] **Fifth Army History,** "The Second Winter," VIII, 6-23.

[23] Fry, **Combat Soldier,** 225-227.

[24] Delaney, **The Blue Devils in Italy,** 173.

[25] Feder, "The Blue Devils Stumped the Experts," 27.

[26] 350th Infantry Regiment History, December, 1944.

[27] Fry, **Combat Soldier,** 228.

[28] **Ibid.,** 229-238.

Chapter Eight

Patrolling and Defense:
January-March, 1945

Aggressive patrolling describes the activity of the Regiment for the month of January, 1945. As the year came in, the Regiment occupied reserve positions. [1] For the first six days of the new year the First Battalion served as reserve for the 351st Regiment in the vicinity of Mt. Delle Formiche, with the command post established at Maceratoio, Italy. After relief by elements of the 351st Infantry on January 7, the First Battalion then marched approximately eight miles cross country to the new positions near Mt. Fano, Italy, where it relieved elements of the 92nd Infantry Division. From January 8 to 12 the battalion occupied positions in the vicinity of Castelvecchia with the front line defensive positions near Mt. Fano. Ambush patrols continued active. The patrols investigated road blocks; moved into new areas to prevent the enemy from using the draws in the vicinity; engaged the enemy in firefights to inflict casualties and secure prisoners or identify actions; and secured estimates of enemy strength.

On one occasion the battalion commander, Major Holland, and the S-3, Lt. Boatner, moved forward to company positions to follow the activity of the patrol for that evening. This particular patrol from Company B had the task of determining enemy strength in Parrocchia di Vignale. The description of the action is typical of the patrolling on the "Forgotten Front" during these winter months of 1945:

Patrol reached objective in extended formation in anticipation of hostile fire which materialized to the extent of two rifles and two grenades. Patrol leader ordered assault on church, launched under protection of grenades, bazooka and rifle fire. Despite two enemy machine pistols, rifles, and grenade launcher patrol reached church, made search, and found it clear of the enemy. Movement was heard on ridge behind church but malfunctioning of some weapons decided patrol leader to discontinue advance due to uncertain fire power. Patrol returned to battalion at 0130 hours intact reporting one probable enemy casualty and estimating enemy strength at one squad with close support behind ridge.[2]

In preparation for the move to Montecatini, the battalion left its positions in the vicinity of Castelvecchia on January 13, marched cross country approximately six miles to the en-trucking area at Fiumetto, and then drove approximately 85 miles during the night and arrived at the Montecatini rest area on the morning of January 14.

During the first two weeks of the month the Second Battalion occupied positions in the San Benedetto area. To reach this area, the battalion had marched seven miles from C. Rocca after relief by the 349th Infantry. A new officer replacement, Captain Powers, joined Company G; also reporting for duty at this period were 1st Lts. Gillette and Furlo and 2nd Lts. Bat-lett, Bende, and Harhaugh. After engaging in training and rehabilitation for approximately one week, the battalion then proceeded by trucks on January 8 to Fiumetto where the men then marched cross country three and one half-miles to C. Vaglia to relieve elements of the 349th Infantry. Although the movement was hampered by a severe snow storm, no casualties were sustained. While the Second Battalion was in the San Benedetto area, General Paul Kendall, commander of the 88th Division, awarded the silver star to First Lieutenant Charles E. Lesnick, T-Sgt. Joseph E. Silva of the Medical Detachment, and S-Sgt. Fernand M. La Croix.

From January 1 to 6 the Third Battalion was in reserve in the vicinity of Boschi, Italy. Beginning on January 2, the men began digging defensive installations for the secondary MLR. During a continuous snow storm on January 5, battalion officers reconnoitered the positions of the 365th Infantry, 92nd Division, in preparation for relief of that unit. Upon relief by elements of the 351st Infantry Regiment, the Third Battalion then marched seven miles through heavy snow to relieve the Second Battalion, 365th Infantry, in the vicinity of C. Aie, Italy. In these positions the Third Battalion spent a period of relative quiet before its relief for movement to Montecatini. On January 15 the men marched approximately six miles to the area of Cripple Creek, where they then entrucked for the journey of 96 miles due southwest to Montecatini.

Although operating under extremely adverse weather conditions in manning its positions in the Appenines during the first two weeks of January, the Regiment operated with maximum efficiency. (See attached sketch for front-line positions.) The Regimental History for this period describes well the conditions under which the regiment operated:

> Heavy snowstorms hamperd patrol activity. Roads were icy and dangerous. The regiment's stay in these positions near Mt. Fano brought no exceptional activity. Regular but moderate artillery and mortar barrages fell in the general area of these positions and proved of great value since only 6 wounded were reported for this month.

Once again the Regiment savoured the pleasures of Montecatini - dances for all with the guests drawn from the civilian population. On separate nights different battalions sponsored dances for officers of the regiment at the regimental command post at the Hotel Belloni. In addition larger quotas of officers and enlisted men enabled the Blue Devils to visit Rome and Florence. These passes continued even while the regiment served in front line positions. Stream lined and stream-heated trains left Montecatini regularly for the Rome Rest Center.[3]

The presentation of awards highlighted the Regiment's second visit to Montecatini. Colonel Fry presented awards to members of the First Battalion on January 18, 1945. The day previously the Second Battalion had formed in review to receive from Lt. General Mark W. Clark the War Department

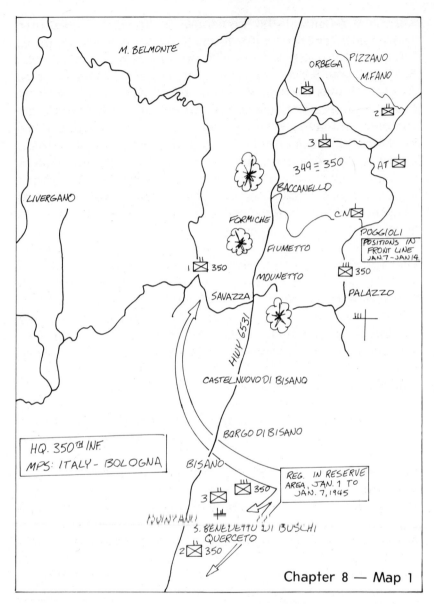

M. BELMONTE

ORBEGA PIZZANO
M.FANO

1

2

3

349 = 350   AT

BACCANELLO

LIVERGANO

FORMICHE

C.N.

POGGIOLI
POSITIONS IN
FRONT LINE
JAN.7-JAN.14

FIUMETTO

1 350

MOUNETTO   350

SAVAZZA   PALAZZO

HWY 6531

CASTELNUOVO DI BISANO

BORGO DI BISANO

HQ. 350TH INF.
MPS: ITALY - BOLOGNA

BISANO

REG. IN RESERVE
AREA, JAN. 1 TO
JAN. 7, 1945

3   350

MOUNTANI

S. BENEDETTO DI BUSCHI
QUERCETO

2 350

Chapter 8 — Map 1

Distinguished Unit Citation for its struggle in seizing and
holding strategic Mt. Battaglia in the September battles. At
this same time Second Lieutenant Charles Shea received the
Congressional Medal of Honor for his actions in May, 1944, in
the battle for Rome. The next day, January 18, at the Excelsior
Theater Colonel Fry addressed the battalion and awarded the
Distinguished Service Cross to Second Lieutenant Steven M.

Kosmyna of Company E and the Silver Star Oak Leaf Cluster and three Silver Star awards to other members of the battalion.

Colonel Fry also awarded many members of the Third Battalion with Silver Stars and Bronze Stars on this occasion. At the previous awards' presentation on January 17 the commanding generals of the Fifth Army and Fifteenth Army Group witnessed the awards ceremony, including Lt. General Mark W. Clark; Lt. General Lucian G. Truscott; Major General Geoffrey M. Keyes; Brigadier General Paul W. Kendall; Colonel Champney and other officials of Fifth Army, II Corps, and 88th Infantry Division. In addition to the presentation of the Congressional Medal of Honor to Second Lieutenant Charles W. Shea, Jr., two other Blue Devils, Major Erwin B. Jones and Technical Sergeant Manuel V. Mendoza, were presented the Distinguished Service Cross decoration.

While in Montecatini the Regiment received 310 replacements; although the men were assigned to the companies, they were not taken to forward positions when the Regiment again moved to the front line but instead engaged in a rigid training program in a rear training area. These replacements received training from a cadre of officers and enlisted men to insure their correct duty assignments.[4]

The new assignment on the front for the 350th Infantry after rest and recuperation at Montecatini was the former positions of the 363rd Infantry of the 91st Division in the area of the small villages of Monzuno, La Valle, and Anconella. For the rest of the month the First Battalion operated from the vicinity of Monzuno.

In preparation for a company sized raid to be made on the night of February 1, the First Battalion moved 1500 yards south of Monzuno to a new position approximately 600 yards northeast of the town. The patrol activity for the next day had been co-ordinated with the British unit on the left. The companies continued patrol training throughout the evening, and the sector remained quiet and free of enemy activity.

The Second Battalion had relieved the First Battalion of the 363rd Infantry by January 24. In this area the battalion assumed forward defensive positions on the left flank of the Fifth Army front. To insure the maintenance of high morale, the battalion instituted a program of sending a proportion of each company to the rear at which point a shower and clothing exchange unit was situated. These combat-tried Blue Devils also found welcome relief in the motion pictures and hot meals provided at this position.

The Third Battalion left Montecatini on January 23 and reached its new area on the front late in the afternoon. After detrucking on Highway 65 about two and one half miles southeast of Anconella, the troops marched toward the front to take over the positions of the 3rd Battalion, 365th Infantry. As the traffic moved over the wet, slippery trails, it was impossible to eliminate congestion on the icy roads. Had the enemy only known the situation, he would have had a picnic as his artillery could have easily zeroed in on some of the congested points along the road. By 2300 hours, though, the battalion had effected the relief and located its command post at La Valle, Italy.

The enemy atop Monterumici was in an excellent position to observe all activity during daylight hours. To reach the forward companies, the supply personnel had to pack all supplies on back. Men had to wear white clothing to avoid detection by the enemy. The difficulty of supplying was aggravated by the swollen streams. The river near the positions of Company L flooded, washing out all bridges and thus necessitating supplying across the river on cable strung by the engineers.

It was in the latter days of January that Margaret Bourke-White visited the Regiment. Arriving with Colonel Fry at the Third Battalion command post on the morning of January 28, she immediately photographed various battalion activities with the purpose of publishing a sroty on winter at the front in Italy. She followed all the details of a patrol from start to finish. Although she was to have published a story, no reporting of the 350th Infantry's activities appeared in print from her visit. Presumably the films she took were lost in Rome.[5]

For supplying the front line companies, the S-4 section set up in the town of Loaiano, literally a pile of rubble in the winter of 1945. Hundreds of telephones lines crisscrossed along the road in the vicinity, attesting to the method used by communication sections of following the quick and simple method of laying lines along the protected areas rather than exposing themselves for lengthy periods of time while trying to find broken ones or those cut by artillery fire. From the cellars of that town the supply personnel operated effectively throughout the remainder of the winter.

The headquarters of the Regiment, approximately two miles north of Loaiano, was the village of Anconella, well hidden under the crest of a hill. The pattern of life for the rest of the Regiment, however, was even grimmer than that experienced in the former positions in the winter line. East of Loaiano a stream flowed down a lush valley past the nose of the long sloping ridge of Monterumici and the high vertical cliffs of Mt. Adone. From these dominating positions the Germans looked down on every daylight movement of the front line companies. For the most hazardous positions in the area, Colonel Fry purposely chose the Third Battalion, because its commander, Major Witter, had the most experience in combat of any other battalion commander at that time. The battalion's area extended across the Savena stream onto the edge of Monterumici. The deep valley, only about 150 yards in rear of the company on the left, made retreat or reinforcement a hazardous and difficult problem. The smoke generators used for concealment of positions indeed proved to be of inestimable value to these exposed troops.

As the supplies moved forward at night on men's backs over the slippery, muddy trails, or in some places on mules, the wounded, who had frequently remained in battalion aid stations until darkness, were brought back down. The more serious cases, however, that had to be moved during daylight hours were evacuated under the banner of the Red Cross, which the Germans generally respected.[6]

Beyond Loaiano stood the battered village of Livergnano, where a group of tanks nestled behind buildings for use in a counter-attack. On occasion these tanks delivered fire across the valley against the Monterumici ridge and the crest of Mt. Adone. At one point the lines were separated by only about 100 yards from those of the enemy, with a limited defense of wire and mines in front. Once, while investigating this exposed position, Colonel Fry and Major Fingerhut moved toward the knoll of a hill only to be pinned down by machine gun fire. As an enemy flare lit up the entire area and as they hugged the ground from the previous fire of a machine gun, the Kraut gunner suddenly ceased firing. Both these officers could easily have met their fate on this occasion, but for some unknown reason the gunner ceased firing, perhaps for fear of exposing his position also.[7]

Even amidst these treacherous and menacing situations, the 350th Infantry operated with such expert efficiency that casualties of all sorts remained at a minimum. The Medical Detachment for this month evacuated only 333 casualties; of these, six were wounded in action, 30 injured, 21 carried as administrative admissions, and 276 evacuated for disease, 123 cases alone for hepatitis.[8]

The first week of February witnessed greatly accelerated and aggressive patrol action. The First Battalion in its defensive secondary positions, with the battalion command post established approximately 600 yards northeast of Monzuno, prepared for a company sized raid for the night of February 1-2, 1945. The company chosen for this assignment, Company A, occupied positions in the Second Battalion area. The company had the mission of proceeding to enemy-held territory at Castel Furcoli, 600 yards ahead of the most forward foxholes, to capture prisoners for interrogation.[9]

As spring approached and plans were developing for the inevitable offensive to drive the enemy from Italy, II Corps and 88th Infantry Division planned this raid to capture prisoners to learn of the enemy's intentions for future operations. Captain Ray Stroup was assigned the leadership of this bold raiding party.

Prior to the raid Colonel Fry had worked out plans for artillery support with Colonel George T. Powers, III, the executive officer of Division artillery. They decided that only a routine number of rounds of artillery were to be fired before the raid was to take place, with a heavy concentration on the night of attack. Machine gun and rifle fire was to distract the enemy's attention from the Furcoli area.[10]

Since Company A would be attacking Furcoli from the Second Battalion area, the First Battalion Commander, Lt. Colonel James G. Holland, assumed command of the area for the period of operation. For this novel raid the supply officer had supplied the patrol with clothing and equipment needed in the sub-freezing temperature, with the ground covered with snow approximately twenty-four inches deep. For camouflage the men were outfitted with white parkas and had even been issued white gasoline soluble paint for possible use in painting the weapons and helmets. For support on the slippery snow-covered trails the men received issues of clampons for scaling the ridges around Furcoli. [11]

The objective in capturing a number of the enemy hinged on the success of diversionary tactics to confuse the enemy about the raid. To accomplish this goal, the officers in command on the regimental and division level stipulated that nothig was to fire at the outset on the nose of Monterumici. It was hoped that Germans would be standing up in their trenches and possibly walking about in their area to get a better view of what was going on only a short distance away. Machine gun and heavy rifle fire was to distract the enemy's attention from the Furcoli area. During this diversion Company A had the task of moving as close to the enemy line as possible without alerting the Jerry outguards; then on signal from Captain Stroup the artillery was to come down with two battalions of VT fuse explosives. After pounding the area for ten minutes, they were then to lift to the crest of Monterumici. [12]

Captain Stroup spent a large part of the afternoon at the battalion command post and made a thorough check and review of the proposed raid with the battalion staff.[13] Before Company A left their positions for incursion into enemy territory at approximately 1930 hours, Division artillery barraged the primary objective for approximately 15 minutes. The platoons then employed a column of squads, in single file, echeloned on either side of the road. At the first objective A (see attached map) the raiding party found no Germans, whereupon the monitoring headquarters ordered another barrage on Castel Furcoli, the final objective, and the company again moved out. To reach the scattered buildings there, the entire company had to pass along a narrow trail on an explosed ridge, covered by German 50-millimeter mortar fire. There was no alternative route. Under the impact of mortar fire on this ridge the company suffered most of its casualties for the evening's raid. [14]

After the platoons had failed to find Germans in the buildings in different sections of the small mountain hamlet and after receiving fire from four enemy machine guns and other aumoatic weapons, they moved on toward the well-entrenched dugouts and caves.[15] By this time, approximately three hours after the patrol had left the line of departure, the company had suffered two killed and two seriously wounded with nine

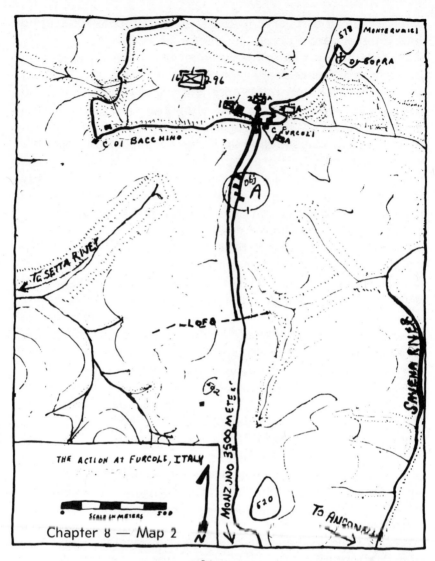

THE ACTION AT FURCOLE, ITALY

SCALE IN METERS

Chapter 8 — Map 2

casualties slightly wounded. [16] In this second phase of the raid 2nd Lt. Henry G. Smith, of Memphis, Tennessee, a rifle platoon leader, lost his 535 radio as he hit the dirt under the impact of fire from a German machine gun in a hidden cave. He then led his platoon to a safer position. Now a bazooka team and a browning automatic rifleman neutralized the machine gun position, whereupon Lt. Smith crawled to a position near the cave, drove five Germans from their position with smoke grenades, and took them prisoner at the point of a carbine.

Although three of the four German machine guns opposing the Blue Devils were silenced, no definite count of the casualties was possible, but the partol definitely accounted for six German dead found in the machine gun positions. 1/

It was shortly after midnight that the company effected the capture of five of the enemy, all Bavarians, before withdrawing. After reaching the company area and discovering that one man was missing, a volunteer group attempted to recover the missing comrade but were unsuccessful; enemy machine gun fire accounted for the wounding of another Blue Devil in this attempt. In addition to the number of enemy known to have been killed, five were captured and an unknown number wounded at a cost of two killed, twelve wounded, and one missing.[18]

As the prisoners were brought into Colonel Fry's headquarters, they came in on the run with hands above their heads. The Blue Devils quickly relieved the enemy of watches and other insignia for souvenirs of the night's raid.[19] Neither Colonel Fry nor the Division Commander, Major General Paul W. Kendall, on hand to follow the progress of the raid, objected to the seizing of the customary rewards of war.

The next day General Kendall personally presented medals in a special ceremony to two officers and thirty-three enlisted men, including eight silver stars and twenty-seven bronze stars. Major General Geoffrey M. Keyes, II Corps Commander, sent his personal congratulations to General Kendall and Colonel Fry and commended all the men and officers who had participated in the action. Others were granted pass privileges to Rome and the Montecatini Rest Center.

Until February 6-7 the regiment remained in front line positions. On February 2 the First Battalion relieved the Scots Guards of the 24th Scots Brigade and took up positions on the extreme left flank of II Corps Army front.[20] In their area around Monzuno, the First Battalion engaged in rather extensive patrol activity. By Februay 7 the battalon had moved from its front line positions into Division reserve in the vicinity of Trasasso, after having been relieved by the Third Battalion, 349th Infantry. The Second Battalion was likewise relieved on the same date by elements of the First Battalion, 349th Infantry, and moved to the regimental rear area in the village of Bibulona. No casualties were sustained in the maneuver.

For the period February 1-6 the Third Battalion also engaged in extensive patrol activity. New replacements arrived at battalion headquarters and were dispatched to various companies. On February 5 guides from each platoon were called to battalion headquarters to lead the relieving British contingents to front line areas in the relief to be accomplished the next day. By February 7 the battalion had moved to the rear at Anconella.

While in reserve positions in Trasasso the First Battalion underwent a few temporary changes in command structure. Major Jones left for temporary duty with the Fifteenth Army Group for an estimated month tour of duty, while Major Holland, the Battalion Commander, departed for a four-day rest period to Florence on February 9. In his absence, Major Cussans, Executive Officer of the Second Battalion, assumed temporary command of the battalion. Major Holland returned on the night of February 14 from Florence and re-assumed command of the battalion.

Preparatory to taking over reserve positions of the First Battalion, an advance group from the 351st Infantry Regiment arrived at the command post on February 16 for orientation. On the next day, February 17, Major Holland and Captain Haegstron left the command post for the new area to be taken over by the First Battalion, and Captain Stroup arrived at the command post and assumed temporary command. During late afternoon of February 18 the battalion traveled by trucks to the new sector, Livergnano, a distance of approximately twelve miles. The battalion command post located in the rubble of Livergnano itself.

The most significant event for the Second Battalion during this period occurred on February 13 when the battalion assembled in official formation for the presentation of the Distinguished Service Cross to Second Lieutenant Steven M. Kosmyna of Company E. The presentation was made by General George C. Marshall, who had stopped at Fifth Army Headquarters on his return from the Crimean Conference. Along with General Marshall for this important occasion were Lt. General Truscott, Lt. General McNarney, Lt. General Mark W. Clark, and Major General Paul W. Kendall. On February 19, the battalion proceeded by truck five and one half miles forward to defensive positions, relieving the First Battalion of the

351st Infantry. It closed into its new area in the early hours of February 20.

From their area around Anconella the Third Battalion engaged in usual training schedules. In addition to relaxation at Rome and other rest centers, the men enjoyed movies shown in "the theater of the cave" in their area. The battalion would remain in the reserve positions until February 23. Another means of relaxation from military duties was afforded by the visit of the Special Service Division accordionist who entertained on February 14.

After relieving the Second Battalion, 349th Infantry, on February 23, the Third Battalion set up a propaganda program via loud speakers to the Jerries in the front lines. It was hoped that some enemy soldiers could be induced to desert. After each broadcast, the battalion withheld all shelling of enemy positions for 45 minutes to give any deserters a chance to come into the battalion's lines safely. Then the big guns to the rear would open up with heavy concentrations.

For their period in the front lines in the vicinity of Livergnano from February 18 to the end of the month, the First Battalion engaged in continued patrol activity primarily from the rifle companies. Occupying positions astride Highway 65 south of enemy-held Pianoro, Companies A, B, and C patrolled the areas of Barchetta, Canovetta, and C. Nuova. Major Holland generally made nightly visits to the companies scheduling patrols for that particular evening. The difficulty of finding suitable routes of approach toward enemy areas was frequently given as "due to density of foliage and steepness of banks flanking draw on route. Only practicable way found to be along Highway 65." Beginning on February 21 and continuing generally until the end of the month, the battalion headquarters delivered a series of propaganda broadcasts to the enemy approximately four times nightly. The Krauts often retaliated by increased mortar and artillery shelling of forward positions.

The Second Battalion experienced similar activity as the First. While in this forward area, units were subjected to enemy harassing artillery fire; however, active defence of the sector continued with patrols operating from the advance elements.

After leaving its reserve positions to relieve the Second Battalion of the 349th Infantry on February 23, the Third

Battalion extended its defense line almost 200 yards. Some of the areas patrolled by the Third Battalion would be the scenes of the fiercest fighting in the final drive in April, 1945-the area on Monterumici between Di Sopra and the cemetery. The numerous details and plans for successful patrolling required expert co-ordination by all elements, and no better resumé of these requirements is found than that for the Third Battalion's history for February 28, 1945:

> Patrol in at 0300, did not make any contact with the enemy, no casualties. Battalion Commander and S-3 now going over last minute details for tonight's raid, making a check on the needed supporting fire, to make sure everything will go off according to plan. The weather today is very clear. Enemy artillery very active...Men who will go on raiding party have been cleaning and zeroing in weapons all afternoon. Also last touching of camouflaging (blacking of hands and faces) before dusk. Received final instructions from Commanding Officer; Raiding party left CP at 1940 hours...to start on their mission. [21]

After moving back into defensive positions around the middle of February, the 350th Infantry Regiment Headquarters located in La Guarda. The left flank of the Regiment tied in with the 349th Infantry, with the 361st Infantry of the 91st Division on the right. On February 22 the Regiment received notification that the Congressional Medal of Honor had been awarded posthumously to Captain Robert E. Roeder, the second member of this Regiment to receive the award. (Lieutenant Charles Shea had been awarded the Medal of Honor in January.) The presentation of Captain Roeder's medal would be made in the United States to his mother, his next of kin. [22]

For February the Medical Detachment reported evacuations as an all-time low, only 177. Various diseases rather than battle casualties were the major cause of hospitalization. As the month of February marked the completion of one year in combat for the medical group, it could look back with satisfaction on its performance. Its personnel had been awarded one Legion of Merit, eight Silver Stars, 45 Bronze

Stars, and more than 60 purple hearts, although only half the original group remained. Five enlisted men had been given battlefield commisions for meritorious work and were then serving as capable assistant battaion surgeons. During the past year the Detachment carried out 7,412 evacuations for the Regiment, a feat that was ample proof that the non-combatant medics had done their job and done it well. [23]

The Information and Education program scored well during February. Under its sponsorship a "Barber Shop Quartet" contest created considerable competition. After eliminations in the battalions and special units, the winners gathered in Loaiano on February 14 to compete in the finals. The winner, an exceptionally capable quartet from the Second Battalion, was privileged to travel to Montecatini on February 20 for Division eleiminations. Although this quartet, coached and led by Lt. William G. Bell, performed admirably and won by a unanimous choice of the Division judges in Montecatini, it came out third in Fifth Army finals. The success of this competition, however, encouraged the men to plan a Regimental Glee Club when the organization moved into more favorable positions. [24]

As the Regiment completed one year of combat on March 3, 1945, a number of significant changes occurred. It was with mixed emotions of pride and sadness that the Regiment received the news of the promotion of its valiant leader, Colonel J.C. Fry, to the position of Assistant Division Commander. Not only was Colonel Fry an expert leader in combat, but also he was endowed with the sincere quality of genuine and sincere understanding of the problems of the individual soldier - his times of despair and confidence; of anguish and relief; of fear and hope. [25]

For the first five days of March the Regiment occupied positions astride Highway 65. The First Battalion held the right flank south of Pianoro. Ambush patrols continued probing enemy lines in the vicinity of Barchetta, Ca Nuova, and Canovetta. After being relieved by elements of the 168th Infantry, 34th Division at approximately 2230 hours, March 5, 1945, the battalion moved to an entrucking point for travel to a bivouac area in the vicintiy of Florence. In this area near Prato, the Regiment would engage in intensive training, including battle tactics with emphasis on river crossing techniques.

The Second and Third Battalions in the early days of March pursued similar training. The Third Battalion, located at Scascoli with the command post in a church, received harassing fire from the vicinity of Di Sopra atop Monterumici. Elements of the Second Battalion, 168th Infantry, marched from Sabbione in the evening of March 5 to the Third Battalion's positions in preparation for its relief, which was completed about 2400 hours. The Third Battalion then traveled by truck for approximately 55 miles to its rest area in the vicinity of Gonoriana, Italy, arriving around 0600 hours.

While undergoing intensive battle training for the coming offensive, the Regiment maintained a keen competitive spirit by instituting a program of contests including rifle firing, machine gun firing, mortar tests, close order drill, and sports competitions. For the first week all passes and leaves to Florence, Rome, and Montecatini were canceled so that all men could engage in this extensive training program. [26]

On Sunday, March 11, 1945, the men of the 350th Infantry "Battle Mountain" Regiment honored their members who had died in action. The highlight of the memorial services, held in the regimental rest area, was the principal address by Colonel James C. Fry. Miss Ann Moray, of Scotland and the British Red Cross, and Corporal Robert F. Hartman of Philadelphia, were soloists for the occasion. The newly formed 40-man Regimental Glee Club sang "Be Still My Soul." [27] The memorial services were conducted by the Regiment's chaplains, Captain Pressley, Captain Newman, and Lieutenant Marleau. Colonel Fry's impromptu address inspired the men as the Commander's words elicited a vivid recollection of the "Battle Mountain" Regiment's past year in combat. The Commander closed the address by reminding the troops of their duty to their God and country.

After the first week of intensive training the men again resumed their visits to Rome and Montecatino. There were USO shows and late movies, along with boxing contests and spirited competition among the volley ball teams. For the non-commissioned officers of the first three grades, the club at San Donato provided dances and parties. In addition to recreation in the immediate area eight enlisted men each evening attended shows and movies at the Apollo Theater in Florence during a seven day period. For the officers dance parties were held every Wednesday, Saturday and Sunday nights at the Regimental Command Post with music furnished by the special service orchestra. [28]

With regular training scheduled for the third week, the various battalions engaged in river crossing training on the Arno River. Competitive firing on the range for all companies caused the discontinuance of pass quotas for March 20, but the prize of a one day pass to Florence for the best dismounted drill platoon and the best machine gun section encouraged the maximum effort among the men.

During the latter days of March, Captain Romano, formerly of the First Battalion who had been captured in September and later liberated by the Russians in the Spring 1945 offensive, returned to his old battalion for a visit. All companies curtailed their training at 0930 on March 28 to listen to the captain describe his experiences as a prisoner of war. The talk and session lasted until midday.

When Colonel Fry bade farewell to the regimental staff on March 28 and departed to assume his duties as the assistant division commander, his officers and men responded with wishes of great success in his new undertaking and assurances of confidence in the continued brilliant leadership of their former commander. Lieutenant Colonel Avery M. Cochran, the Regimental Executive Officer, then assumed command of the Regiment. His excellent leadership and significant achievements in the past left no doubt among all regimental personnel that the Regiment would still be ably led and continue to operate at its accustomed high standard of efficiency.

Along with these changes toward the end of the month, the Regiment practiced for an entire Division review to be held on Saturday, March 31. After this date the Regiment would no longer wear its division insignia as it prepared to move to a new area for additional specialized training. At the Division review, probably the first to be held in the Italian theater, a number of Army Group, Army, Corps, Air Force, Division, and Assistant Division Commanders and other dignitaries honored the Division with their presence, including General Mark W. Clark of the Fifteenth Army Group; General Truscott, commanding Fifth Army; General Keyes, of II Corps; General Cannon, commander of the Twelfth Air Force; General Kendall and Colonel Fry, the Division and Assistant Division Commanders respectively.

After the presentation of the colors, General Clark gave a short address wherein he praised the Division for its excellent work in the Italian campaign. He recalled the Blue Devils' glory-filled campaigns: "From the Garigliano to Rome, through Volterra and the successful push through the Gothic Line, the 88th has covered themselves with glory in every operation." 29

After this review the Regiment made final preparations for the move to the new training area. All Division insignias and all regimental designations were removed from clothing, vehicles, and equipment. The Regiment now prepared to engage in a short but highly specialized training, yet with no indication of its real nature or exact purpose. As the war in Europe entered its final stages, the Blue Devils would be ready to engage the enemy in any situation and would continue to display their resourcefulness, tenacity, and courage that had characterized their valorous activities throughout the Italian campaigns of 1944-45.

Mount Adone, February, 1945.

Livergnano area, Italy.

A winter patrol in the Belvedere sector...

U.S. Fifth Army ambulance is evacuating wounded over icy front line road which is under heavy enemy shell fire. The Loaiano area, January, 1945.

Infantrymen march around a curve in the road near Mt. Grande, Italy. The men are on their way back from the front lines, February, 1945.

Lt. Gen. Mark W. Clark, CG, 15th Army Group, awards the Medal of Honor to Lt. Charles Shea, New York City, New York. Lt. Gen. Lucian K. Truscott, CG, Fifth Army, in foreground. Montecatini, Italy, January, 1945.

White tents and guns huddled on the snowy slopes...

Sketch by Gus Fagerholm—Italian Theater, 1945 - 350th Infantry Reg't. from the collection of William Gardner Bell.

Footnotes to Chapter VIII

350th Infantry Regiment History, January, 1945.
First Battalion History, 350th Infantry Regiment, January, 1945.
350th Infantry Regiment History, January, 1945.
Ibid.
Fry, **Combat Soldier,** 259.
Ibid., 252-256.
Ibid., 257-258.
Medical Detachment, 350th Infantry Regiment, January, 1945.

Times-Herald News, Dallas Texas, February, 1945.

Fry, **Combat Soldier,** 261.

Personal Experiences of Captain Ray Stroup, in Monograph, Advanced Infantry Officers Course, 1949-1950, The Infantry School, Fort Benning, Georgia, "The Operations of Company A, 350th Infantry at Furcoli, Northwest of Loaiano, Italy, Night of 1-2 February, 1945."

Fry, **Combat Soldier,** 261.

Times-Herald News, Dallas Texas, February, 1945.

Stroup, Personal Recollections, 16.

Times-Herald News, February, 1945.

Stroup, **Personal Recollections,** 16.

Times-Herald News, February, 1945.

First Battalion History, February, 1945.

Fry, **Combat Soldier,** 261.

350th Infantry Regiment History, February, 1945.

Third Battalion History, February, 1945.

350th Infantry Regiment History, February, 1945.

Medical Detachment History 350th Infantry Regiment, February, 1945.

350th Infantry Regiment History, February, 1945.

Ibid., March, 1945.

350th Infantry Regiment History, March, 1945.

"Battle Mountain Outfit Honors Own Dead," **Stars and Stripes,** March 12, 1945.

350th Infantry Regiment History, March, 1945.

Ibid.

Exchange building where all the lines coming into Livergnano branch off. Sgt. George Nemergut and Pfc. Earl Hackbarth, Company H, check a phone line running into an "exchange building." February, 1945.

Tired soldiers scrub off the mud of the Apennines.

Behind the front—litter bearers, pack mules, and infantry moving up.

Chapter Nine

The Final Offensive:
From the Appenines and into the Po Valley, April, 1945

As plans for the final offensive in Italy were being finalized, the 350th Infantry engaged in a vigorous and highly specialized training program. On Easter Sunday, April 1, 1945, the Regiment moved by convoy almost seventy miles from the area near Prato to a staging area near Pisa, Italy, where it would engage in boat drills and river crossing exercises. The area for this specialized training, a site on the Arno River a short distance from the western coast, had originally been the royal hunting grounds. In this beautiful pine wooded area, the combat team participated in river crossing training, including actual crossings by "Ducks," "Weasel" assault boats, and storm boats. Included also in the amphibious exercises was actual movement of artillery pieces and anti-tank guns across the river. Attached to the Regimental Combat Team at this time were Company "B," 313th Medical Battalion; Company "B,", 313th Engineer Battalion; and the 338th Field Artillery Battalion. Having completed this phase of training in preparation for the coming offensive, the Regiment departed the area on April 6 and traveled to its new area where final preparations for the spring offensive were made. [1] (See Map 1 for allied and enemy positions.)

After traveling a distance of 95 miles, the First Battalion set up camp about 5000 yards northwest of Firenzuola, approximately 800 yards southeast of Pietramala, Italy. From April 6 to April 11 the battalion underwent ordinary training.

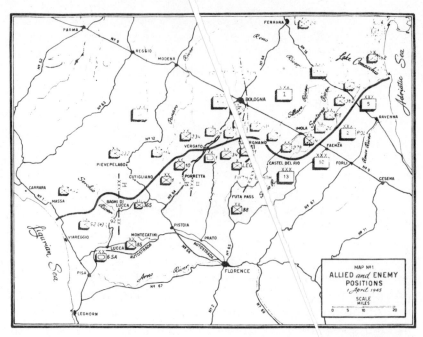

On April 10, Lt. Col. Holland led an advance group to the forward area to be occupied by the battalion; however because of a 24 hour cancellation of movement orders, the First Battalion bivouaced for the night; under the command of Captain Haegstrom, the Battalion Executive Officer, the battalion advanced the next day a distance of approximately sixteen miles, arriving at Anconella in the evening, where it relieved the Second Battalion, 362nd Regiment. The battalion command post, set up in the town of La Valle, came under direct observation of the enemy entrenched on Monterumici.

During the period April 6-13, 1945, the Second Battalion occupied positions also in the Pietramala area. After resting on Sunday, April 8, and enjoying the luxury of showers, the battalion the next day engaged in platoon and squad problems and observed a demonstration in the use of flame throwers. On April 11 the battalion was alerted and traveled by truck approximately sixteen miles to the reserve position at Anconella. At this time Company E was attached to the First Battalion, and Company H assumed forward positions to prepare for the coming attack.

While the Third Battalion followed river crossing training in the vicinity of Pisa during the first five days of April, a number of officers received battlefield promotions: Lt. Ochenkowski and Lt. Heady from second to 1st lieutenant; and Lieutenant Pope of Company L from first lieutenant to captain. By evening of April 6 the Third Battalion had arrived in its new area in the vicinity of Boschetto, Italy, after having traveled a distance of approximately 90 miles. To understand the terrain better over which the Third was scheduled to attack in the near future, all company commanders flew in a liaison plane over the enemy positions. As a quartering party from the 351st Regiment arrived to take over the Third's positions on April 11, the Third Battalion received orders of cancellation of movement for 24 hours, but by evening of the next day, April 12, it had arrived at Sabiano where it then walked a distance of five and one half miles to Mollinoli, and occupied buildings previously held by the 362nd Infantry Regiment.

While the Regiment trained near Pietramala, each rifle company was divided into three eight-man squads, plus heavy weapons personnel, and a regimental replacement pool was set up in the vicinity. The Regimental Headquarters took up front line positions on April 11, with the rear command post installed at Anconella. With the First Battalion (under Lt. Col. Holland) in the front line positions at La Valle, along with the regimental forward command post; the Second Battalion (under Lt. Col. Yongue) in a rear assembly area near Anconella with Company E attached to the First Battalion and Company H in forward positions where all fire data for maximum support of the attack was compiled and checked; the Third Battalion (under Lt. Col Witter) in its assembly area by April 12; and Service Company south of Monghidoro-the Regiment utilized these last few days prior to attack to perfect its vital supply routes and transportation. In keeping with blacked-out conditions for purpose of secrecy to deceive the enemy relative to the whereabouts of the Division, Cannon Company took up positions near Anconella but refrained from firing of any sort to insure the enemy's continued confusion about the movement of the Regiment into the front lines; however, artillery, mortar, and air observation posts were established at La Valle and Scascoli. 2 All plans had been completed for the imminent offensive, which was to begin momentarily.

The role allotted to the 350th Infantry in the plan of the coming offensive to drive the enemy from the mountain strong points into the Po Valley was perhaps one of the toughest assignments of any other regiment. The Regiment had the unimposing task of scaling the heights of Monterumici and driving the Krauts from strongly fortified caves, interconnecting passageways between concrete pillboxes and towns atop the peak of Monterumici, and strongly entrenched mortar, rifle, and machine gun emplacements - all of which the fanatical enemy had prepared to the final degree of perfect defensive positions throughout the winter months. The Division had been given this disheartening assignment just a couple of days after the parade at the end of March just outside Florence. Colonel Fry later wrote of this almost suicidal task: "That stark-grim, shell-marked elevation, with its barren cliffs high above the ridges which we were supposed to capture, boded ill for our forthcoming advance." With the Division poised for the push-off, with division headquarters at Monzuno, three miles south of Monterumici, he recalled:

> Only a photograph can convey appreciation of the terrain. From the almost vertical heights of Mt. Adone, a long undulating ridge runs southward to the less formidable hill mass of Monterumici. Stark, grim and pick-marked with caves and artillery shell holes, it overlooked the low ground to its immediate front. Many of our men had died there during the winter as we probed the enemy's defenses. [3]

The general outline for the push into the Po Valley-Operation Craftsman, the title designation of Fifth's Army plan for its part of the offensive-had been completed by the middle of March. The plan of attack called for the main effort to be made initially astride Highway 64 until the valley of Setta Creek had been cleared and the road junction of Praduro, fifteen miles north of Vergato, had been captured. A secondary effort would be made along Highway 65 to the east of 64 and generally parallel to it, while the units with IV Corps reduced the dominating positions west of the road and came up abreast. Thereafter the weight of the Army would be concentrated west of Highway 65. [4]

This plan to attack just east of Highway 64 was in reality a modified plan of the Pianoro Operation but differed greatly from the original, which had envisioned a frontal assault by all of the Fifth Army's available strength against the most heavily defended part of the German lines - the area south of Bologna along Highway 65 extending westward to the Reno River. To try to catch the enemy off guard and to insure surprise, Fifth Army Headquarters had initiated a coverplan or ruse called **Big Game** to create the illusion that the American II Corps with the 85th and 88th Divisions was moving from the Fifth Army to the Eighth Army front. For the 350th Infantry as well as for the other regiments of the division, the plan, carefully worked out, included reconaissances of fictional headquarters lay outs, establishment of simulated command posts, and a fictional assumption of II Corps sector by the IV Corps. General Truscott described the various details involved in the plan:

> Full use was made of camouflage, activity in supply dumps shrewdly controlled, radio activity limited, traffic restricted, artillery support reduced and then gradually built up again. Small preliminary stabs were made to pin down and confuse the enemy, and add to the illusion. And limited air activity contributed to make **Big Game** very effective.[5]

For the men of the 350th, however, it was somewhat a grueling experience to intiate still another all-out offensive at a time when Hitler's forces were being rapidly over-run throughout other sectors, by the Russians from the east and the Allies from the west, racing toward a junction with the Russians at Torgau on the Elbe. At the crucial period in April just before the war would end in Europe on May 8, 1945, Allied Military Headquarters still persisted in the assumption that Hitler might hold out for an extended period in the so-called Southern Bavarian Redoubt; and there were still in Northern Italy alone twenty-five German and five Italian Fascist divisions. General Clark surmised that if the Nazi forces in Germany withdrew southward in the Bavarian Alps and the thirty divisions in Italy joined them in that vast mountain stronghold, they might hold out indefinitely.[6] This view, coupled with the information from prisoners that the industrial machinery was being moved from Milan and Turin into the sheltered valleys of the Alps, apparently in preparation for manning the Southern Redoubt, tipped the scales in favor of the attack-an attack that in retrospect in some ways seems to have been askew of the soundest military principles; yet the task of the battle-tried 350th Infantry was not to question why the plans to attack, and with its usual elan and devotion to the highest ideals of duty, the Regiment, along with the 91st Division on its right before Mt. Adone, would press the attack with unflinching dedication to duty.

In the zone facing II Corps were four crack German divisions of the XIV Panzer Corps, all committed in the narrow sectors astride Highway 64 and east to Mount Grande - the 94th Grenadier Division, 8th Mountain Division, 65th Grenadier Division, and 305th Grenadier Division. Of these the 350th Infantry would face elements of the 8th Mountain Division, reinforced by the 3rd Independent Mountain Battalion and the 7th GAF Battalion, made up of German Air Force personnel serving as infantry. In this main line of defense, the Genghis Khan Line, the enemy defenses ran east of Vergato, crossed the Reno River, and thence over the guardian peaks of Mount Sole and Mount Adone in the area between Highways 64 and 65, and then continued eastward of the latter road along the mountain tops north of Mount Belmonte and Mount Grande until it reached the line of the Senio River. The 350th zone of operations was festooned with every type of formidable defense mechanisms imaginable:

> The mountain line was made up primarily of mutually supporting strongpoints, featuring automatic weapons and anti-tank guns. Machine guns were liberally distributed to cover all possible approaches to the summits of the mountains; anti-personnel minefields were laid along all the paths, ravines, and creek beds. Dugouts had been constructed to shelter the garrisons of the various strong points, which were connected by communication trenches and further protected by bands of barbed wire. All roads and cross-country avenues of advance

were strewn with mixed anit-tank and anti-personnel minefields. Many of the existing stone farmhouses were fortified and incorporated into the line, while many of the small villages also were organized for defense and surrounded by firing positions. The suburbs of Bologna itself contained many concrete pillboxes and antitank gun emplacements.

The role of the 350th in the attack emanated from the II Corps plans of attack in two main prongs - one on Mount Sole (to the west of the 350th Infantry's positions) and another on Pianoro and in the hill masses to the west of Highway 65 (350th's positions) including Mount Adone. The staggered attacks called for the attack on Mount Sole (and the Monterumici hill mass) at 2230, April 15, and the drive on Pianoro at 0300 the following morning.[7]

After the attack of the IV Corps on the left, extending to the Ligurian Sea in the west, had reached the Green Phase Line, then II Corps planned to attack. In this operation, called Brown Phase, the 88th Division had perhaps the toughest assignment-the envelopment of Monterumici, with the South Africans on the left moving against Mount Sole; the 91st Division on the right against Mount Adone, Mount dei Frati, and the village of Pianoro; and the 34th Division east of 65 against Dei Mori Hill. The Italian Legnano group received orders to patrol aggressively on the extreme right of II Corps.[8]

As the 350th prepared to attack on April 15, the 349th Infantry held the ground on its left. In this area, running south and west from Monterumici, the terrain dropped off in boot-toe contours to make a long hill where the houses of Furcoli were located; this, too, was a German stronghold. Immediately to the south in this area, a deep ravine represented no-man's land between the 88th Division's lines. Further to the east the ravine sloped down into the Savena Creek, which flowed generally northward along the east of Monterumici past Mt. Adone. The front line here barely reached across the stream, against the sharply rising hills.

At first the 350th Infantry exhibited an abundance of optimism; to their front an artillery smoke screen could contain enemy observation from Mt. Adone to a minimum; and the view that the enemy facing the 350th would perhaps fight only a delaying action, inasmuch as he needed forces to prevent the envelopment by the 91st Division on Mt. Adone, seemed to support the cause of optimism.[9] In retrospect, the military analyst could hardly plan for any attack against Monterumici other than a diversionary effort,; but the over-all plan at that time envisioned wearing down and defeating the enemy also at this strong point. In the final event, the 350th encountered a savagely determined enemy.

The entry of the 350th and 88th Division into the lines came as a complete surprise to the enemy; the plan of deception had worked magnificently. To shield the entry of the 350th into the lines, the 34th Division kept its command post signs in place, along with a light screen of its troops for patrol purposes.[10] Taking up front line positions, the 350th immediately perceived that the battle for Monterumici would be similar to the battle for Mt. Battaglia, with the exception that here the enemy upon the peaks of Monterumici observed each movement of the Regiment. Only tortuous trails served as avenues of advance; no aid would be forthcoming from the armor sections until the regiment descended into the Po Valley.

The deception plan for the 88th Division Artillery followed similar lines as that for the infantry. The movement of the artillery preceded that of the rifle companies, since the artillery moved into position on April 7, followed by the first infantry elements on April 10. By the period April 13-14 all sections had relieved the screening elements in their zones.

In the order of battle for the attack against Monterumici, the First Battalion, in regimental reserve and occupying frontline positions, received orders to make a diversionary move along the trail to La Tombe, while the Third Battalion, from its rear assembly area near Anconella, moved to La Valle, in preparation to charge enemy positions along the trail from LaPiano to LaTorre, with one company scheduled to move towards Fazanelli, and then to Hill 416, Le Mandrie, and Casarola. (See Map 2.) The Second Battalion received the following orders: Attach one company to First Battalion until H hour plus 30, then move from the assembly area near Anconella, and attack up Fazzano Ridge. Upon securing this feature, the Second was to continue up the ridge to seize San Lucia and Casa di Mazza and then progress toward Querica and finally to Val del Fossa.[11] In simplified form the Third Battalion was to seize the crest of Monterumici, while the Second on the right was to capture the long ridges extending to the base of Mt. Adone.[12]

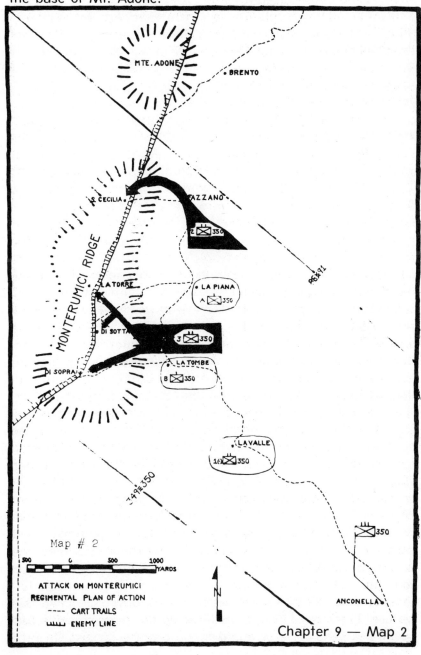

Map # 2

ATTACK ON MONTERUMICI
REGIMENTAL PLAN OF ACTION
- - - - CART TRAILS
⊔⊔⊔⊔ ENEMY LINE

Chapter 9 — Map 2

Preceding the attack of II Corps on the evening of April 15, 765 Flying Fortresses and Liberators blasted targets on the main highways south of Bologna. In the general area of the 350th Infantry zone, 211 medium bombers blasted away on Highway 64 while 120 fighter bombers worked over Monte Sole on the left from 4:30 until light began to fall. Incendiaries, rockets and machine guns blackened the surface of the hill, driving the enemy deep into the rocky caves. One 88th Division observer remarked, "I wonder if they remember Rotterdam?"[13]

The over-all plan of attack of the 350th obviously hinged on the Division's objectives. After capturing Monterumici, the 88th planned to relieve the 91st on Mt. Adone and Dei Frati to the east of Monterumici and then continue to the Black Phase Line, which included the key communications center short of the Po Valley, Praduro, plus Mount della Capanna.[14] Although this phase of the attack later would be altered to changing battle situations, it does partially explain the tactics of the over-all plan in attacking Monterumici. In addition to battling against perfectly prepared defensive positions, the 350th faced an enemy almost its equal in infantry and artillery; only in armor and air power did the Americans have a clear-cut advantage.[15]

After the 91st Division had cleared the ridge extending between Mount dei Frati, it was to move on Corps order to relieve the 88th Division east of Setta Creek, whereupon the 88th Division was to swing left to seize Mount Mario, dominating the road center town of Praduo at the confluence of the Setta Creek and the Reno River. The 88th Division at that time was to relinquish its zone to the 91st Division in order to assume the zone left vacant on the west side of the Reno River, thus pinching out the 6th South Armoured Division (which should have captured Mount Sole, the peak to the west of Monterumici); the 6th South African Division had the task then of clearing the high ground between the Reno and Setta Creek north to Praduro, establishing a bridgehead across the Reno River south of Praduro, and then assisting the 88th to pass through it.[16] (See map 3.)

The attack of the 350th against Monterumici, originally scheduled for April 13, was postponed; on the next day it was again postponed. Early on April 14, General Truscott's Fifth

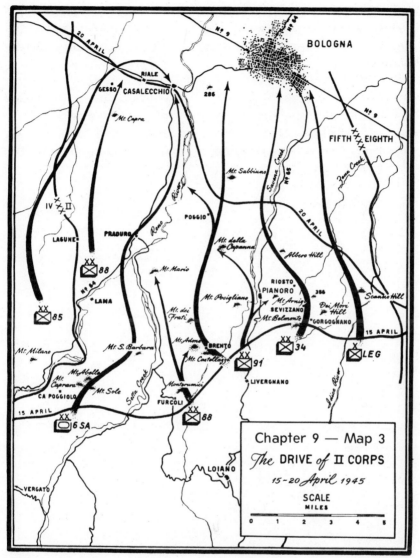

20 APRIL

N° 9

N° 64

BOLOGNA

RIALE

GESSO CASALECCHIO

286

N° 9

Mt. Capra

FIFTH / EIGHTH

Mt. Sabbiuno

Savena Creek

N° 65

IV × II

20 APRIL

LAGUNE

PRADURO

Reno River

POGGIO

Mt. della Capanna

Albero Hill

XX 88

RIOSTO

PIANORO

386

Scanno Hill

N° 64

LAMA

Mt. Mario

Mt. Posigliano

Mt. Arnig

Dei Mori

Hill

XX 85

Mt. dei Frati

SEVIZZANO

Mt. Belmonte

GORGOGNANO

15 APRIL

Mt. Milano

Mt. S. Barbara

Mt. Adms

BRENTO

Mt. Castellazz

XX 34

XX LEG

Mt. Abello

Mt. Sole

Mt. Caprara

CA POGGIOLO

Montcrumici

Mt. Castellazz

XX 91

LIVERGNANO

Idice River

15 APRIL

Setta Creek

FURCOLI

XX 88

XX 6 SA

LOIANO

Chapter 9 — Map 3

The DRIVE *of* II CORPS

15–20 April 1945

SCALE
MILES

0   1   2   3   4   5

VERGATO

Army front was blanketed in mist and fog from the Tower of Pisa to Mt. Grande. Anxiously the attacking forces awaited a break in the heavy clouds. At dawn the weather again appeared hopeless, but by 8:00 o'clock the clouds began breaking up and by 8:30 the troops heard the welcome roar of fighter-bomber engines. At 10:45 in the IV Corps zone the 10th Mountain Division moved forward. The next night, April 15, II Corps attacked against Monte Sole and Monterumici after a 30 minute artillery saturation of 75000 rounds fired by regular artillery units and tanks. [17] The 350th Infantry began its attack at promptly 2230 hours after the fury of artillery, mortar, tank, tank destroyer, machine gun, and AAA gun fire had blasted Monterumici.

At 2300 Companies K and I led the assault for the Third Battalion with Company L in reserve, with Company K moving from LaPiana and L moving to the right. In the attack of the Second Battalion, Company F led the assault with Company G following. The attack developed according to plan and the

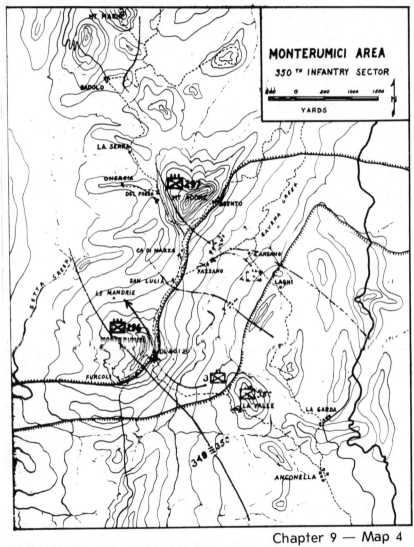

Chapter 9 — Map 4

infantry troops successfully crossed the Savena River without any untoward incident; but when the troops attempted to move up the slopes of Monterumici, they were met by intense and extremely accurate mortar and machine gun fire from deeply entrenched positions.[18] (See Map 4).

While the rifle companies of the Third Battalion attacked, the battalion command post was located at La Piana with the rear command post at Mollinoli. In the early movement of the companies, some casualties resulted from booby-trapped foxholes. The next day, April 16, found Company K still at Di Sotto, with Company I at La Torre and Company L now entering the lines. By 1700 hours Company K's radio had been knocked out. By the next day, April 17, the company had lost two platons surrounded by the enemy and had suffered heavy casualties due to mines and mortars. The company thus pulled back to the protection of the river bed. With Company I still at La Torre and Company L yet on line 100, the artillery pounded Di Sotto, Company K's objective, and Company C of the First Battalion entered the lines to replace Company K.[19]

Not until April 18 would the Second Battalion be able to continue the attack, that is, after the capture of Mt. Adone by the 91st Division. On April 17 the battalion remained in its forward offensive positions until 2030 when it attacked toward Fazzano and C. di Mazza; but because of extremely heavy enemy counter fire and mine fields, the battalion halted after suffering severe casualties, some 52 being sustained. (See Map 5 for 2nd Bn. Sector.)

Before Company K moved out on the evening of April 15, Colonel Fry, recently promoted to Assistant Divisional Commander, gave last-minute instructions to Captain Stroup, Company Commander: "We must have the top of that hill, come what may." Captain Stroup grinned as he answered: "We'll get it." Immediately the attacking force was met by a heavy concentration of enemy mortar rounds. In the jet blackness of the night the men hugged the hillside for protection. By 0400 the company had occupied a cemetery on the very crest of Monceruuumici, the only company in the Regiment to have reached the ride of the mountain.[20]

In conducting this attack toward the town of Di Sotto on April 15, the company was stopped by the intense German fire coming from the ridge down the slope. Atop this ridge, actually

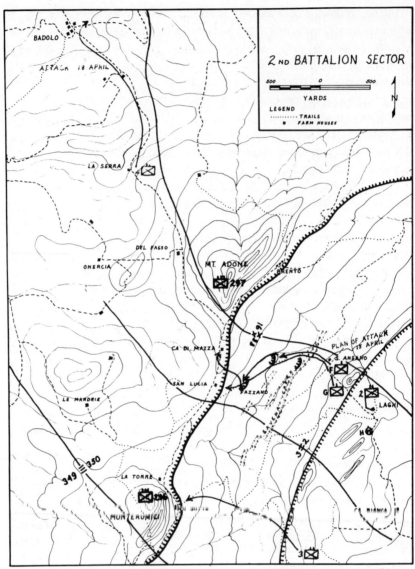

a finger of the mountain chain, perched the town of La Torre on its northern portion and Di Sotto on its southern, the latter being the objective of Company K. Because this company was stopped by the fire from the ridge, it was ordered to swing around to the north and attack the town of La Torre, a movement that failed because the Germans were also strongly defending the northern portion of the ridge.

Because of the two failures, Company K decided to send one platoon to hit the ridge west of La Torre and one platoon to attack Di Sotto simultaneously. Although successful in getting up the steep bluffs to the towns, both platoons were driven back by automatic weapons on the crest. On the morning of April 16, the company was able to occupy the towns because the enemy had apparently abandoned them. Actually the Germans had hidden in the ruins, and when the platoons of the company were on the exposed slopes, the Krauts came out of hiding and completely disorganized the company to the point of killing or capturing most of the men. [21]

Facing the 350th and Company K as it attacked toward its objective, the enemy 297th Mountain Regiment occupied a well-fortified position based on the towns of Di Sopra and Di Sotto; and from the deep strong cellars of these towns and with all usable slopes literally sprinkled with schu and other anti-personnel mines, their positions appeared to be well-nigh impregnable. [22]

Not only from the fortified cellars and the thickly sewn mined approaches to the towns but also from an elaborate system of interlocking caves, dug-outs, and cleverly concealed gun positions, the enemy had done an excellent job of organizing the defenses on Monterumici; in addition to these formidable defenses, the enemy could blanket all the approaches with deadly machine gun and mortar fire. The narrow, tortuous trails were impassable to armor, but yet were the only means of advance on the enemy positions.

By 0100 hours, April 16, Company K, after suffering casualties from schu mines, occupied positions about 400 yards below La Torre, where it was held by accurate enemy machine gun fire directed at the men from hitherto unsuspected enemy positions. By this time, Company L, striking to the right of Monterumici, had been able to advance against very light resistance until it reached a point just short of the road west of Fazzano. Then Company K tried to outflank the enemy by sending one platoon to the left of La Torre while another attacked Di Sotto. It was at this time that the company scaled the crest, only to be driven back by point-blank automatic weapons fire delivered at them from cellar positions in the ruined houses. [23] .(See Map 6.)

Company L had taken Fazzanello by this time, well down on

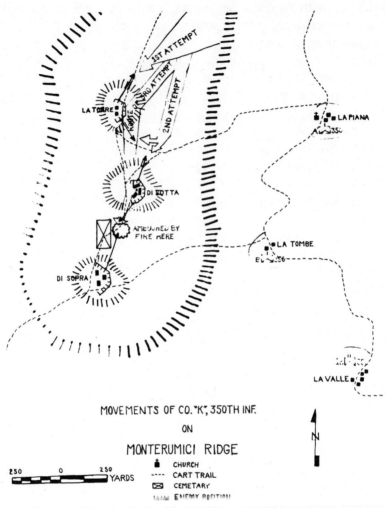

MOVEMENTS OF CO. "K", 350TH INF.

ON

MONTERUMICI RIDGE

250   0   250
YARDS

🛆 CHURCH
---- CART TRAIL
⊠ CEMETARY
⫪⫪⫪ ENEMY POSITION

Chapter 9 — Map 6

the eastward slope of Monterumici ridge; when the company attempted to proceed further, however, it encountered machine gun and small arms fire from Santa Cecilia that halted them abruptly. Since the 91st Infantry Division had not taken the dominating height of Mt. Adone, direct enemy observation from this peak subjected the 350th to heavy artillery and mortar fire from that sector.

In the early morning hours following these actions, the 338th Field Artillery blanketed Mt. Adone with a heavy smoke screen. The Second and Third Battalions, now reorganized and reinforced with new replacements, continued the attack with the aid of increased mortar and machine gun support.[24] And strangely enough with the coming of daylight (April 16) enemy automatic weapons fire ceased completely, so Company K was able to move three platoons into the village of Di Sotto and La Torre without any resistance other than an occasional sniper shot.[25]

Elated by their apparent success and continuing forward without checking ruins for enemy soldiers, the company moved directly through the two villages in preparation to assault the two remaining enemy positions on Monterumici crest-Di Sopra and the cemetery in the saddle between that village and directly above Di Sotto. As soon as the men reached the exposed slope between Di Sotto and Di Sopra, they were greeted by a hail of fire from machine guns, machine pistols, rifle and hand grenades from Di Sotto beneath them, Di Sopra to their left, and the cemetery directly above them and to their front.

Hit now by mortar fire directly on them, the disorganized company tried to take cover in the fox holes in the vineyards on the slope to the right and left of the trail but found them mined and booby-trapped, whereupon the enemy launched a short, furious attack from the cemetery, completely disrupting the company and resulting in the death, wounding or capture of most of the men and capture of all their radios, and thus for all practical purposes taking them out of the fight.[26] Company I, now sent in to support Company K, moved on Di Sopra under cover of fire from supporting tanks, while Company L, meanwhile, had been driven back by heavy mortar and machine gun fire; under these circumstances the Second Battalion returned to Fazzano.[27] The two attacking battalions melted into every available space erosion had prepared. As the sun shone brightly upon the attackers, a cloud of smoke hung steadily above the front line.[28]

In the attack of Company K through Di Sopra and Di Sotto, the company suffered heavy casualties but not as great as the reports indicated at the time. One platoon which was cut off was found later to be in caves occupied by the enemy. Included in the wounded in action were Captain Stroup, commanding; Captain MacDonald, of Company I, who refused to be evacuated; and Lt. Humphrey, killed in action.[29]

At the time of the attack on April 15, the Second Battalion

command post was set up at Laglia with the rear units at C. di Boscia. In its move to capture the dominating ridge line be tween Monterumici and Mt. Adone, the latter the 91st Infantry objective, the Second Battalion sent Companies F and G in the lead with Company E initially in reserve. Because of intense mortar and machine gun fire, the Second Battalion command now called the reserve Company E into the attack to help consolidate the position when it was captured. Although German attacks were beaten off and the positions were held, the battalion suffered two enlisted men killed in action, 26 wounded, Lt. Hunter injured, and the loss of Company F's commander, Captain Laurent A. Charbonnet, who was struck by machine gun bullets. Lt. Drogowski then assumed command of the company.

In the attack to the right of Monterumici by the Second Battalion just west of Fazzano and S. Lucia, Company F had bypassed Fazanello on the move to Fazzano when the men were pinned down by machine gun fire from Casa di Mazza. After halting before the accurate enemy machine gun fire from Casa di Mazza, Company F split up and attempted to approach the position from the left and right but was unsuccessful and, at 0500, after a heavy fire fight in the vicinity of Casa di Mazza, returned to defensive positions at Fazzano. Company E then prepared to launch an attack on the flank of Company F. Company G likewise had been forced to dig in near Fazzano after attempting to pass through Company F.[30]

In its attempt to take Le Mandrie, Company L encountered intense machine gun and small arms fire before reaching half way to the objective. The men continued to fight, however, making their way to within twenty feet of the ridge before being forced to withdraw after suffering one enlisted man killed and one officer and one enlisted man wounded. After digging in, the company was later forced to withdraw also to Fazzanello, after having suffered four casualties, one of whom was the platoon leader, Lt. George Wheeler.

Although held in reserve during the first hours of the attack, the First Battalion early was ordered to relieve the Third Battalion after Company K had failed to clear the rubble heap of the town of Di Sotto atop Monterumici. Company C had orders to seize Di Sopra and then to be relieved by Company B. The battalion moved out at 2300 hours, April 16, up the ridge line from La Tombe toward Di Sopra. After Company C had moved into Di Sopra and secured the objective, Company B followed and made contact. The next objective for Company C, the cemetery north of Di Sopra and the main Monterumici ridge line, could be approached only from the narrow ridge. Moving along this ridge, the company was brought under a withering crossfire from machine guns in Di Sotto, an emplacement near the cemetery, and also from a gun to the rear. The intrepid company commander of C Company, Captain Lynch, moved all available automatic weapons and rifles of his company into a position to lay down an effective base of fire. With the first light of day he led his company in the assault of the cemetery amidst extensive schu-mine fields on the right and intensive automatic weapon fire and succeeded in capturing the ridge. Largely because of his heroic leadership and indomitable courage, Company C attained the objective but just short of the goal, Captain Lynch was killed.

Orders to continue the attack were received later in the day after Company A to the right had cleared Di Sotto of the enemy. Company A now pushed the attack on the ridge, with Company B on the trail to the right past La Torre, where it ran into a serious ambush and suffered over 40 casualties before being forced to retire to the vicinity of La Torre, while Company A met little opposition and consolidated gains farther up the ridge. The reason for the heavy casualties of Company B was the tactic of the enemy in permitting large parts of the company to advance before opening up with a crossfire from well-placed machine guns.[31]

After the debacle of Company K in bypassing Di Sotto and La Torre, the fanatical enemy now came out of their hiding around 1400 hours on April 16 and occupied the village of Di Sotto. From this position the Krauts directed their heaviest fire. Meanwhile Company L had managed to place one platoon within a few feet of the ridge from the right, just short of Le Mandrie, in the morning around 0800 hours and had knocked out two enemy dug-outs on the south side of the ridge. The second platoon was now sent to aid the third only to be pinned down and suffer heavy casualties in its attempt to gain the crest before being driven off by sniper and machine gun fire.[32]

After withdrawing under cover of friendly machine gun fire and after suffering heavy casualties, the second and third platoons of Company L again attacked at 2230 hours and managed to infiltrate a few men to Hill 100 before moving back under a heavy mortar and machine gun fire attack. After Company F had withdrawn to Fazzano, Company G now attempted to advance towards the ridge line north of this village but was halted by a fifty foot cliff around which movement was impossible, since machine gun and mortars were zeroed in on all approaches. At least fourteen were wounded in this drive, including Lt. Duane Cordiner. It was in this disheartening situation that Regimental Headquarters decided to commit the Firt Battalion. [33]

The plan now called for Company A to attack Di Sotto from La Piana, Company C to move out from La Valle and take Di Sopra and the cemetery, and Company B to remain in La Tombe as the battalion reserve. Company C moved out after darkness, scaled Monterumici bluff from the left, and at dawn on April 17 moved through Company I and assaulted Di Sopra. [34]

Before Companies A and C moved out abreast to make up the assault, Colonel Fry visited the First Battalion headquarters, where he found the young Colonel Holland intently studying the situation maps under the flickering candles on the crude and long-neglected fireplace, supplementing the light of the field lantern which the operations sergeant held above the map. Colonel Fry moved over to join two combat-tried officers, Captain Walter Scott of Company A and Captain Charles Lynch of Company C, to wish them well and told them that they had proved their courage already; someone else should be the lead points of the advance guards for a change. Captain Lynch laughed quietly in his usual way. [35]

As fighting died down on the night of April 16, the First and Third Battalions were in position to execute the plan of attack for the next day. The hell of shelling by mortar and automatic weapons fire is shown by the fact that by 1000, April 16, over 1000 rounds of mortar ammunition had fallen alone on the 350th Infantry. [36]

The situation by the end of April 16 was that on the left boundary of the 350th sector no progress had been made, with the 349th Regiment 700 yards to the west on the ridge and in Furcoli; the 350th had four companies up against enemy positions on the northern and eastern slopes of Monterumici, with some elements of the Second Battalion some distance up the eastern slopes of the saddle just below Mt. Adone. There were some devastated villages on the slopes of Monterumici partly in American hands, but the peak was by no means cleared of the enemy. He still held many of his major positions as well as comanding observation and control of the ridge line. Between the most advanced positions held by the Americans, there were yet wide gaps occupied by the fanatical enemy. Neither was the right flank secure; the 91st Division still struggled toward Adone; but on the left of the 88th Division sector, the South Africans had won the Monte Sole-Mount Capara-Mount Abelle traingle. [37] The fighting for Monterumici, the 350th sector, would reach its greatest intensity on the next day, April 17.

The attack of Company A the next day, April 17, on Di Sotto can be described in no other terms than as a masterful execution of assault against a strongly held and fortified position on seemingly unassaultable positions. Company A officers and non-commissioned officers had worked out a plan of attack based on information from observing the attacks by Companies K and I the day previously and from interrogating the wounded brought down during the nights of April 15 and 16; further the company had access to detailed air photos of the area. The company officers were convinced that the best assault positions ran along a slope directly east of Di Sotto and containing a rocky ledge of about one-foot in width that could accomodate about 30 men moving in single file. Moving out at 2345 hours, April 16, the men moved in single file and followed a trail from La Piana to La Torre along a cliff with a deep ravine just below it. By 0300 hours they had reached a point about 500 yards east of La Torre. Then three men of Mexican-Indian descent, who had proven their amazing ability to move swiftly and silently over difficult terrain at night, reconnoitered the off-the-trail route to Di Sotto. After they had returned and reported the discovery of the route along the bluff, the company then sent a platoon along this route; as the men halted to allow negotiation of a troublesome spot, each man in turn would have to hand his weapon and equipment to the man behind him, cross the gap by jumping or clawing his way, and then have his weapon and equipment thrown to him. To negotiate the 500 yards took fully one and one-half hours. (See Map 7.)

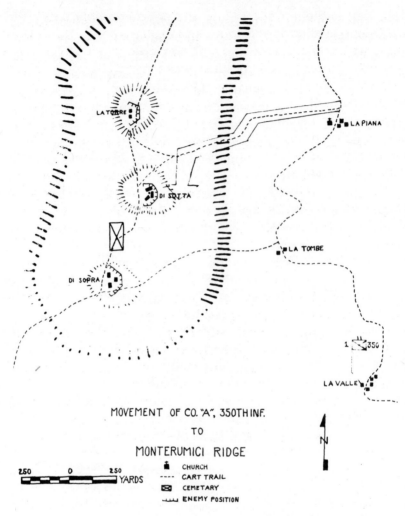

MOVEMENT OF CO. "A", 350TH INF.

TO

MONTERUMICI RIDGE

250   0   250
YARDS

🏛 CHURCH
---- CART TRAIL
⊠ CEMETARY
⊔⊔⊔ ENEMY POSITION

N

Chapter 9 — Map 7

As the platoon began this tortuous climb around 0500 hours, April 17, Mount Adone, the main observation point to the right rear, still remained in enemy hands. After enemy mortar fire had zeroed in on the company, it called for smoke shells on Adone, so that in the early morning hours no enemy mortar fire came close to the company's dispersal area. This latter point was separated from Di Sotto by a vineyard slope about 250 yards long, with an incline of about 30 degrees. It was at this time that the reconnaissance party returned with word that a very small rock ledge, about long enough to accommodate 30 men and about one foot wide, existed on the rock face of the bluff, well to the left of Di Sotto and approximately under the short slope leading to the south end of the village. The reconnaissance party also reported that, by ridding themselves of all equipment other than individual weapons, one platoon could make its way to this ledge, using the roots and bushes growing out of the face of the bluff to draw themselves along.[38] Colonel Fry, newly arrived at the observation post, appeared worried at the situation facing the company.

A short while before, Colonel Fry had received the news of the death of Captain Lynch from Colonel Holland. Colonel Fry immediately turned from the sorrowful news to command Colonel Holland to get the attack rolling; he himself would move forward to Company A's headquarters to see that Scotty (Captain Scott, Company A commander), moved abreast of Company C. Moving through a ravine toward Di Sotto, Colonel Fry found Captain Scott studying the approaches to the shattered village. A broad smile creased his features, but tears welled in his eyes as he mentioned Captain Lynch's death; perhaps having a premonition of his own death later, Captain Scott told Colonel Fry that he was not as optimistic as he once was and that the going forward became harder every day. A half hour later the attack began, with Lt. Daniel Swett swinging his platoon wide to the left and moving swiftly into Di Sotto. The 350th would again regain the top of Monterumici.[39]

The plan for the attack on Di Sotto called for the Third Platoon to work its way along the ledge, and after arriving at its destination, it was not to assault until the rest of the company had fired for about five minutes to divert the enemy's attention, then to lift the fire and continue firing from light machine guns and individual weapons during the assault, shifting to the right end of the village. They were to lift their fires only when the third platoon was observed actually in the left end of the village; then the second and first platoons were to move in from the front slope into the village and prepare for a counterattack. Further plans called for the company then to reorganize on the ridge and take La Torre. (See Map 8.)

After the third platoon had successfully traversed the ledge, moved toward Di Sotto, and silenced a machine gun in its path, it then moved right on into the village, whereupon the other two platoons quickly came in and immediately hurled grenades into the cellars and other strong points. The cry of "kamerad"

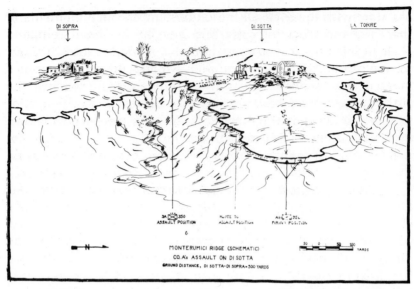

DI SOPRA   DI SOTTA   LA TORRE →

3A ⊠ 350
ASSAULT POSITION

ROUTE TO
ASSAULT POSITION

AN ⊞ 350
FIRING POSITION

N

MONTERUMICI RIDGE (SCHEMATIC)
CO. A's ASSAULT ON DI SOTTA
GROUND DISTANCE, DI SOTTA-DI SOPRA=500 YARDS

50 0   50   100
            YARDS

Chapter 9 — Map 8

came from all quarters; however, the enemy counterattacked with about 60 men moving from La Torre to Di Sotta. The company held its fire until the enemy closed in on the north; again the cries of "kamerad" and "surrender" betokened the defeat of the former fanatical enemy. After taking these Krauts prisoners, who ran into the village with hands in the air, Company A then quickly took La Torre, after having given the Krauts holed up there less than thirty seconds to come out. [40]

After the first platoon had occupied La Torre, clearing parties, sent into the network of tunnels that existed between the two village and connecting them and Di Sopra, discovered a part of the Mt. Adone galeria system, an ancient tunnel going completely through Mt. Adone and Monterumici. In these tunnels where the Germans had lived rather comfortably during the winter were found a number of enemy and Company K wounded. It was learned from these men the reason for the debacle suffered by Company K previously. There were no German officers among the captured enemy; they had given instructions to the non-commissioned officrs to fight to the last and then surrender. During the attack, Colonel Fry was heard to remark to the commander of Company A: "This is just like an attack demonstration at Fort Benning." [41]

On April 17 after the partial success of the 350th Infantry on

Page 232

the right with the First Battalion passing through elements of the Third and attacking south and west up the slope, Company C about this time lost 10 killed and 31 wounded in the stiff fight for the cemetery, an enemy major strongpoint, whose capture yielded 45 prisoners. By 1000 the company had reached the summit and turned it over to the Third Battalion to organize for defense, whereupon the First Battalion now moved north down into the saddle. Company B during this day suffered approximately 40 casualties in an ambush, but the battalion by the close of the day had made considerable progress astride a ridge which ran northwest to the Setta behind Monterumici.[42]

On this same day, however, the Second Battalion made very slight progress in its efforts to knock out the strongpoints under the steep southern slopes of Mount Adone. Because of the suicidal aspects of attacking under enemy observation, the battalion was ordered to hold until darkness. Moving again into battle at 2130, two companies attacked toward two strongpoints on the ridge, one right up under the slopes of Adone, but after suffering approximately 50 casualties (the enemy was entrenched on a ledge above the attacking troops who had to pick their way through minefields), the Regimental Command decided to discontinue the attack until it became lighter.

It was in this attack on April 17 on the cemetery to the north of Di Sopra that Captain Charles P. Lynch, Jr., was killed. As Captain Lynch led his company in the attack, they encountered a strong German point covering the trail they were following. When the sergeant and two other men had crawled around the flank and were almost in position to open fire, the sergeant observed the exposed silhouette of Captain Lynch, and instantly there was the chatter of a German smyser. Captain Lynch fell. Only a second later the sergeant and his men killed the three Germans who had delayed the advance.[43] Lt. Charles Dornacker now assumed command of Company C and prepared the company to continue in battalion reserve. After the troops had dug in to insure this vital high ground, they were subjected to mortar and machine gun fire all day.

After Company A had cleaned out Di Sotta, Company B attacked to the right past La Torre and captured St. Cecilia without sustaining any casualties; but when the company continued to Le Mandrie, it was ambushed and suffered heavy casualties. The enemy had allowed two platoons to pass through them before they opened fire with five machine guns. The company then received orders to return to La Torre for reorganization. In the meantime, Company A had continued to consolidate gains further up the ridge, and by 1030 hours the Regiment had succeeded in capturing Monterumici but only after a heavy toll of casualties in the long battle.

The action of Company L highlighted the activity of the Third Battalion on April 17 after the debacle suffered by Companies K and I. As Company L attacked again at 0300 in the morning to try to capture hill feature 100, fierce machine gun fire forced them to withdraw three more times. After suffering heavy casualties in their numerous attempts to take this feature, the company waited for cover of darkness to withdraw and at 2000 hours moved through La Piana into Di Sopra, whereupon the Third Battalion then went into battalion reserve.

The Second Battalion continued the almost impossible task of capturing enemy strongpoints around Mt. Adone. Companies F, E, and G attacked in the vicinity of C. di Mazza, but when it became obvious that the ojbective could not be reached before daylight, Company E returned to positions at Laglia and decided to launch an attack later under cover of darkness. At 2130 hours, Company G launched an attack against S. Lucia, synchronized with the attack of Company E once more on Ca di Mazza, proceeding northwest from Fazzano. As the company moved toward the ridge line, it was halted by machine guns set on ledges directly above them. Even though the enemy dropped hand grenades on them from the ledges above, the men yet attempted to work themselves up the hill by grasping vines to pull themselves over the top.

WIth Company F wIthin 300 yards of their objective although suffering sixteen casualties, Company G, meanwhile, had advanced over 400 yards in the vicinity of Mt. Adone with light casualties. As resistance decreased, the whole line moved with grim determination forward. The 361st Infantry, however, had not succeeded in capturing Adone. Yet, a swift advance was anticipated, so aid stations prepared to move forward. While enemy artillery fire increased, supporting units of the 350th Infantry employed VT fuzes on rear slopes and ridges to cut off supplies or reinforcements from being brought up to these fanatical enemy troops. [44]

Among the individual exploits of heroism and courage during

these difficult days of attack against Monterumici was the inspiring example of Pfc. Orville G. Warren of Company K and Belleville City, Illinois, who crawled through a minefield to flank Kraut riflemen who were holding up his squad's advance; after accounting for a number of enemy dead with rifle shots and fire from a delayed grenade, he stayed in position blazing away until his company moved up. S-Sgt. Ernest C. Hardesty of Tulsa, Oklahoma, calmly worked through a minefield in disarming enough of the mines to clear a path for his quad, even under the hell of machine gun and mortar fire. He then retraced his steps to carry out the wounded. First Lieutenant George Fumich, Jr., of Pursglove, West Virginia, tossed hand grenades into the air to create bursts like an air bomb, in full view of the enemy. He then disposed of a box of grenades in this manner, along with a score of enemy soldiers. Lt. Col. Donald A. Yongue, Second Battalion Commander, of Summerville, North Carolina, won the nickname "Bare Fist Colonel" when he surprised a Kraut with a machine pistol and knocked out the startled gunner with two staggering blows.

As Colonel Yongue led his battalion toward the town of Badolo on the morning of April 18, the lead platoon came under heavy machine pistol fire from a defilade behind a large rock. Since he hardly had time to draw his pistol and attempt to return the fire, Colonel Yongue instead rushed forward into the face of the deadly barrage, vaulted the rock, and grappled the enemy with his bare hands. After dealing the Kraut a number of tremendous blows with his fist, Colonel Yongue then tore the machine pistol from the enemy's fingers and took him prisoner. He then relieved the Kraut of eleven grenades.

The medics, as usual, won accolades from all the units. Pfc Henry Perkins of Philadelphia cared for the wounded of Company K. When a GI tripped a mine on a steep slope and fell seriously wounded, Perkins rushed into the minefield, staked the wounded man into a position to keep him from sliding, and then reset both his legs in the middle of a barrage that drove others to cover. He then treated other casualties and aided litter bearers in moving them over minestrewn trails to the aid stations. Pfc Marshall R. Weigott, Jr., of Cincinnatti, Ohio, and attached to Company B, worked until he collapsed from exhaustion but helped evacuate twenty wounded amidst the hail of machine gun and mortar fire. The next day he was back on the job.[45]

The change in plans of direction of attack of II Corps on April 18 would determine the action of the 350th Infantry in the move out of the mountains into the plains below. On this day, about half-past nine, General Keyes and his G-3, Colonel Bob Porter, came to see General Truscott. At that time the 88th Division had taken Monterumici, but the pursuit of the enemy from the remaining peaks before the valley remained impeded since the 91st Division had not yet captured Mt. Adone. General Keyes wanted to withdraw the 88th Division, move it to the west, and send it up the east bank of the Reno River on the right of the South Africans. General Truscott agreed and immediately moved to implement the plan. [46] The first elements of the 85th Division had already moved up on April 16 from its reserve area in the Arno Valley to the vicinity of Africa, near Vergato. Because of the lessend enemy resistance in front of II Corps, however, the 88th Division by April 18 had moved to take over a good part of the zone originally planned for the 85th Division.[47]

Up to a point, there was a parallel between the action of II Corps in its attack to that of the piercing of the Gustav Line in May, 1944. The II Corps attack could be likened to the action of the British Corps in front of Cassino in 1944, while farther to the west, the action of IV Corps paralleled the action of the FEC in traversing the mountainous terrain (along with the 88th Division) west of the British in the Gustav battles. The parallels were not complete, however; for the 350th Infantry and other elements of II Corps had cracked the tough enemy defenses in its sector in April, 1945, although Mt. Adone and the area west of Furcoll still remained in enemy hands.

On the left, the ridge west of Furcoli was taken in the morning, and by afternoon the 349th Infantry had cleared the triangular area between Furcoli ridge and Setta Creek. The 361st Infantry on the right finally won the top of Mount Adone a 1000, April 18, whereupon the 350th Infantry, which had seized the top of Monterumici the day before, was now secure on both flanks and began a rapid progress to the northwest. The First Battalion on the left followed a ridge line northwest from Monterumici to the Setta and thence moved up the creek bottom; the Second Battalion skirted around the lower slopes of Mount Adone and followed a road leading northwest from the height. By midnight, after an advance of three miles, the 350th Infantry held an east-west line extending east of Setta Creek one mile south of Mount Mario, the 88th Division's Black Line objective. Resistance had been scattered and consisted chiefly of small rearguard detachments and bypassed elements.48

During these attacks on April 18 the Third Battalion remained in reserve. The Second Battalion began to move rapidly after the capture of Mount Adone at 1000 hours. About this time Company E, which had moved out in the attack on C. di Mazza at 0800, reported occupying this position along with S. Lucia. Attacking now in platoon column, the company followed the trail around the western edge of Mount Adone and after moving through the unoccupied town of Vale di Fasse pressed forward to Quercia. By 1400 hours, the regiment began to move forward in a column of companies after capturing a number of prisoners and generally breaking enemy resistance. Making contact with the 91st Division on the right after attacking cross-country to Tre de Barto, the Second Battalion set up its command post at Badola and in a fire fight at Pianazza sustained 55 casualties. In this are around Pianazza Captain Nicholas R. Brooks, the battalion S-3, was wounded and evacuated, whereupon First Lieutenant William G. Bell then assumed the duties of S-3.

As Company A, First Battalion, marched forward, it captured 166 prisoners but encountered snipers around one RP. In leading one section of the company in search of these snipers, First Sergeant Plank was killed. With the assistance of tanks, the company cleared the houses facing them and prepared to continue the attack. Company B at this time moved along Highway 6428, capturing thirty prisoners. By 1730 the Regimental CP located at Badola. The companies dug in for the night and held their gains. Prisoners reported that they would have held out longer but for the fact that American artillery concentrations had prevented supplies and ammunition from reaching them.49

Company A advanced swiftly down the ridge branching to the northwest, with the rest of the battalion following in its path. In the advance in the direction of Sasso Bolognese, Company A moved on the left in the valley with Companies B and C in the hills on the right. As the battalion command post and Company B moved down the valley road south of Company A, Company C went forward to clean up the ridge south of Mount Mario. [50] When Company A discovered a bridge blown out, the men, previously riding tanks, descended and took their objective along with 24 prisoners. In this engagement the company suffered three killed and three wounded from fire from SP guns and mortars. [51]

On the afternoon of April 18, the 350th Infantry was ordered to extend its left flank to replace and cover the withdrawal, under cover of darkness, of the advance elements of the 349th Infantry. This operation was accomplished with smoothness and efficiency.[52] The 350th Infantry could swing its flank in this direction partially as a result of the enemy's orderly retreat all along the line facing II Corps. Although there had been no breakthrough on Highway 65, the fact that Monte Sole and Monterumici were in Fifth Army's possession put the German front lines in jeopardy. The morale, too, of the Germans was low-by the end of April 18 the 8th Mountain Division alone had lost 1000 prisoners, so by April 18 II Corps faced gradually reduced resistance. [53]

While the rest of the 88th Division moved to the left across the Reno to be recommitted on the right of the 85th Division, the 350th Infantry still engaged the enemy before Mount Mario. This move resulted from the action of the 91st Division's shift to the left toward the Reno while the 6th South African Division, further to the left, crossed the shallow stream of the Reno at Praduro. II Corps had now reached the Black Line attack line west of the Reno, with the 88th Division and the South Africans on the west and the 91st Division and 34th Division on the east of the river. The main effort now envisaged on attack to cut Highway 9 and capture or isolate Bologna. Meanwhile, the 350th Infantry, still engaged at Mount Mario, came under control of the 91st Division. [54]

As the First Battalion moved in the direction of Sasso Bolognese around 0500, April 19, with Company A leading, Company B, in battalion reserve, moved from Della Leone to Mol Albano to make contact with Company A. The Second Battalion still engaged in the struggle for Mt. Mario and the high ground at Villa Guiete. Company F suffered only one casualty in its attack against stiff enemy resistance and dug in at night at C. Nuova. Company G cleared the hill south of Sasso Bolognese, capturing 33 prisoners after suffering four casualties. In pursuing the enemy, Company E attacked toward C. Vota, clearing enemy pockets in the way and capturing a number of prisoners. After the capture of Mt. Mario, the company went into battalion reserve and Companies F and G moved through it. At the Black Phase line, the 350th Infantry was to pass into division reserve after being relieved of its positions by the 362nd Regiment of the 91st Division. [55]

After capturing Villa Quiete on the important height outside Sasso Bolognese, the Second Battalion went into reserve and spent April 20 in rehabilitation of men and equipment. [56] The Third Battalion rested in the vicinity of Sasso Bolognese, where it received new replacements.

The description by General Fry of the rolling plains of the Po as the division marched out of the mountains on April 20 expresses completely the feelings of the entire Regiment:

> The view of the broad Po Valley, as we were descending from the rolling hills, was a beautiful picture to the eyes of everyone. Green as far as one could see, we knew instinctively that this area would not witness any serious battle. More than anything else, human endurance would determine the degree of success. [57]

On Mt. Adone the Germans had excellent observation of Fifth Army activities.

Charles P. Lynch, Jr., Captain, Infantry

Killed in action in the final battle of Italy, Captain Lynch was posthumously awarded the Distinguished Service Cross for extraordinary heroism in action.

Fifth Army, Monturmici area, Italy 88th Div., Infantry squad ready to take off on mission gets last minute pep-talk by officer. April, 1945.

Monterumici, April, 1945

Blue Devils advance past wrecked tank after the breakthrough at Monterumici.

This cave, an arsenal for German weapons and ammunition, was taken by troops of the 88th Div., U.S. Fifth Army, during the break-thru at Monterumici, Italy.

Bailey bridge eased supply problems for 13 corps.

British artillery plows through mud and water on the 13 Corps front

Close-up view of caves and gullies which characterized the Monterumici area

Mount Adone off Highway 65. View from Loiano-
Livergnano area.

Footnotes to Chapter IX.

[1] 350th Infantry Regiment History, April, 1945.

[2] Ibid.

[3] Fry, **Combat Soldier,** 267-277.

[4] **19 Days from the Apennines to the Alps: The Story of the Po Valley Campaign**
(Milan, Italy: Pizzi and Pizio, 1945), 21.

[5] Truscott, **Command missions,** 482.

[6] Clark, **Calculated Risl,** 426.

[7] **Fifth Army History,** IX, 11-24.

[8] **Ibid.,** 24.

[9] Fry, **Combat Soldier,** 277-278.

[10] **Ibid.,** 279.

[11] 350th Infantry Regiment History, April, 1945.

[12] Fry, **Combat Soldier,** 279.

[13] **19 Days from the Apennines to the Po,** 32.

[14] Fifth Army History, IX, 63.

[15] **Ibid.,** 28.

[16] **Ibid.,** 65.

[17] Clark, **Calculated Risk,** 423.

[18] 350th Infantry Regiment History, April, 1945.

[19] Third Battalion History, April, 1945.

[20] Fry, **Combat Soldier,** 282.

[21] "A Rifle Company in Mountain Terrain," **Infantry School Quarterly (April, 1949), 83.**

[22] Personal Knowledge, Captain Daniel H. Swett, Advanced Infantry Officer Course, 1949-1949, "The Operations of Company A, Northwest of Anconella, Italy, April 17, 1945," in "Infantry Company Attacking Village in Mountainuous Terrain," IAIO Class No. 2.

[23] Statement by Captain Ray Stroup, **Ibid.**

[24] 350th Infantry Regiment History, April, 1945.

[25] Statement by Captain Stroup, "The Operations of Company A, April 17, 1945."

[26] **Ibid.**

[27] 350th Infantry Regiment History, April, 1945.

[28] Fry, **Combat Soldier,** 282-283.

[29] Third Battalion History, April, 1945.

[30] 350th Infantry Regiment History, April, 1945.

[31] First Battalion History, April, 1945.

[32] 350th Infantry Regiment History, April, 1945.

[33] **Ibid.**

[34] Personal Knowledge of Captain Swett, April 17, 1945.

[35] Fry, **Combat Soldier,** 285.

[36] **Fifth Army History,** IX, 69.

[37] **Ibid.,** 70.

[38] Personal Knowledge, Captain Swett, April 17, 1945.

Fry, **Combat Soldier,** 287.

[40] 350th Infantry Regiment History, April, 1945.

[41] Statement by Captain Stroup, "The Operations of Company A, April 17, 1945."

[42] **Fifth Army History,** IX, 70-71.

[43] Fry, **Combat Soldier,** 207.

[44] 350th Infantry Regiment History, April, 1945.

[45] Delaney, **The Blue Devils in Italy,** 199.

[46] Truscott, **Command Missions,** 489.

[47] Starr, **From Salerno to the Alps,** 405.

[48] **Fifth Army History,** IX, 71.

[49] 350th Infantry Regiment History, April, 1945.

[50] Fifth Battalion History, April, 1945.

[51] Company A History, April, 1945.

[52] Fry, **Combat Soldier,** 293.

[53] **Fifth Army History,** IX, 83.

[54] **Ibid.,** 84.

[55] 350th Infantry Regiment History, April, 1945.

[56] Second Battalion History, April, 1945.

[57] Fry, **Combat Soldier,** 294.

Page 246

Chapter Ten

Through the Po Valley and
Into the Alps Mountain

As the Regiment marched out of the last of the hills overlooking Bologna, green stretches of the Po Valley rolled far into the distance. By 1600 April 21 the command post established in the town of Gesso. Prior to this date the Regiment had been alerted to move to the west on April 20, at which time it went back under Division control. Moving a distance of 12 miles on April 21, the Second Battalion arrived at Malcantone, while the First Battalion marched more than fourteen miles to reach Gesso and after a short rest continued for five more miles and bivouaced on Highway 9. The Third Battalion likewise marched 12 miles to arrive at Gesso and by 2000 again moved out for approximately eight more miles to arrive at the town of Anzola dell Emilia. The Third Battalion still remained in Division reserve.

The Regiment was now ordered to secure the line of the Panaro River. To implement this order, Regimental Headquarters established its command post in Crevalcore. At this area the First Battalion received the orders to move forward in the attack to the north after relieving the 351st Regiment; the Second, after a road march of fourteen miles, moved to the vicinity of Villa Nuova. While on the march the Second Battalion suffered 21 casualties from bombing by enemy planes. The Third Battalion, facing north, marched approximately 21 miles this day, first to Scuola and then on to San Bernardino near Crevalcore. [1] (See Map 1.)

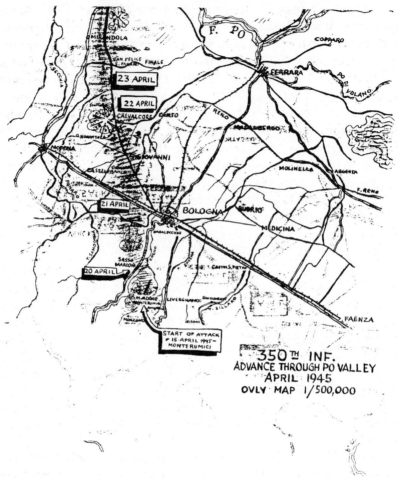

Chapter 10 — Map 1

By April 23 the Regiment was in swift pursuit of the enemy trying to reach the Po and cross rapidly for the retreat further north. The new division zone of advance was west of Bologna, following generally Route 12 toward Ostiglia and Verona. It was here that Major (later Lt. Colonel) Croyden M. Woodbury again joined the Division with his 752nd Tank Battalion and continued to supply superbly efficient direct tank support to the front line riflemen throughout the remainder of the Italian campaign. [2] Everywhere the theme of the pursuit, "Hurry, hurry, hurry," rushed the Blue Devils along as they captured numerous prisoners trying to escape the encircling pincers of II Corps. The 88th Division and the 350th Infantry were indeed

Page 248

fulfilling their task in implementing the plans of Fifth Army after capturing Bologna - two corps, each with one armored and two infantry divisions to press on boldly and rapidly, seizing the line of the Panaro RIver, and then pressing on to the Po to secure crossing sites and thereby cutting off German forces still south of the river.[3] The 350th Infantry was slated to pass through the 351st Infantry, which had reached the Panaro east of Camposanto in the middle of the afternoon on April 22, and then with the 349th Infantry on the right and the 350th Infantry on the left to dash toward the Po, first northeast and then north when the corps boundary was shifted west past Revere.[4]

On this date Colonel Fry received orders from General Keyes: "Elements of the Division must reach the Po tonight." The reply from Colonel Fry was short and to the point: "I'll wash my hands in the Po today."[5]

After relieving the 351st Infantry in the vicinity of Camp O Santo on April 23, the 350th Infantry moved forward rapidly and encountered only scattered enemy resistance. With the First Battalion on the right and the Third Battalion on the left flank and the Second Battalion following the Third about 1000 yards, the Regiment presented a motley group as some rode bicycles, tanks, horses, and enemy vehicles. All companies captured numerous prisoners while suffering comparatively light casualties.   Initially in the campaign, however, the Third Battalion engaged the enemy in a fierce fire fight of about a half hour's duration.[6]

Approximately an hour after the battalion had left San Bernardino, it spotted two enemy motorcyclists driving from under a bridge onto the highway that the battalion column was following. Captain Ashton, at the head of the column with two radio operators, jumped to the side of the road to radio the other commanding officers to be alert. At that time one round from a rocket gun landed near the small group, killing Captain Ashton and Pfc. Weintraub and wounding Pfc. Austin.[7]

On this date also the Second Battalion suffered a number of casualties when the rear of the company column was bombed by enemy air craft. Six casualties were sustained, including the executive officer, First Lieutenant Ure, and First Sergeant Fink, both of whom were replaced by First Lieutenant Furlo as executive officer and Technical Sergeant Bernier as first sergeant respectively. Moving on at a rapid pace, the Second

Battalion reached the Po River by nightfall. With Company E in the lead, the battalion reorganized approximately eight miles from the Po and went on towards the river. In this move the battalion captured a field hospital and approximately 200 prisoners and then proceeded to the Po. Occupying the south bank of the river and mopping up enemy positions in the vicinity, the company added fully another 300 prisoners to the total and thus brought the prisoner total for the company for that day to 600. [8] In addition the company captured uncounted numbers of weapons, vehicles of all types, horses, and great stocks of ammunition. [9]

By 2000 on April 23 and 349th Infantry had reached the Po north of Carbonara and fanned out along the river bank to gather in the thousands of German stragglers in the vicinity. The 350th Infantry, shifting over to the left astride Highway 12, arrived at the river a little latter. [10] (See Map 2.)

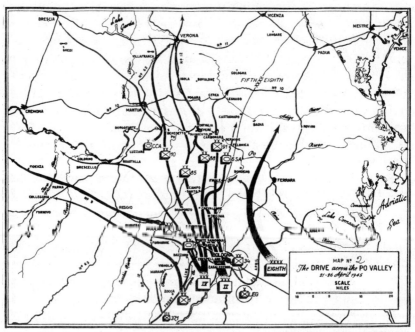

Chapter 10 — Map 2

The jaunt of the Second Battalion on bicycles toward the Po River and beyond had its genesis in the requisitioning by the Regimental Commander, Colonel Cochran, from Italian civilians all the bicycles in the vicinity. The enemy, now completely disorganized, was employing horses, mules, and oxen to draw tanks and even vehicles. The 350th troops advanced so rapidly that they surprised the Krauts in the town of San Felice where they had left a whole train load of supplies, containing food, cigarettes and cheese at the railroad station. The whole town-men, women, and children-welcomed the liberators by throwing flowers, offering wine, and wishing them God speed. Their enthusiasm was unbounded when the soldiers were able to linger in a town for a short time. By this time partisans aided willingly and did good work in rounding up bypassed enemy soldiers and in guarding prisoners.

So rapid was the advance at this point that it was impossible to keep an accurate account of prisoners. To permit the attacking companies to pursue the enemy without pause, sometimes a solitary American soldier, mounted on a beautiful horse either leading or following a double column of two or three hundred enemy prisoners, directed the captured Krauts to the rear.[11]

The Regiment reached the Po on April 24. Fewer and fewer personnel walked by this time, and more and more rode on all varieties of transport known, from dog carts to German half tracks. Late at night the First Battalion moved across the Po by DUKW's and shortly thereafter the battalion command post was organized at Pieve di Coriano.

The Second Battalion had preceded the First across the Po. At 1945 hours it moved out to cross the Po on alligators, meeting no enemy resistance. By 2300 it closed into the area of Serravalle after having continued across the valley for eight miles and halted for the evening. The Third Battalion troops, like those of the Second, likewise used everything available in their march to the Po. After crossing the IP at 0630 hours, the battalion marched approximately seven miles to Le Teste, but many rode horses, bicycles, and any other type vehicles they could find. The battalion remained in Le Teste next to the Po River for the rest of the day and crossed at 1930 hours on DUKW's and alligators, whereupon the G-I's proceeded to walk seven miles to Serrabbe. On this day ex-Sergeant Harland, now a Second Lieutenant after attending OCS, returned and was assigned as S-2, with Lieutenant Hebel now taking over as S-3.[12]

The first crossing by the Regiment had actually occurred at

1200 hours on April 23 when Major Cussans and a task force of thirty men made the first crossing of the river, using a varied assortment of assault boats and civilian rowboats.

In its operation of crossing the river, the 88th Division found the Germans assembling shattered forces for escape across the river. The prisoner haul reached its peak in the Division zone. From 1200, April 23 to 1200, April 25, the Division took approximately 11,000 prisoners, the bulk from the 65th Grenadier, 305th Grenadier, and 8th Mountain Divisions. Included in the prisoner haul was the first German division commander captured during the whole Italian campaign, Major General von Schellwitz, commanding officer of the 305th Grenadier Division, as well as the G-3, signal officer, and division artillery commander. [13]

By April 24 the proud Wehrmacht in Italy had only a few days left before surrender. Since the enemy forces disintegrated rapidly after this date, II Corps decided to abandon the set piece assault crossing against an anticipated strongly defended river line and made plans then to move swiftly along the axis of Highway 12, which enters Verona from the south, to seize the west bank of the Adige River from Legnango north to Verona. In addition the Corps had the task of capturing four large towns and road junctions in a rough quadrangle of its zone-Nogara, Isola, Cerea, and Bovalone.

Orders from II Corps Headquarters laid out on April 24 the individual objectives beyond the Po in order to accomplish the mission of clearing the west bank of the Adige from Legnagno, where Highway 10 crosses the river, north to Verona. The 88th Division, one of the two main divisions chosen to make the main effort, received two batteries of 155 mm guns to support the crossing operation. In its orders to attack toward Verona astride Highway 12, the 88th Division had the objective also of clearing the town of Nogara at the junction of Highway 10 and 12 and Isola, seven miles north of Nogara on Highway 12. The bridgehead of the 350th Infantry on the left of the Po at Revere had been established on the night of April 23-24. It was on the following morning that the 88th Division started the march for Verona by foot, jeeps, captured vehicles, and bicycles, even though the armor had not yet reached full scale accompaniment because of the lack of bridges across the river. [14]

The pursuit by the 350th Infantry on April 25 found the battalions moving even 37 miles in one day along Highway 12 before stopping for the evening. (See Map 3.) On this day part of the Second Battalion obtained bicycles, at 2030 hours, to make the advance more rapid. [15] The Second Battalion stopped on the outskirts of Verona around 0145, April 26, after having taken some 135 prisoner amidst light scattered resistance. [16] With Company E in the lead on Highway 12, the company moved through Nogara and then turned to the left and followed the secondary roads to the left of Highway 12 to the outskirts of Verona. The method of march was to mount the first platoon on three TD's to precede the battalion by five or

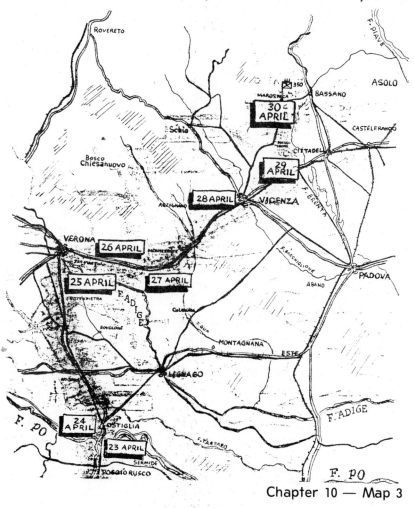

Chapter 10 — Map 3

Page 253

ten miles, clearing out all resistance on the way and thus enabling the battalion to follow without resistance. Included in the POW cache for the day were a German colonel and captain.[17]

The Third Battalion marched along Highway 12 for 37 miles, from 0500 to 2400, from Serrarabbe to Ca di David south of Verona before stopping for rest in the evening.[18] The First Battalion marched across swampy terrain criss-crossed with canals before stopping for the night in the vicinity of San Ferraro.[19]

By April 26 the German forces in Italy had been split into two groups. General Truscott now issued his operations instructions calling for his forces to continue the advance to cut off and destroy German forces in the northwest and to assist Eighth Army in the capture of Padua. The task of the 350th Infantry was to swing eastward on the axis of the Verona-Vicenza highway to assist Eighth Army in the capture of Padua and to block escape routes to the mountains which might be used by enemy forces along the Adriatic.[20]

In implementing this order, the First Battalion on April 26 moved north on Highway 12 to Verona and after remaining a while in Raldon moved across the Adige River to San Martino. The only means of transportation across the river was an old Italian scow. The Second Battalion also crossed the river and proceeded east almost 14000 yards to Musella. After the Third Battalion had crossed the river on the same Italian scow, it engaged the enemy in a fire fight beyond San Martino before capturing the objective, the highway north of the town. Partisans' activity in this area aided the 350th Infantry in its march forward.[21]

Although the main infantry troops were across the river, the tank problem remained unsolved. As Colonel Fry moved on to join the troops, he left a message to Captain Woodbury: "Get your tanks across, if you can, and when you do, move east on Highway 11 until you catch up with us."[22]

Amidst heavy rainfall on April 27 the 350th Infantry continued racing the enemy toward Vicenza, approximately 30 miles east of Verona and 20 miles northwest of Padua. As the Second Battalion moved east almost 22 miles this day, it encountered only light enemy resistance. As the First Battalion marched ten miles along Highway 11 to Perarota during the day, the Third Battalion followed in trace. Since heavy rain impeded movement and visibility and since the First Battalion moved rapidly, it encountered pockets of the enemy at different intervals. At 2130 it was held up by a short fire fight, but tanks came to its assistance and the battalion moved out again shortly thereafter. It was then organized into a task force under the command of Colonel Fry, with the 752nd Tank Battalion and the 805th Tank Destroyers as support.[23]

On this march toward Vicenza, Colonel Fry had caught up with the First Battalion just before it reached San Bonifacio. After taling with his old friend of Company A, Captain Walter Scott, who gave him a dagger the Italians wore with their dress uniforms, Colonel Fry later moved on to his old command post of the 350th Infantry. There Lt. Emmanuel Spano gave him some coffee. About that time a cub plane appeared overhead and dropped the following message from Headquarters 88th Infantry Division:

> Memorandum: Colonel Fry: 1. Assemble at one two companies of tanks, two companies of TD's (now across the river in the vicinity of railroad bridge going up Highway 11), whatever elements of the 88th Reconnaissance Troop you can lay your hands on, one platoon of B Company, 313th Engineers, a battalion of the 350th Infantry, one battery of the 338th Field Artillery now across the river, load up TD's and tanks with men and utilize whatever trucks you can find. Other trucks are enroute but don't wait for them. I believe there are six over there now being used for shuttling. 2. From a task force and proceed without delay and take Vicenza. The 91st Division is also moving on Vicenza. We would like to beat them there." -s- Paul Kendall, Commanding.

A scribbled note in longhand at bottom read: "Watch out for 91st Division coming up from south," and "partisans report that there are no Germans this side of Vicenza."

About this time the commander of the tank unit, Captain Woodbury, drove up. He nonchhalantly explained that his units had moved over to the IV Corps sector in Verona and crossed there. He gave several gifts — a captured luger, pistol, and a few quarts of cognac. When Woodbury told Colonel Fry he would be ready by 9:00 hours, Colonel Fry then asked Colonel Cochran for a battalion. When Cochran suggested the First, then lined up in and along the road in groups opposite tanks, Lt. Col. Holland, commanding, stepped forward and said, "Everything is ready." At that time the Third Battalion was up front guarding the advance route. [24]

The night was just perfect for such an action - clouds that looked as if a rain might be in the offing and through the trees along the road side the picture of relatively flat fields. In only a few minutes Captain Woodbury and Lt. Col. Holland reported that they had agreed upon each one's respective roles and that they were ready to move. [25]

On the march down Highway 11 to Vicenza during the night of April 27, the Regiment met resistance from the enemy as he fired machine guns, sniper bullets, and bazookas at the roving force. By 2300 hours the task force halted for a few hours only about 12 kilometers from the objective and resumed the advance at 0530 the next morning. Since the task force moved quite rapidly, enemy units, moving cautiously and lying in wait at covered positions after allowing the task force to pass through, were able to surprise the long and unprotected columns; at such times a sudden fierce enemy attack would frequently cut a column in two. [26]

Although the enemy was disorganized, he still possessed military virtues not to be lightly disregarded. As the Krauts retreated to the north, they were encountered all along the road. When the 350th's columns broke through one barrier, they would be met only a few hundred yards in the distance by other enemy groups who had banded together to spray the advancing Americans with rifle and machine gun fire. The overwhelming fire power of the 350th's advancing columns would smother the enemy fire out and then move on. Occasionally some one was wounded, and once or twice a man was killed. [27]

As the task force moved on toward Vicenza in the early morning hours of April 28, the Third Battalion received the mission of clearing the town. Although the partisans had control of most of the town and greeted the liberators with bell ringing and cheering, the task of clearing the town proved quite tedious. Approaching the city amidst a light drizzle of rain, the infantry walked for safety after having dismounted from vehicles in the task force. As lightning flashed and thunder rolled, enemy machine guns struck the column and were answered with violent bursts of fire from the Regiment's own tanks. The infantry followed a deep ditch beside the road, and the riflemen fired at every moving object. On the outskirts of Vicenza Lieutenant Joseph Nash was wounded in the stomach and lay beside the road as the troops approached the city limits around 0800 hours.

To aid the American wounded in the fight for the city, an English-speaking enemy doctor provided his services. During this melee an enemy bazooka firing from a window knocked out two tanks within minutes, and machine gun, and rifle, and canon fire deafened the men moving cautiously through the city. As the task force tanks blazed away with their cannon, blankets of smoke filled the streets. The German doctor aided the wounded, including Captain Schwellensattl, as he climbed down from his tank with a bandage pressed tightly against his eye.

Company C especially encountered deadly fire from the enemy. The commander, Lt. Charles Dornacker, told Colonel Fry: "We've got to get some help up here. My men are being murdered. The Jerries have a position in a building where they are cutting us to pieces as we try to advance." Colonel Fry then gave orders for tanks to move through the alleys where they could work on the German-held building from whence the deadly fire emanated. He then sent a message to Colonel Cochran, Commander of the 350th Infantry, to take his available forces and exert pressure north of Route 11, the main highway that the task force had followed in entering the town.

Sometimes around 1000 hours Company C had generally gained control of part of the town held by the fanatical enemy. [28] As Colonel Fry moved along by a tank maneuvered by Captain Woodbury and preceded by two tanks in the lead and a column of infantry on each side of the street watching the windows and doorways opposite them, a blonde woman on a balcony suddenly threw open the window and cried, "Viva Americanos!" Hundreds of people now appeared in the streets; Vicenza had fallen to the 350th Infantry Regiment. [29]

After only a short respite in Vicenza, the Regiment again moved out at dusk. The Third and First Battalions moved east on Highway 53 to San Pietro in Gu.[30]   The Second Battalion became motorized once more, and as a task force struck further into the Po Valley. After riding on tanks and TD's through San Pietro, the battalion column became separated when it met an enemy column at Grantorto. In the severe fire fight that ensued Lieutenant Powers of Company E was hit, but within an hour the enemy was routed and some 125 prisoners taken.

Before the rear column could establish contact with the forward element, German paratroopers launched a surprise attack using interdictory machine gun fire, whereupon the column went into defensive positions. After a two-hour engagement, the battalion again routed the enemy and killed and captured a further estimated 80 Germans. Especially instrumental in routing this attack was the machine gun section under Lt. Tuttle of Company H, along with the well directed fire of machine guns and 57 mm weapons from AT Platoon of Headquarters Company. One officer, Lt. Brand of Company F, was wounded, and Lieutenants Drogowski, Fumich, and Erickson and six enlisted men captured by the enemy, whereupon Lieutenant McCollum assumed command of Company F. [31]

In its swift move astride Highway 53 as it fanned out to the left into the hills toward the Brenta and Piave River valleys, the Regiment left behind thousands of Germans caught in valleys south of the advance. During the day enemy units would hide out and then make desperate efforts at night to escape through the lines. At 0520 hours, April 29, the gun area of Cannon Company was overrun by enemy troops arriving in captured United States vehicles. After engaging the enemy in a rifle fire fight, the company then fell back on First Battalion troops who occupied the vicinity of San Pietro In Gu. Although the majority of the company made contact with Company A of the First Battalion, thirty enlisted men fell captive to a German unit which they had mistaken for Americans. In the battle with the German unit Pfc Dennis Pescod was killed and Privates Bowman and Adams were wounded. [32]

An enemy column that had captured American jeeps now disguised its movements and moved rapidly through the regimental area. The heavy fog, typical of the climate of the valleys west of Venice, helped to screen the movement and to confuse the thinly spread troops of the First Battalion in the area.

One enemy column passed boldly along a road near Company A. The commanding officer, Captain Scott, knew he had received no warning from the 350th Infantry Regiment Headquarters of a movement of tanks and vehicles through his area. When he moved to investigate and cried "Halt!" a German sitting on the hood of the lead jeep cut him down with a smyser. [33] Another valiant officer, carefree, courageous, and happy, who had borne the trials of the Italian campaign for many months, died only a few days before the cessation of hostilities.

On this day the Third Battalion arrived at the Brenta River at 0530 where the convoy stopped. As the battalion had no transportation for the captured along the way, the sergeant-major decided to set up a POW cage in the vicinity; but as he was herding the enemy toward the cage, he discovered great numbers of the Krauts coming from around the building where he had hastily rushed the prisoners. After the sergeant had ordered three machine guns positioned around the building and the prisoners placed on the second floor, the enemy force launched a fierce counter-attack from the right, driving the entire battalion to the river bed approximately 400 yards to its immediate front and thus leaving the sergeant-major, guards and prisoners isolated from the battalion and surrounded by the enemy.

Enemy bazooka teams were knocking out battalion vehicles at the rear of the convoy. Amidst the fierce battle, including tanks firing at the enemy positions from all sides, armor-piercing shells hit the building where the prisoners were held. The captured POW's accepted the opportunity to leave, but the Americans remained in the building. At 0930 hours the battalion tanks once again attacked the Krauts, supported by riflemen, and this time they were successful in driving the enemy back. In this fight Company K sustained six KIA's and two WIA's, and Lt. Rivers of Company I was wounded by machine gun fire and evacuated. After the 91st Division passed through the battalion at 1045, the men rested, having had no sleep in over forty hours. [34]

In the early evening the 350th Infantry was relieved by the 362nd Infantry of the 91st Division and then received the mission of protecting the 88th Division's left boundary from

Vicenza to Bassano, a change of direction now almost due north into the precipitous Dolomite peaks of the Alps.[35] Traveling astride Highway 53, the Regiment fanned out to the left into the hills and into the Brenta and Piave River valleys north of Bassano and Treviso to round up the fleeing enemy there.[36] As the Regiment moved swiftly into the mountains, German units became disorganized and were broken up into roving bands that attacked separate groups of both American soldiers and Italian civilians. The Partisans treated the Germans more harshly than the Allies; thus the German troops generally fought more fanatically against overwhelming Partisan odds. Many of the Germans had changed into civilian clothing in these last hectic days in the Alps mountain.[37]

On the last day of April, 1945, the First Battalion moved to the town of Marostica and relieved the Second Battalion of the 351st Regiment in defense of the town.[38] The Second Battalion moved from San Pietro from its forward reserve offensive positions and proceeded by road march to Dueville, six and one half miles, where it set up road blocks and established patrols.[39] The Third Battalion on this day headed northeast on Highway 53 and then turned north to Sandrigo. After marching approximately ten miles, the battalion established its command post in the vicinity.[40] All men received the much-needed rest after the strenuous pursuit of the enemy beyond Vicenza.

As the month of May came in, the 350th had its battalions located in the same areas as April 30. From Marostica, Dueville, and Sandrigo all three battalions sent out patrols to clear the area of all enemy troops. With the aid of the Partisans, the 350th liberated many small towns in the vicinity. After the Fascists were tried by the Partisans and German soldiers turned over to the Americans, the Regiment took precautions to guard Service Company and the kitchen areas that were almost twenty and thirty miles behind the front lines. This move was considered necessary, because many Germans were found hiding in farmhouses dressed as civilians, and all their efforts were directed toward escaping from the Partisans and delivering themselves into American hands.

Although the Italians had begun to celebrate the end of the war as early as April 29 in some areas, the Americans yet found the enemy to be resisting fiercely and inflicting numerous casualties. Bells were rung continuously in San Bonifacio and

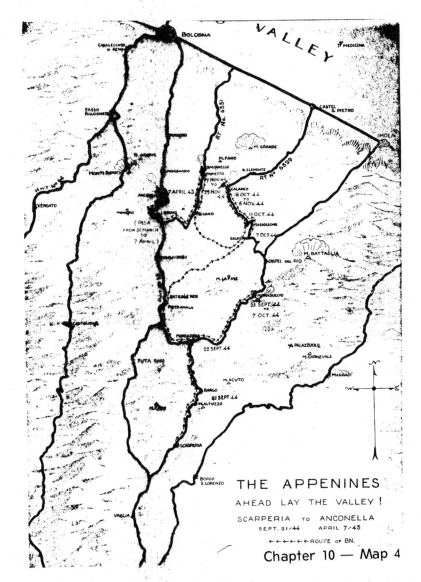

THE APPENINES

AHEAD LAY THE VALLEY!

SCARPERIA TO ANCONELLA
SEPT. 21/44   APRIL 7/45

←←←←←ROUTE OF BN.

Chapter 10 — Map 4

Verona and surrounding villages. The German emissaries had actually arrived at the Royal Palace in Caserta to sign the terms of the surrender.

Even though surrender was expected momentarily, the Germans in some areas resisted fanatically. Many of the captured by this time wore outfits made from shelter halves, some without shoes, and many ill fed. Others were bitter about being deserted by their officers.

On May 2 the Regiment planned to move out of Marostica with the object Innsbruck, Austria, where it would make contact with the Seventh Army driving south into Austria. After leaving Marostica at 0530 and then stopping at 1945 hours at San Marino, the Regiment was informed by the jubilant civilian population that the end of the war in Italy had been officially announced by radio. At 2000 hours, the men themselves heard the news by radio, and the convoy started again and moved to Arsie. The First Battalion bivouanced at Mellame, the Second at Primalano, while the Third occupied buildings in the town of Arsie.

The war in Italy had finally ended.

U. S. Pietramala Cemetery, Futa Pass, Italy, North Appenines.

Advance troop clear out sniper's nest to open way for Po River crossing.

Footnotes to Chapter X

[1] 350th Infantry Regiment History, April, 1945.

[2] Fry, **Combat Soldier,** 299.

[3] Truscott, **Command Missions,** 425.

[4] Starr, **From Salerno to the Alps,** 425.

[5] Fry, **Combat Soldier,** 302.

[6] 350th Infantry Regiment History, April, 1945.

[7] Hq. Co., Third Battalion History, April, 1945.

[8] Second Battalion History, April, 1945.

[9] Company E, Second Battalion History, April, 1945.

[10] Starr, **From Salerno to the Alps,** 425.

[11] 350th Infantry Regiment History, April, 1945.

[12] Third Battalion History, April, 1945.

[13] **Fifth Army History,** IX, 105.

[14] Ibid., 108-117.

[15] 350th Infantry Regiment History, April, 1945.

[16] Second Battalion History, April, 1945.

[17] Company E, Second Battalion, History, April, 1945.

[18] Third Battalion History, April, 1945.

[19] First Battalion History, April, 1945.

[20] **Fifth Army History,** IX, 118.

[21] 350th Infantry Regiment History, April, 1945.

[22] Fry, **Combat Soldier,** 318.

[23] 350th Infantry Regiment History, April, 1945.

[24] Fry, **Combat Soldier,** 319.

[25] Ibid., 320.

[26] 350th Infantry Regiment History, April, 1945.

[27] Fry, **Combat Soldier,** 322.

[28] Company C, First Battalion History, April, 1945.

[29] Fry, **Combat Soldier,** 328.

[30] 350th Infantry Regiment History, April, 1945.

[31] Second Battalion History, April, 1945.

[32] Canon Company History, April, 1945.

[33] Fry, **Combat Soldier,** 330.

[34] Third Battalion History, April, 1945.

[35] 350th Infantry Regiment History, April, 1945.

[36] **Fifth Army History,** IX, 119.

[37] 350th Infantry Regiment History, April, 1945.

[38] First Battalion History, April, 1945.

[39] Second Battalion History, April, 1945.

[40] Third Battalion History, April, 1945.

BIBLIOGRAPHY

A. Unit Reports and Histories

350th Infantry Regiment History, May, 1944–May, 1945.
First Battalion History, 350th Infantry Regiment, May, 1944–May, 1945.
Second Battalion History, 350th Infantry Regiment, May, 1944–May, 1945.
Third Battalion History, 350th Infantry Regiment, May, 1944–May, 1945.

Company Histories
    Company E, April, 1945
    Hq. Col, Third Battalion, April, 1945
    Medical Detachment, 350th Infantry Regiment, January, 1945.

Fifth Army History, Volumes V–IX
G-2 Summaries, 350th Infantry Regiment, May 10-15, 1944
Historical Documents, World War II, AGO Microfilming Job. No. 200, AGO (TIS Library), Fort Benning, Georgia
Narrative, 88th Infantry Division Headquarters 1-31 October, 1944, dated 26 November 1944.
POW Interrogation Report, 350th Infantry Regiment, September 24, 1944
S-1 Journal, 350th Infantry Regiment, November, 1944
S-2, S-3 Journal, 350th Infantry Regiment, November, 1944.

B. Unpublished Sources
The Infantry School, Fort Benning, Georgia

Harwood, Major Richard. "The Operations of the Second Battalion, 350th Infantry (88th Infantry Division) in the Supported Night Attack on the Gustav Line East of Minturno, Italy, 11-13 May, 1944," TIS, Fort Benning, Georgia, Advanced Infantry Officers Course, Class No. 1, 1952-1953.
Jones, Major Erwin B. "Operations of the 2nd Battalion, 350th Infantry (88th Infantry Division) in Clearing a Regimental Supply Route to Roccasecca, Italy, 21-25 May, 1944," Personal Experiences of a Battalion S-3, TIS, Fort Benning, Georgia, Advanced Infantry, Officers Course, 1949-1950.
Matthews, Major Milton A. "Operations of the 350th Infantry Regiment (88th Infantry Division) in the Attack on Mount Damiano, West of Castelforte, Italy, and Subsequent Objectives, 11-15 May, 1944 (Rome-Arno Campaign), TIS, Fort Benning, Georgia, Advanced Infantry Officers Course, 1949-1950.
Mozingo, Captain Roule C. "The Battlefield Commander Must at All Times Assure Himself that his Security is Adequate and Alert," TIS, Fort Benning, Georgia, Advanced Infantry Officers Class No. 99, 1949-1950.
Stroup, Captain Ray. Personal Recollections in reports given at TIS, Fort Benning, Georgia, from the period of combat, February, 1945.
Swett, Captain Daniel H. Personal Knowledge, Advanced Infantry Officers Course, 1949-1950. "The Operations of Company A, Northwest of Anconella, Italy, April 17, 1945," in "Infantry Company Attacking Village in Mountainous Terrain," TIS, Fort Benning, Georgia, Advanced Infantry Officers Class No. 2, 1949-1950

C. Personal Interviews and Correspondence

Personal Interview, Lt. Cary Ashcraft, July, 1976.
Personal Interview, Lt. Col. Corbett Williamson, October, 1976.
Personal Correspondence from Clayton Eighmeny, April 17, 1976.

D. Published Sources—Books, Magazines, and Periodicals

Adelman, Robert H., and Colonel George Walton. *Rome Fell Today.* Boston: Little, Brown and Company, 1968.
"Battle Mountain Outfit Honors Own Dead," *Stars and Stripes,* March 12, 1945.
Clark, Mark W. *Calculated Risk.* New York: Harper & Company, 1950.
Delaney, John P. *The Blue Devils in Italy: A History of the 88th Infantry Division in World War II.* New York: 88th Infantry Division Association, Inc., 1947.

Feder, Sid. "The Blue Devils Stumped the Experts," *Saturday Evening Post,* September 7, 1946.

Von Senger und Etterlin, General Frido. *Neither Fear Nor Hope: The Wartime Memoirs of the German Defender of Cassino.* Trans. by George Malcom. New York: E. P. Dutton & Company, Inc., 1964.

"Four 88th Division Men Hung on Until Bitter End," *Stars and Stripes,* May, 1944.

Fry, General James C. *Combat Soldier.* Washington, D.C.: The National Press, Inc., 1968.

Fry, Colonel J. C., U.S.A. "One Week in Hell, *Saturday Evening Post,* June 25, 1949.

Hall, Walter P. and William S. Davis. *The Course of Europe Since Waterloo.* New York: D. Appleton, Century & Company, 1947.

Jackson, W.G.F. *The Battle for Italy.* New York: Harper & Row, Publishers, 1967. ———. *The Battle for Rome.* New York: Scribners, 1969.

Kesselring, Albert. *A Soldier's Record.* Trans. by Lynton Hudson. Washington, D.C.: William Morrow & Company, 1954.

Orgill, Douglas. *The Gothic Line: The Italian Campaign, Autumn, 1944.* New York: W. W. Norton & Company, Inc., 1967.

"A Rifle Company in Mountain Terrain," *Infantry School Quarterly,* April, 1949.

Starr, Lt. Col. Chester G. (editor). *From Salerno to the Alps: A History of the Fifth Army, 1943-1945.* Washington, D.C.: The Infantry Press, 1948.

Times-Herald News, Dallas, Texas, February, 1945.

Truscott, General Lucian K. *Command Missions.* New York: E. P. Dutton Company, 1954.